Miriam Day Díaz
2009

Iva

" *Mimi* " *Miriam Díaz*
2010

HISTORIC LITTLE ROCK

An Illustrated History

by C. Fred Williams, Ph.D.

Commissioned by the Quapaw Quarter Association

Historical Publishing Network
A division of Lammert Incorporated
San Antonio, Texas

CONTENTS

First Edition

Copyright © 2008 Historical Publishing Network

All rights reserved. No part of this book may be reproduced in any form or by any means, electronic or mechanical, including photocopying, without permission in writing from the publisher. All inquiries should be addressed to Historical Publishing Network, 11555 Galm Road, Suite 100, San Antonio, Texas, 78254. Phone (800) 749-9790.

ISBN: 9781893619821
Library of Congress Card Catalog Number: 2008922764

Historic Little Rock: An Illustrated History

author: C. Fred Williams
dustjacket photography: Arkansas Democrat-Gazette
contributing writers for "Sharing the Heritage": Eric Dabney, Scott Williams

Historical Publishing Network

president: Ron Lammert
project manager: Wynn Buck
administration: Donna M. Mata, Melissa Quinn, Diane Perez
book sales: Dee Steidle
production: Colin Hart, Craig Mitchell, Chuck Newton, Evelyn Hart, Roy Arellano

PRINTED IN KOREA

ACKNOWLEDGEMENTS

The author wishes to acknowledge the following people for their special assistance—Brian Robertson and Rhonda Stewart at the Butler Center, Central Arkansas Library System; Jillian Barnett and Linda Pine at the Archives and Special Collections section of the Ottehenheimer Library at UALR; and Lynn Ewbank and Wendy Recter, at the Arkansas History Commission.

To Tag & Walker
with love

CHAPTER I

ARKOPOLIS OR LITTLE ROCK: THE FORMATIVE YEARS

People began coming before dawn. By daybreak, lines stretched back from each of the entry gates, and a low buzz of hushed, excited voices filled the gray November air. For a brief time world attention was focused again on Little Rock, Arkansas in anticipation of the much ballyhooed opening of the William Jefferson Clinton Presidential Library. It was November 2004, and the typically quiet capital city on the Arkansas River had grown to over twice its normal size as dignitaries and commoners from around the world gathered to pay tribute to the nation's forty-second president.

Much had happened in the 183 years since this, the twenty-second largest state capital, came into being. If those waiting in line had wanted to, by looking a hundred yards or so to the north, northwest, they could have seen an indentation that marked a crossing on the Arkansas River. Three hundred million years earlier, during Paleozoic times, the continent Llanoria drifted up from the south and crashed into North America. This collision wrinkled the earth's strata, pushing its surface perhaps ten thousand feet into the air into a series of long ridges that came to be called the Ouachita Mountains. Over the next two hundred million years the center of the Atlantic Ocean began to spread, causing an underwater uplift that displaced water from the Gulf of Mexico onto the continent. The rising Gulf water created an inland sea called the Mississippi Embayment that extended north to the edge of the mountains. Contact between Embayment waters and the Ouachitas' front range eroded the surface. Further changes in the earth's topography caused the Embayment to recede into the Gulf, leaving an exposed, jagged rock outcropping in its wake.[1]

About a million years ago the earth's climate went through a series of ice ages. Snow accumulated and compacted to form a huge ice cap more than a mile thick that extended out of Canada as far south as St. Louis, Missouri. Over time, the ice melted and formed rivers. One, now called the Arkansas, cut through a valley in the Ouachitas and into the Mississippi Embayment. Along the way it passed the rocky outcropping eroded by the Gulf waters. This "point of rocks" on the south bank of the Arkansas River became a landmark for crossing the river first to the buffalo and other migrating animals, then to humans who followed the roaming wild life and also became familiar with "the rock."[2]

By the time the Europeans arrived in the new world in the sixteenth century, the crossing had been well defined as an intersection of two animal highways—one came from the west following the north bank of the Arkansas River, the other came from the Northeast following the line of demarcation between the uplands and the flood plain along what came to be known as the Southwest Trail. The growing numbers of new immigrants altered the natural environment and added settled communities to the hearths already established by the Indians. One of these new "settlements," New Orleans, was built by the French in 1718 to guard that nation's inland empire on the North American continent. Because it was to be a great "defensive fortress," it was essential that the new city have an adequate supply of food and fuel to support an extended population. Founder Jean-Baptiste Le Moyne, sieur de Bienville dispatched reconnaissance missions throughout the major river systems in the Mississippi River Valley to identify potential sources for supplies and possible uses of the countryside. Some historians have also noted that Bienville had heard "stories" from Indian sources of a "green stone," possibly an emerald, and that made him more curious about the interior.[3]

One of the de Bienville assignments was given to Bernard de la Harpe, an experienced traveler who had previously explored Galveston Bay and the Red River as far west as present-day Oklahoma. His instructions for the Arkansas River were to determine what that region could contribute to New Orleans' support and if possible find the "green stone." La Harpe prepared carefully for his assignment, even taking time to construct a hoist on one of his canoes to extract the precious stone should he find it. Jean-Francois Benjamin Dumont, a surveyor on the expedition, wrote a "considerable manuscript describing his experiences in Louisiana" and explained that the group's "main object was to search out a fabled *rocher de topaz*"—a rock of topaz.[4]

Satisfied that he was fully equipped, la Harpe and his crew of twenty-two men left New Orleans in late February 1722. Three weeks of travel brought them to the rocky ledge on the south bank of the Arkansas River near the animal trails' intersection. La Harpe noted in his journal that this was the first evidence of rock formations since he had left New Orleans and no doubt it served as a reminder to his crew

about the "emerald" and its potential to make them all wealthy. It is significant to note that la Harpe recorded the outcropping in different ways, a "point of rocks," or simply as "the rock" but never used "la petite roche" nor "le petite roche" in reference to the site.[5]

Continuing up the river, la Harpe also observed a sheer rock cliff, rising more than one hundred feet above the river on the north bank. He recorded this site as *le Rocher Francais*—the French Rock. Excitement rose again as the party stopped their canoes, and a contingent of the more daring climbed to the top only to discover green forest but no green stones or jewels of any kind. Disappointing though such failure may have been, la Harpe did succeed in his primary mission and discovered that the forests along the river were teeming with deer, bear, and small wildlife. He also established two of the most important place names in on the river by identifying the "point of rocks" and "French Rock."[6]

Ironically, the origin and meaning for Little Rock, as with the state's name as well, has become something of a controversy. Morris Arnold, the foremost historical authority on Colonial Arkansas, notes that "numerous early nineteenth-century documents attest to [Petit Rocher] as the French name for Little Rock" and he reprinted a map of Northern Louisiana, made in 1799, as evidence.[7] However, anthropologist and journalist Samuel Dorris Dickinson argues that Petit Rocher "would be wrong, because it does not conform to the French language's distinction between the height and shape of the masses."[8] Dickinson also quotes from a French dictionary to note "*Roche* is an isolated rock of considerable size and height...like a block or piece detached..." while "*Rocher* is a very lofty rock, very high, and very steep ...*roche* sometimes is flat, the *rocher* comes to a peak."[9] Evidence seems to indicate that the original name of "rock" or "point of rocks" had evolved to "*la petit rocher*" in common usage by the late 1700s.

During the hundred years following la Harpe's Arkansas expedition, French settlement increased in the Arkansas River Valley, particularly as many of the newcomers intermarried with the Quapaw Indians. The Quapaw were also relative newcomers to the

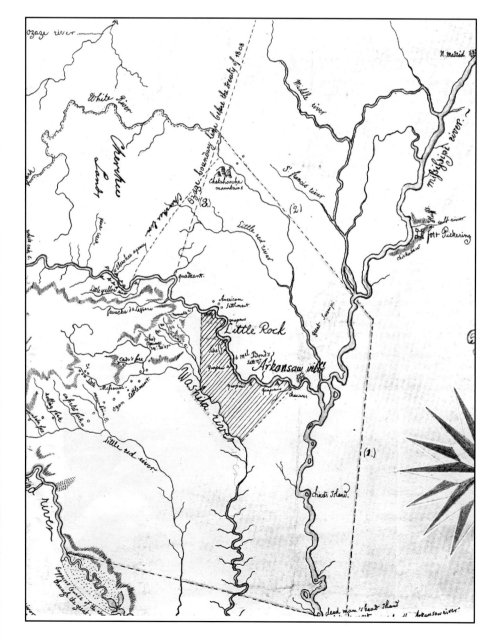

region. They began arriving in the sixteenth century and claimed the territory between the Arkansas and Red River as their homeland. Decimated by disease and alcohol addiction from their contact with the Europeans, the tribe had been reduced to a few hundred people by time of the American Revolution. Originally concentrated in four villages near the confluence of the Arkansas and Mississippi Rivers, the tribe became increasingly scattered.[10] Those with French ancestry frequently settled on individual home sites away from the traditional villages. One of these individuals, John Baptiste Imbeau, Sr., brought his family to settle just downstream from the "point of rocks," perhaps as early as 1769. One of his sons, Francis Imbeau, built a house at the "point of rocks" in 1803 and cultivated a garden there until 1808. Over the next decades he was joined by several other similar settlers including Francis Coussatt, Sr., and Louis Bartholomew. Being primarily hunters, they were hardly "settlers" and frequently moved in and out of the region depending on the hunting season.[11]

The area around the Petit Rocher did not become settled in the traditional sense until after the United States acquired the property in the Louisiana Purchase of 1803. Even with U.S. acquisition it was difficult to establish clear title to the region. In addition to the Quapaw Indians claiming the area, Spanish officials had rewarded

soldiers by making numerous grants along the river after acquiring Louisiana from France in 1763. The grants were rewards for service in the Seven Years War, and, even though most were never taken, their existence presented a legal challenge to would-be developers.[12]

Anticipating rapid settlement in the Louisiana Territory, U.S. officials moved quickly to establish procedures whereby new immigrants could secure clear title to the land. As a first step, Congress agreed to honor all Spanish grants. Those not holding a Spanish claim were able to secure clear title provided they could prove they had resided on the grant for a minimum of ten consecutive years prior to 1803—and had made improvements. These were known as "settlement or improvement" claims. Both the Spanish and settlement/improvement sites had to be recorded with the General Land Office to be valid. To facilitate filing on those claims, Congress passed the Pre-Emption Act of 1814, which gave the first Anglo settlers in the Louisiana Territory first option to purchase their "settlement" claim. The law went into effect April 12, 1814.[13]

Quapaw claims to the area proved a bit more complicated. Traditionally, U.S. officials extinguished Indian claims by

✧

Below: Formed more than two hundred million years ago when the continent Llanoria collided with North America, the earth's surface wrinkled into the long west to east ridges of the Ouachita Mountains that stretched from the Oklahoma border to the "little rock" on the Arkansas River.
COURTESY OF M. J. GUCCIONE, GEOLOGIC HISTORY OF ARKANSAS THROUGH TIME AND SPACE.

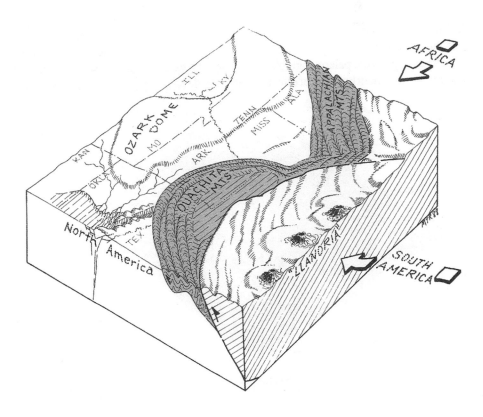

treaty, and, in August, 1818, representatives from Washington sought to do this to much of the area south of the Arkansas River. Principal Chief Heckaton and a delegation of Quapaw warriors were invited to St. Louis, where they were lavishly entertained and invited to sign an agreement limiting their settlements to an area bounded on the west by a line beginning on "the Saline fork [of the Ouachita River] to a point, from whence a due north course would strike the Arkansaw river at the Little Rock."[14] The Quapaw "reservation" was east of that line and presumably lands west of the Little Rock were open to settlement. While it is uncertain when the "point of rocks" evolved into Little Rock, according to the treaty it had become a part of the official language by 1818 —even though Arkansaw was the spelling used for the region.[15]

While federal officials were moving to establish legal title to the Louisiana Territory, the anticipated Anglo migration west of the Mississippi River began. By 1812 the advance guard had reached the little rock on the Arkansas. In July of that year, William Lewis, a buffalo hunter, descending the river in a canoe with his unnamed family, became ill and stopped at a spring on the south bank. He erected a crude "hunter's cabin" perhaps a hundred yards or so upstream from the "Rock."[16]

Whether Lewis' building qualified as a "homestead" under the General Land Office definition, thus entitling him to the right of preemption, became a matter of dispute. A delegation of Quapaw visited him soon after he completed his cabin and he assured them his stay was temporary. Also, Chester Ashley, a rival for the site, claimed that Lewis "...cleared no ground (except cutting the bushes covered by his camp), made no fence, nor planted anything and cultivated nothing whatever..." Ashley went on to report that Lewis lived off the "charity of his neighbors, on the north bank of the river...." To complicate matters, Lewis left his family in October to hunt buffalo. When he returned almost six months later, he moved his family to the north side of the river and lived for a time with William Mabbett, a slave trader who had recently moved to the area from Arkansas Post. A short time after returning, Lewis quarreled with Mabbett, separated from his wife, and left again.[17]

In Lewis' absence his original campsite was all but abandoned. According to Ashley, while Lewis was gone "some persons happening at the site...found a flourishing crop of weeds...one pumpkin vine, of stunted growth...that contained one pumpkin about the size of one's fist and one sickly cucumber vine containing two cucumbers of the size of one's little finger, both growing from seed accidentally covered in the dirt floor of the [Lewis'] cabin the previous year...."[18] Clearly Ashley did not believe Lewis' work met the minimum qualifications to be considered a homestead. But it remained for a federal court to decide the issue.

In March 1814, Lewis returned to the Rock. He patched up his differences with Mabbett and reestablished his relationship with his wife. However, in only a few months his restlessness took over and he left again— taking his wife with him. Before leaving, Lewis sold his claim to the point of rocks area—which he now called "Little Rock Bluff," to Elisha White for $10. After Lewis made his final exit from Arkansas, he apparently traveled to Nashville, Tennessee, and filed a preemption claim with the federal land office for his camp at Little Rock Bluff. White and his wife Martha were recent immigrants from Cape Girardeau, Missouri. They settled on the north bank of the Arkansas in the shadow of what was then being called "Big Rock Mountain," (later shortened to Big Rock) but only stayed four years before returning to Cape Girardeau in 1818. He died not long after returning to Missouri.[19]

Seven months after the U.S. Congress approved the Quapaw Treaty (August, 1818), its Committee on Territories recommended that the five southern-most counties of Missouri be separated and recognized as "Arkansaw Territory." Residents of those counties had petitioned for such and celebrated when President James Monroe signed the bill on March 2, 1819. The legislation stipulated that Arkansas Post was the "temporary" capital but left it to local residents to choose a permanent site. That action was an invitation for speculators and town developers to descend on the new territory. Even as Congress began a divisive debate over whether Arkansas should be organized as a slave or free territory, a small group of men in St. Louis, Missouri, launched plans to develop a new town at the Little Rock on the Arkansas River. Using land certificates which Congress authorized in 1812 to compensate individuals who lost property in the New Madrid Earthquake of 1811-1812, this band of "associates"—Stephen Austin, James Bryan, William O'Hara, and their agent Amos Wheeler, began plans to secure the site.[20]

The Associates' plan called for Wheeler to proceed to Arkansas and make enough "improvements" to allow them to "prove" their claim. Before leaving St. Louis, Wheeler hired two workers, Daniel Whitter and William Starkweather, to follow him and build structures as he surveyed the lots. Wheeler arrived shortly before Christmas in 1819. However, before he could begin any serious work, he had a visitor: William Russell. He is described by historian Margaret Ross as "the shrewdest and most successful of all the speculators in Arkansas lands...."[21]. Russell was also from St. Louis and had been traveling the backcountry since 1812, searching for future development sites. The Lewis/White property caught his attention and sometime after Elisha's death, he located

Martha White and got a verbal commitment from her to sell her deceased husband's claim. He also bought several other preemption claims at or near the site.

Russell made no effort to develop the property in 1819 but did tell Wheeler that he had preemption claims to the best part of the property. He offered to sell his interest in the site for $25,000. Wheeler, who by that time had been joined by James Bryan, refused the offer and ordered Russell to leave. Less than two weeks later, Russell returned with a copy of two property deeds. The first was signed by William Lewis to Elisha White and dated May 25, 1814. The second was signed by Martha White to William Russell and dated June 1819. When Wheeler and Bryan again refused a settlement, Russell went to the Pulaski County justice of the peace and filed a lawsuit against the two "for forcible entry" to his property. A jury in the Justice's court ruled in

✧

Above: In 1884 three railroad companies joined forces to build the Junction Bridge across the Arkansas River, anchoring its southern base at the little rock. More than half of the historic rock was excavated to make room for a pier for the new bridge.
COURTESY OF THE ARKANSAS HISTORY COMMISSION.

Below: The excitement of the Bernard de La Harpe party was greatly stimulated by their sighting of this rock cliff on the north bank of the Arkansas River from the "point of rocks." Commonly referred to as Big Rock, to distinguish it from its smaller neighbor, the outcropping was also referred to as French Rock in recognition of LaHarpe's recording the site as a place name.
COURTESY OF THE ARKANSAS HISTORY COMMISSION.

type of physical work he could do in building a new town.

While Austin and Russell were vying to see who would control the Little Rock, Governor James Miller called the Territorial Legislature into special session. Legislators convened at Arkansas Post on February 7, 1820, with a single agenda item—where to locate the permanent capital. Speaker of the House Joab Hardin of Lawrence County appointed a select committee with himself as chair and Thomas Tindall and Radford Ellis, the two Pulaski County representatives, to do the investigation. The committee considered two sites—Crystal Hill, founded in 1807 by John and Jacob Pyeatt in the shadow of Big Rock Mountain about ten miles above the Little Rock, and Cadron, a fur trapping post built by John Standless in 1778, some thirty miles upstream from the Rock.[23]

During its deliberation, the committee faced enormous pressure from both Russell and Wheeler to add Little Rock to the list of possible sites. Wheeler made a written offer to provide the territory with:

> ...a public square of nine hundred feet square and a half square of one hundred and fifty feet...to furnish...for the use of the legislature of said Territory, (if so ordered) a room of about eight two (sic) feet by thirty two feet square, and a chamber over the same of the same dimensions, gratuitously for the time of three years, and also to furnish the said Rooms of said term of three years for the use of any public courts which may needed to be held in them.[24]

Wheeler also offered to provide space for a "county court house, public market, schools, churches, and a cemetery" if the legislature would designate Little Rock as the capital. Finally, he committed to build enough houses to accommodate "at least one hundred people by August 1," in preparation for the legislature meeting in October. Russell was more subtle but also persistent.

Despite this pressure, the committee recommended Cadron as the new capital. The full House adopted the committee's bill with a 6-3 vote on February 22, 1820. Russell,

Russell's favor, but Wheeler and his associates hired Chester Ashley, a Massachusetts lawyer who had only recently arrived at the Rock, to appeal the decision to the Pulaski County Court of Common Pleas. The common pleas court on "a writ of certiorari" set the Justice's court decision aside. Russell countered by appealing to the territory's Superior Court at Arkansas Post. With the case on appeal, Russell then prepared to lobby members of the Territorial Legislature to select the Little Rock site as the permanent capital.[22]

Wheeler, in addition to Russell's challenge, faced problems with improving the property enough to satisfy federal land office officials. His associates had managed to get him appointed postmaster of the Little Rock site, but his two hired hands, Whitter and Starkweather, were delayed in their travel to Arkansas. Low water on the river forced them to stop at Arkansas Post. After waiting several days without success for the river to rise they decided to walk to Little Rock. Unfortunately the weather turned cold and began to snow soon after they left the Post. Whitter suffered extreme frostbite on his feet, but, with the aid of those he later called "stranger friends," he made it to Little Rock. For some four months thereafter he was unable to walk without the aid of crutches and was quite limited in the

unable to influence the House vote, did get the Council to amend the bill by substituting Little Rock for Cadron.

However, before the legislature was able to resolve the differences between the Assembly's and Council's version of the bills, Governor Miller became involved in the issue. He questioned whether the Assembly was legally constituted because the elections the previous November were held before he arrived in the territory. Although appointed governor in March 1819, he did not arrive in the territory until December, just days before he called for the special session. His question may have been a bit disingenuous since he was the one who called for "an extraordinary" session and set the date for it to convene. Furthermore, Miller's role in the capital issue may have also been influenced by his ownership of property at Crystal Hill. In the days leading up to the special session, he openly expressed his desire to see that site chosen. Faced with the governor's question, the Assembly decided to delay a vote on the issue until they convened in regular session in October.[25]

Between March and October real estate around the little rock changed ownership

several times as each side tried to strengthen its position. Wheeler dropped into the background as William O'Hara and James Bryan became more active, Governor Miller was added to the Associates, and Stephen Austin, even though he had officially severed his relationship with the group, continued to show interest in the new town. More significantly, a new member, Chester Ashley, became a part of the Associates. Born in Massachusetts and trained in law at Williams College, Ashley was a relative of O'Hara and quickly became the strategist for the group.

Russell moved to neutralize Wheeler's "offer" and the momentum gained by the Associates. He hired Batesville attorney Townsend Dickinson as his agent and cultivated his friendship with key members of the legislature. In May he also published a notice in the *Arkansas Gazette* which read in part:

> To Stephen F. Austin, William M. O'Hara, Amos Wheeler, James Bryan, Austin Elliott, Chester Ashley, and all concerned or interested in any...
>
> Of the lands joining the southwardly margin of the Arkansas River, at and near a place called Little Rocks (sic).... Take notice, that I ...have a better right and claim to and for the lands.... Therefore I will not pay for any improvements upon any part of said lands;

✧

Above: A native of Massachusetts, trained as a lawyer, Chester Ashley came to Arkansas in 1820 just in time to become involved in the land disputes surrounding the site for a permanent Territorial Capital in Arkansas. He used real estate investments to become one of Little Rock's most wealthy citizens by 1840.

COURTESY OF THE ARKANSAS HISTORY COMMISSION.

Left: Arriving in 1819 to edit and publish Arkansas's first newspaper, William Woodruff moved his press to Little Rock within weeks after the Territorial Assembly designated Little Rock as the permanent site for the Capital. He became one of the Little Rock's most influential citizens with his activist editorial policy and criticism of political opponents. He also established the city's first lending library.

COURTESY OF THE ARKANSAS HISTORY COMMISSION.

and I will claim damages for the trespasses committed by you and others thereon.[26]

Russell also focused on getting a clear title to his preemption claim. Researching the various transactions, he traced ownership of William Lewis' original claim and discovered that Elisha White had sold the Lewis claim to Benjamin Murphy before the Whites moved back to Missouri. Moreover, Murphy had filed the claim with the General Land Office in Batesville and had been issued a certificate. The GLO had opened in 1815, the first federal land office in the territory. Rather than dwell on Martha White's deception in selling a fraudulent claim, Russell concluded that he had no choice but to buy Murphy's claim and he found Murphy ready to sell. Russell then subdivided the claim among several key politicians. Among those receiving "deeds for town lots" at the Little Rock were Robert Crittenden, the Territorial Secretary, Andrew Scott, a member of the Superior Court, and legislators Robert Oden and William Trimble. Joseph Hardin, brother to the Speaker of the House Joab Hardin, also received a grant.[27]

When the legislature reconvened on October 2, there was a noticeable difference in attitude on the capital issue. The Council's bill was amended to substitute Little Rock for Cadron and was taken up by the House. With little debate, Hardin, Tindall, and Ellis switched their votes, and the bill passed 6 to 3. Governor Miller signed the amended bill into law on October 18. It became effective June 1, 1821. Russell seemingly had won the contest with the Associates. However, on October 21, the lawmakers threw some doubt on the matter when they voted to accept Wheeler's offer to build the Capitol and courts building along with his promised donation of public land. They also required Wheeler to post a $20,000 bond with Governor Miller to insure his good faith with the development. Russell saw the potential for trouble and tried to get lawmakers to stipulate that the building must be placed on "undisputed lands." But the legislature adjourned without addressing that issue.[28]

Where the capital was to be located was settled. But who owned the land around the Little Rock was not, and the contest for control became even more heated. Russell seemed

confident that the steps he had taken to shore up his preemption claim solidified his standing with the Superior Court, and he concentrated on getting the name Little Rock identified with the site. The Associates, with lawyer Chester Ashley increasingly becoming the spokesman for the group, tried a new tactic. On February 3, 1821, the Associates held a public meeting and, with considerable fanfare, named the site Arkopolis. The *Arkansas Gazette* covered the event in a letter to the editor dated Arkopolis (formerly Little Rock) February 5:

Gentlemen—On the 3d inst. we had a large and respectable meeting of all the citizens of this place and its vicinity, for the purpose of giving it a name; and we unanimously adopted the above [Arkopolis] a combination of the first syllable of Arkansas, and the Greek word for polis for 'city'. Notwithstanding the weather was very unfavorable the day passed with much cheerfulness and mirth; and it gave me peculiar pleasure to witness the cordial expressions of good will, and the wishes of all present for the improvement of our new seat of government....[29]

Despite the Associates' fanfare, Russell made no effort to survey new lots or build additional buildings. Such was not the case for his rivals. Prior to the legislature's decision on the permanent site of the capital, Wheeler built two additional buildings on the New Madrid claim. One, a frame building made from cypress boards approximately 18 by 30 feet in size, was about 200 yards upstream from the "rock" fronting on the river. A second building made from logs built about thirty feet downstream from the frame house was used by workers as they prepared the site. With the governor now holding his performance bond, Wheeler turned his attention to having Arkopolis ready for the next session of the legislature. His work crews cleared some timber, built four "huts from round pine logs," but did not survey any additional lots. Apparently, the New Madrid Associates gambled on winning their claim to the "rock" on the strength of the cypress board building Wheeler had erected when he first arrived. By 1821 the structure had been divided into two sections, one used as a general merchandise store and the second, smaller room served as Wheeler's office. Matthew Cunningham, the town's first physician and also the first mayor, described the inventory as "a scanty stock of drugs and medicines and a liberal supply of whiskey."[30]

For undetermined reasons, plans for preparing the Little Rock site for the permanent capital were slow to materialize. The two-story capitol and courts building Wheeler promised was never built, and, while numerous trees were cut to build "a half a dozen" log buildings, no streets were laid out. The public square had been surveyed on parts of four blocks with the capitol designated to be near the intersection of Main and Orange (Fifth Street). Observers noted that in the daytime "20 or 30 men could be seen working around the town site or loafing around the main building" where the supply of whiskey was kept. At night the scene became a ghost town as the workers sought lodging on the north side of the river or slept in the woods.[31] However, in early April there were signs that the control of

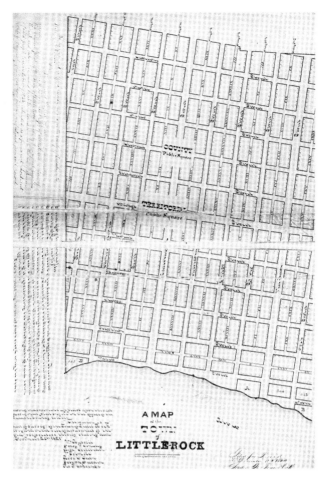

A MAP of the TOWN of LITTLEROCK

the site had shifted in a new direction. William O'Hara sold his share of the New Madrid claims to Chester Ashley for $4,000—a very low price considering the stakes in the contest.[32]

Another indication of a power shift came in June. The first day marked the "official" beginning for the new capital location, but it passed without fanfare. Governor Miller was away, the acting governor, Territorial Secretary Robert Crittenden was still at Arkansas Post, and there was no celebration to mark the event. It remained for the Superior Court to officially christen the site, with the name still in doubt. The Court opened its June session at the new capital, Little Rock or Arkopolis, and, as one of its first items of business, took up Russell's suit against the "New Madrid trespassers."

Addressing the Russell case was a delicate matter for the Court. After the original Court was appointed in 1819, two justices refused to serve. Joseph Selden and Benjamin Johnson were appointed as their replacements, but

Selden had not arrived in the territory when the new Court session began. The decision was left to Johnson and Andrew Scott, a member of the original Court. As noted previously, Scott had "purchased" lots at the Little Rock site based on Russell's claim. Scott excused himself from the case and Johnson, an uncle to Henry Conway, who had also purchased land using Russell's claim, handled the case himself.

Without addressing what constituted "improvements," a decision more properly left to the General Land Office, Johnson found sufficient errors in the lower court's ruling to remand the case to the Court of Common Pleas. The question on the merit of the two claims was left to the GLO. It seemed apparent that Russell had the advantage—at least he had access to his property at the Little Rock.[33]

The Court decision was the death knell to the Associates' partnership. Austin and Bryan had already moved on to Texas, Wheeler had been dropped as agent after Ashley became the group's legal counsel, and O'Hara had sold his interest to Ashley. None seemed willing to continue the fight, but neither did they want Russell to gain the "improvements" they had made to the property. Within hours after learning of the Court's ruling, the workers reversed their efforts to build and began dismantling their weeks of hard work. Some of the structures were put on logs and rolled off the town-site onto the Quapaw Reservation, others were burned and at least one "was blown up" while in the process of being burned. By nightfall, the town of Arkopolis ceased to exist.[34]

With his title to the Little Rock secure, Russell busied himself through the summer getting ready for the fall session of the legislature. More a speculator than developer, he nevertheless had a "two-pen" log cabin ready for occupancy by the time the lawmakers arrived in October. With the permanent site for the capital settled, Little Rock played much less of a role than in the previous special session. Russell and Ashley concentrated on reaching a compromise over their conflicting claims. Both still stood to lose if the matter stayed in the courts. To avoid that, the two met at the General Land Office in Batesville on November 22, and worked out a compromise to jointly share the property. For now the two rival groups were at peace.[35]

William Woodruff, publisher of the first newspaper in the territory, had committed to move his press to the permanent capital site when the dispute over title was settled. He was now free to do that and, over the next month, he rented property and moved to Little Rock. He published his first issue in the new capital on December 29, 1821, and editorialized that:

> Until within the last few weeks, the title to the tract of land selected as the town site has been in dispute; but happily for the place and the territory generally, the parties concerned became sensible of the propriety of settling their conflicting claims in an amicable manner. This circumstance places the prosperity of the town beyond doubt and we feel satisfied…in a few years we shall have the most flourishing and pleasant town west of the Mississippi.[36]

Being designated as the territorial capital and with the land disputes settled, at least momentarily, Little Rock seemed poised to become a boom town. Even as a raw wilderness area, visitors saw the potential for a major city.

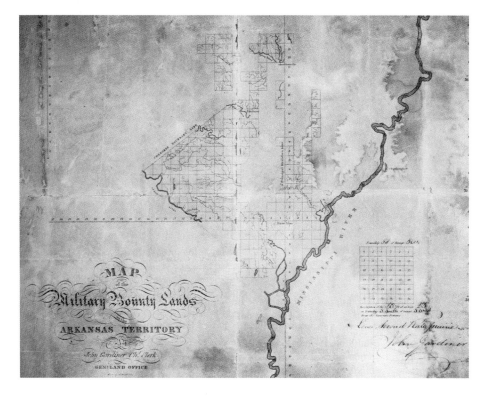

CHAPTER I ENDNOTES

1. M. J. Guccione, *Geologic History of Arkansas Through Time and Space* (Fayetteville: University of Arkansas Department of Geology, 1993), 30-34.
2. Thomas Thomas and Gerald Hanson, *Arkansas and the Land* (Fayetteville: University of Arkansas Press, 1992), 22-24.
3. Morris S. Arnold, *Colonial Arkansas, 1686-1804* (Fayetteville: University of Arkansas Press, 1991), 20-22.
4. *Ibid.*, 16, 79.
5. Margaret Ross, "Old Story of the 'Big' and 'Little Rocks' Not Borne out by La Harpe's Own Report," *Arkansas Gazette*, February 25, 1968.
6. *Ibid.*
7. Arnold, *Colonial Arkansas*, 185.
8. Samuel Dorris Dickinson, "Colonial Arkansas Place Names," *Arkansas Historical Quarterly*, 48 (Summer, 1989), 165.
9. *Ibid.*
10. David Baird, *The Quapaw Indians: A History of the Downstream People* (Norman: University of Oklahoma Press, 1980), 7-10.
11. Margaret Ross, "Three Families Settle at the 'Little Rock' Around 1769 But no Exact Date is Known," *Arkansas Gazette*, April 17, 1966.
12. Arnold, *Colonial Arkansas*, 107-110.
13. Malcolm Rohrbough, *The Land Office Business: The Settlement and Administration of American Public Lands, 1789-1837* (New York: Oxford University Press, 1968), 10ff.
14. Quapaw Treaty of 1818, Article 2.
15. Baird, *History of Downstream People*, 56-59.
16. Margaret Smith Ross, "Squatters Rights: Some Pulaski County Setters Prior to 1814," *Pulaski County Historical Review*, XLVII (Fall, 1999), 60.
17. *Ibid.*
18. *Ibid.*
19. *Ibid.*
20. S. Charles Bolton, *Remote and Restless: Arkansas 1800-1860* (Fayetteville: University of Arkansas Press, 1998), 24-25.
21. Margaret Ross, "June 21—Arkansas' Capital City is Born," *Arkansas Gazette*, June 6, 1971.
22. Dallas T. Herndon, *The Highlights of Arkansas History* (Little Rock: The Arkansas Historical Commission, 1922), 31-34.
23. *Ibid.*
24. Amos Wheeler to the Territorial Government of Arkansas, February 21, 1820, Secretary of State, Miscellaneous Papers Collection, Box 1, Folder 1, Office of the Arkansas Secretary of State.
25. Margaret Ross, *The Arkansas Gazette: The Early Years, 1819-1866* (Little Rock: Arkansas Gazette Foundation, 1969) 34-36.
26. *Arkansas Gazette*, May 20, 1820.
27. Herndon, *Highlights of Arkansas History*, 34.
28. *Ibid.* Both Ashley and Austin co-signed the note with Wheeler.
29. *Arkansas Gazette*, February 2, 1821.
30. Margaret Ross, "Little Rock's First Mayor," *Arkansas Gazette*, September 9, 1951.
31. Ross, "Arkansas Capital City is Born," *Arkansas Gazette*, June 6, 1971.
32. Ira Don Richards, *Story of a River Town: Little Rock in the Nineteenth Century* (Benton, Arkansas: Privately Printed, 1969), 8.
33. New Madrid Certificates, as defined in the enabling legislation, could only be applied to land that was already in the public domain at the time the law was enacted. The Little Rock site was still part of the Quapaw Nation until the 1818 Treaty and therefore ineligible for settlement when the certificates were created. Stated in another way, Russell's pre-emption claim established by the 1814 pre-emption legislation did not have a time limitation and was a superior document to that held by the Associates.
34. Thomas James, *Three Years Among the Indians and Mexicans* (St. Louis: Missouri Historical Society, 1916), 100-101.
35. Russell never recorded his deed, and, in 1839, Roswell Beebe, a newcomer to the city, discovered the omission and claimed title to the entire city. Matthew Cunningham placed a notice in the *Arkansas Gazette* stating that any one who tried to honor Beebe's claim would face a lawsuit. Rather than go through a lengthy legal battle, Beebe used a quit claim deed and went block by block and purchased enough property to make him the largest landowner in the city.
36. *Arkansas Gazette*, December 29, 1821.

CHAPTER II

BEFORE THE ROSES BLOOMED:
LITTLE ROCK BEFORE THE CIVIL WAR

With the land claims settled at least temporarily, speculators turned to town developers. No effort was made to revive the name Arkopolis, and residents seemed content with Little Rock. Despite the tenacious defense of his claim to the site, William Russell did not stay around after the Superior Court ruled in his favor. Ever the individualist, he chose instead to seek speculative ventures elsewhere. Ironically, Chester Ashley emerged as a key player in promoting the town. Blending real estate deals with an emerging law practice, he rapidly increased his standing and was the town's wealthiest citizen by the end of the decade.[1]

Ashley was joined in promoting the town by Matthew Cunningham, a physician trained at the famed Philadelphia School of Medicine. Cunningham sought a career in medicine on the frontier and came to Arkansas Post in the summer of 1819 only days after the new territory was organized. When the legislature moved the capital to Little Rock, he relocated along with most of the other residents at the Post. Less loquacious than Ashley, Cunningham preferred to stay in the background and lead the more quiet life of a professional. He built an unpretentious pine log cabin near the 'little rock' and practiced medicine as best he could. His wife Eliza came from St. Louis to join him soon after he got the cabin built, and the couple had the distinction of being the parents of the first child born in Little Rock. Politics was a thriving business in the territorial capital. However, Cunningham steered clear of the various factions and was rewarded for his evenhandedness by being elected the town's first mayor when the territorial legislature authorized Little Rock to incorporate in 1831.[2]

William Woodruff was another individual who played a pivotal role in Little Rock's early history. A native of Long Island, New York, he gave up a potential career in whaling for editing and migrated west to Arkansas to publish a newspaper. Woodruff arrived at Arkansas Post on October 31, 1819, and three weeks later published the territory's first newspaper, the *Arkansas Gazette,* issued on November 20. As previously noted, he moved his press to Little Rock two years later when the legislature voted to relocate the capital. Woodruff was somewhere between Ashley and Cunningham with respect to personality and public affairs. A firm believer that "the pen is greater than the sword," he used his newspaper to express opinions and promote causes and individuals while keeping Little Rockians informed on the major issues of the day.[3]

Ashley, Cunningham, and Woodruff reflected the dominant themes that came to define Little Rock's identity. Ashley represented the business and political interest that fed off first territorial then state politics. Cunningham symbolized the community's ties to professional groups, particularly in medicine and education. Woodruff reflected the town's cultural interests, and, while he was also mindful of politics, he promoted literature and the fine arts through the pages of his paper. Throughout its history Little Rock set the tone for the state's political, economic, professional, and cultural activities.

The energy that brought Little Rock into existence did not extend into helping it grow into a city. Numerous citizens commented on the town's potential. For example, in 1820, even before he relocated, Woodruff commented in the *Gazette* that:

> The land at Little Rock...for natural beauty and advantages is not surpassed by any west of the mountains. It...has a rocky-bound shore with an excellent harbor for boats. On the spot, and in the immediate vicinity, is a heavy growth of pine and cypress timber for building, and what renders it valuable as a site for a town, there are several perpetual springs of good water issuing from the hills—a blessing seldom to be met west of the Mississippi.[4]

✧

Another indication of Little Rock's strategic position on the Western frontier prior to the Mexican War was a decision by the U.S. War Department to build a military arsenal in the capital city in 1838. The "Arsenal" served as a repair shop and munitions storage depot for the U.S. Army.
COURTESY OF THE UALR ARCHIVES &
SPECIAL COLLECTIONS.

Despite that potential, real growth was slow in coming. Historian Charles Bolton in his book *Remote and Restless* has noted that the entire Arkansas region lagged behind other states and territories in population, and this extended to Little Rock. While it was the region's leading community from the first year it was founded, the capital city remained more a village than city well into the third decade of its settlement. The 14 Anglo residents in 1820 increased to a little more than 1,500 in 1840 but the town still had fewer than 4,000 residents at the time of the Civil War.[5]

Part of Little Rock's slow growth lay with the uncertainty of the Arkansas River. In a time when all the major population centers were dependent on water transportation, Little Rock was all but land-locked for much of the year. Its main water source was unreliable. Rising in the Rocky Mountains some six hundred miles west of Little Rock, the Arkansas snaked across the arid plains too far south to benefit from the annual snow melt that fed the Missouri River. Its slow, sluggish current was too slow to sweep its channel clear of driftwood, and its frequent switchbacks often altered the channel and left sandbars in its wake. Approximately four miles south of Little Rock the river bent sharply to the southwest and created a rough stretch of water that steamboat crewmen named "Dog Tooth Bar." In summer, late fall, and winter, it was all but impossible to get by the bar, except by keel boat or canoe. Steamboat captains typically unloaded their cargo there and the goods were transshipped to Little Rock. Cargo handling for transshipment was one of the city's major

occupations until the 1870s, when railroad companies were finally able to bridge the Arkansas and provide continuous transport for goods to all sections of the state.

The first steamboat to dock at Little Rock, the *Eagle*, did not come until 1822, and even then the town was simply a drop-off, rather than the primary destination. The boat was delivering supplies to the Western Cherokee nation and the Christian missionary school, Dwight Mission, near present day Russellville. Throughout the 1820s, boat traffic on the river was limited, with fewer than a dozen vessels running anything approaching a regular schedule. While a national policy was adopted to improve the interior waterways in 1824, Congress did not consider funds for the Arkansas until 1829, when an appropriation of $15,000 was included in a House bill that failed to pass the Senate. The next year both houses passed the bill only to see President Andrew Jackson veto the measure.[6] Little Rock merchants did not allow this action to go unnoticed in the 1836 presidential campaign.

The cost of consumer goods was another factor shaping the slow growth of Little Rock. The difficulty of traveling the Arkansas River often caused suppliers to more than double the price of trade goods shipped to Little Rock. Insurance rates for vessels traveling on the Arkansas were among the highest in the nation, surpassed only by the Red River, because of the frequent run-ins with sandbars, sawyers, and snags. During the depths of summer and winter when the River was low, area merchants found it more profitable to hire freight haulers or keelboat operators to meet the steamboats at Montgomery's Point on the Mississippi River, and haul their supplies back to Little Rock.[7]

Mail service was also affected by Little Rock's remoteness. Residents complained often and sometimes in strident tones about the mail deliveries. Some years they went an entire winter without receiving any postal service due primarily to the town's dependence on the river. Prior to 1827, the town's primary overland connection with the east came via the Southwest Trail from St. Louis. This previously mentioned animal trail was progressively defined by a growing number of travelers who

❖

Beginning in 1820, when the Comet *navigated the Arkansas River to Arkansas Post, the steamboat was a vital link with the outside world. The first boat to stop at Little Rock, the* Eagle, *came in 1822. By the time of statehood in 1836, more than one hundred boats had docked at the capital city.*

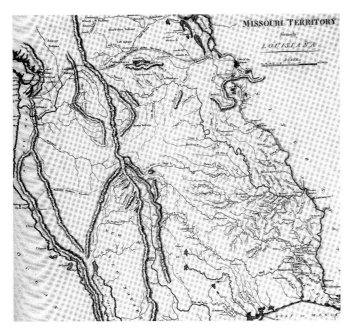

improvised improvements on the trail without public assistance. The road connecting Little Rock with Arkansas Post was even more unreliable because it was often jeopardized by the flooding on the Arkansas River.[8]

Clearly, public assistance was necessary for a region to have a reliable transportation system. But, prior to the 1830s, about the only way Congress could be persuaded to fund "internal improvements" was for an area to call attention to its need for mail service. Little Rockians used this argument in 1824 and were gratified to learn that Territorial Delegate Henry Conway was able to persuade federal officials to appropriate funds for building a road between Memphis and Little Rock. However, the road was not completed until 1827, and even then it provided only limited service—in part because Congress did not authorize enough money to keep the road in good repair, but also because it traversed some of the most difficult terrain in the nation. Flooding almost every year by the Mississippi River turned its flood plain into a quagmire for weeks at a time, making long sections of the road impassable. Little Rock's transportation systems did not materially improve until well after statehood. Even then there were improvements only in a comparative sense.[9]

The Little Rock of the 1820s struggled to establish an identity. One reason for this was that the area earned a reputation early for being a challenge to traditional settlers. In addition to the usual artisans, mechanics, business, and professional classes, the city attracted an unusually large number of outlaws and would-be law breakers. Thomas Nuttall, a naturalist commissioned by the Academy of Natural Sciences in Philadelphia, was one of the first to observe and record this problem. He visited Little Rock in 1820 when the land speculators were still in the process of organizing the town. He noted that as far as he was able to observe: "all inhabitants beyond Arkansas Post could be classed only as renegades fleeing from society." Noted geographer Timothy Flint wrote of Arkansas and Little Rock that, "The people of this region are certainly more rough and untamed than those in the state of Missouri. The valley of the Arkansas is 'sickly' to such an extent that if a person had only a fever he was hardly allowed to complain."[10]

Slow population growth allowed a small group to dominate the settlement. Most were more concerned with personal enrichment than with community development. Travelers who visited the town frequently commented on this "hyper individualism," and it was a source of some concern for those of a more progressive bent who wanted to make the town more worthy of being the territorial capital.

Boston adventurer Hiram Whittington, one of the "progressives," came to Little Rock in 1826 and commented that he could not see many areas where the town had improved. He observed that:

> Little Rock is situated on the south bank of the Arkansas, contains about 60 buildings, six brick, eight frame, and the balance log cabins…. The town has been settled about eight years and has improved slowly. The trees are not half cut down in the town yet. Instead of streets, we walk in one cow path to another from house to house.[11]

Whittington chose to move on rather than contend with the "original" settlers. He could not accept the level of violence in town and what he

✧

The Arkansas River, the middle of three major western rivers that flow into the Mississippi River, was both boom and bane for Little Rock. It was the primary contact to outside markets, both in shipping and receiving. However the river's uncertain channel, filled with snags and sandbars, caused insurance rates on freight to be among the highest in the nation and greatly added to the costs of consumer goods.

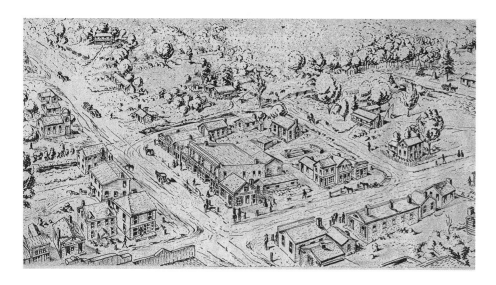

considered a lack of general interest in reforming the community. In 1830, in another letter to his family in Boston, he noted: "When I came here…vice and immorality went hand in hand through our streets; the Sabboth (sic) was not kept …justice had fled our courts; every man carried arms, either for murdering his enemy or for his own defense; and murders were an everyday occurrence."[12] Two years later, he gave up on Little Rock and moved to Hot Springs.

British geologist George W. Featherstonhaugh stopped in the capital as Whittington was preparing to leave and expressed a similar opinion of the town. After complaining for having to spend the night in the same bedroom with two "professional gamblers," Featherstonhaugh commented that the town was a refuge for "Gentlemen who had taken the liberty to imitate the signature of other persons; bankrupts…homicides, horse-stealers, and gamblers." He went on to write that individuals of this nature "admired Arkansas on account of the very gentle and tolerant state of public opinion which prevailed there in regard to such fundamental points as religion, morals, and property."[13]

Professional gamblers were typical of the "undesirable" element that moved into town soon after the first lots were sold. Gambling was not illegal; however, "cheating" was considered a form of thievery and of even more concern it frequently led to violence and sometimes death. Lawlessness connected with gambling became such a problem that the territorial legislature in 1835 voted to remove such crimes from the justice of the peace courts and place them under the jurisdiction of the Superior Court. The Legislature also authorized Little Rock to establish a municipal court in 1835 and that, too, helped curb some of the more objectionable behavior of the "blackleg gentry."[14]

Ironically, Whittington may have left Little Rock too soon. The decade of the 1830s began a period of prosperity that continued almost uninterrupted until the Civil War. Appropriately, the growth was led by improvements in transportation. The catalyst came not from local initiative but from the federal government and was not targeted for Little Rock. Even so, town leaders took advantage of federal officials' sudden discovery of the southwestern frontier. Beginning with Lewis and Clark, and for twenty-five years thereafter, national leaders as well as those engaged in private enterprise, had been enamored with the Missouri River Valley. However, beginning in 1830, that interest was re-focused to the Arkansas River Valley and remained there for almost two decades. Little Rock was a big beneficiary of this rediscovery of the lower regions in the Louisiana Purchase. It served to jumpstart the local economy and move the Arkansas capital from a village to a frontier city. The newfound federal interest was based on two independent but congruent issues. On May 28, 1830, Congress passed the Indian Removal Act that initiated closure to a plan originating with Thomas Jefferson—to remove Indian Tribes east of the Mississippi River to a new Indian Country carved out of the Louisiana Purchase. The second issue was a new colonial policy put in place by the government of Mexico. Following a series of insurrections by citizens of its Texas Province, Mexico adopted a colonization law that closed its borders to further immigration—except in special cases. However, rather than calm the agitation, the new policy further inflamed the Texans. Many of those "rebelling" had been recruited for Texas by Stephen Austin after he abandoned his plans for Arkopolis. By law, they were required to become Mexican citizens, but most did so in name only and retained their loyalty to the United States. Some threatened war with Mexico, others advocated independence, but in either event, odds were the United States would also be involved should conflict come.

These two events had a significant impact on the Arkansas capital. Being at a crossroads on the Arkansas River meant that Little Rock was positioned to receive traffic destined for Indian Country west of Fort Smith as well as for Mexico to the southwest. To the normal civilian travelers on those routes was now added a growing number of military troops as War Department officials moved to meet two potential threats, Mexico and the re-located Indian nations. There was some concern in Washington that Mexico and at least a fragment of the Indian nations could potentially form an alliance to block anticipated U.S. encroachment beyond the Louisiana Territory.

The Removal policy greatly increased the Indian presence in the Arkansas River Valley in a short time. Between 1830 and 1838, more than thirty thousand Indians passed through Arkansas after exchanging their homes east of the Mississippi River for new lands in Indian Country. The migrating Indians presented local residents with some important choices. On the one hand the tribes had money and were ready to purchase a wide variety of supplies. But, they also brought disease and a threat of violence that created ambivalence among Little Rock residents. The *Arkansas Gazette* editorialized in 1832 that:

> The cholera has got to this out of the way place at last. We have about two thousand Indians (Choctaws) camped at the edge of town, who have the cholera among them, and from 10 to 20 die daily.[15]

Typically, the merchants found ways to sell merchandise to the immigrants, even as town political leaders adopted ordinances to keep them outside the community. The Removal was accompanied by numerous military personnel and civilian contractors as well and represented over $100,000 injected into the frontier economy in less than a decade.

As Indian removal neared an official end in 1838, federal officials finally yielded to pressure from Arkansas's new Congressional delegation to recommission Fort Smith—in reality to build a new fort on the Arkansas border. This was

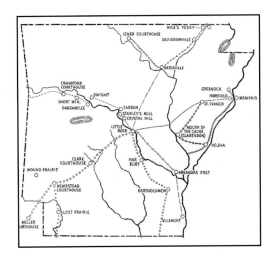

done to place U.S. Army troops between the relocated Indians and Arkansas residents. Prior to the Removal policy, the War Department had determined to build a network of forts approximately sixty miles beyond the Anglo line of settlement. The original Fort Smith was built in 1817 and had been replaced by Fort Gibson farther west on the Arkansas River. With Removal, however, Arkansans now faced a significantly larger Indian population between the old Fort Smith and the newer Fort Gibson. Pulling the defense line back, closer to the western border now seemed a desirable thing to do, at least to many Arkansans. Recommissioning Fort Smith did not directly affect Little Rock, but the indirect effect of the growing military buildup on the state's western border did help the city's businessmen by giving them access to an increasing volume of federal dollars spent to supply the army.

The second decision, to build an arsenal in Little Rock, had a more direct impact.

Mayor Cunningham and other town leaders began requesting a military installation soon after the Indian Removal policy went into effect. At the time Little Rock was a gateway to the western frontier. Not only was it a key supply station between Memphis and Indian Country, but it was also a portal to Mexico and that nation's generous land policies. Plans to build the Arsenal began in the spring of 1836, when project manager, Lieutenant F. L. Jones came to Little Rock and selected thirty-six acres south of Hazel (Ninth) Street and bounded on the west side by the first Quapaw Treaty line. Jones paid the owners, the firm of Hawkins, McLain and Blodgett $3,000 for the site, part of which had

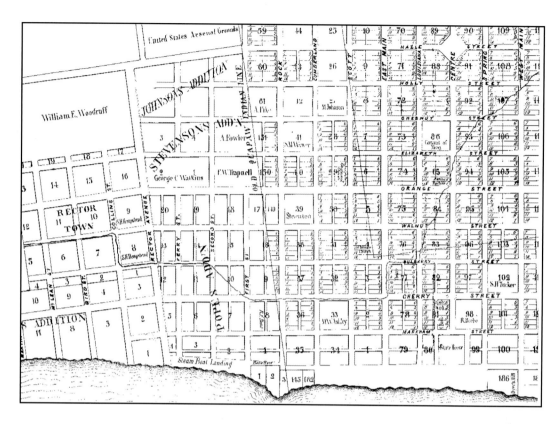

previously been used as the town race track. As an arsenal, the new military installation was small in comparison to other military posts at the time. However, it still represented a substantial investment to Little Rock's approximately fifteen hundred citizens. After an initial appropriation of $14,000, Congress authorized supplemental funds to increase the total construction costs to almost $100,000. By the time the complex was finished, it included a barracks for enlisted men, an officers' quarters, a series of gun repair shops, and enough storage facilities to house some one hundred tons of ordinance that arrived in Little Rock on May 15, 1838. The installation was formally commissioned on June 23.[16]

Not only did the arsenal provide a federal payroll to a starved local economy, its symbolic presence represented a commitment from the federal government to provide protection to the region. Beginning with the Choctaw Treaty of 1824 (Treaty of Dancing Rabbit Creek), *Gazette* Editor Woodruff kept a constant reminder to the citizens, and officials in Washington, that Indians posed a danger and Arkansans needed federal troops for protection. The arsenal represented a pre-positioning of essential

weapons and reassurance to area residents that the U.S. Army intended to defend its borders, whether against Indians or the nation of Mexico.

The Jackson Administration's military interest in the Southwest also led to improvements on the Arkansas River. As previously mentioned, in 1830 Jackson vetoed a bill that provided limited funds for the Arkansas. However, he signed a similar bill in

1832 that not only offered funding of $15,000, but also authorized the construction arm of the War Department (soon to become the Corps of Engineers) to "maintain a channel on the Arkansas River." This legislation not only ensured that the river would receive continued attention but it also allowed the Arkansas to join the Ohio, Mississippi, and Missouri Rivers as part of the nation's strategic infrastructure.[17]

Following up on the legislative mandate, War Department officials assigned Captain Henry M. Shreve to work on the Arkansas. He arrived at the mouth of the river in August 1833, and removed twenty snags before low water forced him to suspend operations. Returning in January 1834, he worked for six weeks to clear the channel up to Little Rock. On February 22, he noted that in the 250 miles from the mouth of the river he had "removed 1,537 snags" from the channel and had cut another "3,370 snags and logs" from dry sandbars and under the banks in the river bends an average of almost 200 obstructions, or potential obstructions per mile.

At Little Rock, a party of local citizens greeted Shreve at the wharf on First Street and went aboard his lead vessel to watch the captain demonstrate his work. He obliged by removing a large cottonwood log from the bank on the north shore. In less than an hour, he "raised the tree...sawed off the root system, cut the trunk into three pieces...and set all adrift in the deep water."[18]

Obviously, Shreve's work did not eliminate the risk, but it temporarily reduced the hazards and reduced travel time. In 1830 it typically took a steamer more than two weeks to reach New Orleans, but by 1840 that time had been reduced to four or five days. More importantly Shreve's work signaled steamboat operators that the Arkansas was now in the system for continued maintenance. Traffic began to increase almost immediately, and Little Rock was one of the largest beneficiaries.[19]

The federal expenditures for military preparations on the frontier could not have come at a better time for Little Rock. In addition to an immediate boost, the new funding allowed the city business community to largely escape the Panic of 1837. That recession became a full-fledged depression that lasted for

almost five years, and much of the nation had a sluggish economy well into 1842. However, Little Rock avoided much of that and grew both economically and demographically. For example, the 1830 federal census showed Little Rock with 527 residents, and by 1840 the population had increased to 1,531. Though small when compared to Atlantic Coast cities, compared to Memphis' population of 1,799 in 1840, it showed how rapidly the Arkansas capital had developed.[20]

A growing population increased interest in local government and community improvements. The Legislature passed "An act for the regulation of the Town of Little Rock." In October 1825, that authorized the town to elect five trustees and provide some measure of local control. Although given a mandate to "levy taxes, not to exceed $20 annually, appoint a tax commissioner and street overseer, erect a market house, and pass laws for public morals," the Trustees took a minimalist approach to government, focusing on public morals and neglecting economic issues. Elected in January 1826, the Trustees met soon thereafter and

Above: As originally designed, the state house had both north and south porticos, with the north side facing the Arkansas River. However, in the 1880s, with steamboats being rapidly replaced by rail locomotives, attention shifted away from the river, and the north portico was replaced by an addition to the capitol to provide space for the House of Representatives and state offices.

COURTESY OF THE ARKANSAS HISTORY COMMISSION.

Below: A large number of the some 60,000 Indians living east of the Mississippi River and south of the Ohio River were moved through Arkansas and Little Rock during the 1830s. Money spent by federal officials under this policy of Indian Removal played a vital role in stimulating the region's economy for almost a decade.

COURTESY OF JOHN L. FERGUSON AND JAMES H. ATKINSON, *HISTORIC ARKANSAS*.

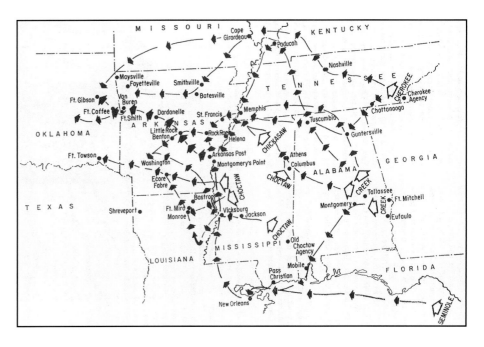

adopted an ordinance to regulate the "conduct of Negro slaves and free Negroes," prohibited gambling between "Negroes and whites, gambling in public taverns," and "to shoot upon the streets on Sunday." Later in the year, the Trustees signed a contract to build a Market House at Mulberry (Third) Street and Main and approved its hours of operation from "daylight to 10:00 am." However, they also included a provision that prohibited "citizens purchasing articles offered at the market" if the same article was available at "some other place" in town.[21]

The trustee model was not acceptable to those wanting a more pro-active approach to local government, and, in 1827 the Legislature approved a bill to allow the town to be incorporated and establish a mayor-town council system of government. It was this law

that Cunningham and others used to call for town elections November 2, 1831, to incorporate the community, and elect a mayor and four council members. Following those elections, the Legislature issued a charter for the City of Little Rock, and, in the 1835 session, legislators authorized the new city to have its own court system. The once small village had taken important steps toward modernization.

At the time of incorporation, Little Rock stretched some twelve blocks south of the river and twelve blocks east to west beginning at Rock Street near the little rock and followed the old Quapaw Line. Rock was the only street that ran the full length of the town plat. Cunningham led the Council in an aggressive move to develop a tax base and generate revenue that would enable them to address some the town's pressing needs.

Taking up economic needs first, the Council passed a series of ordinances setting schedules for personal, property, and franchise taxes. Each voter was accessed a 50 cents poll tax, merchants and liquor dealers were assigned annual franchise taxes of $10 and $20 respectively, and property was assessed, 25 cents per slave, 12 ½ cents for horses, and 6 ¼ cents for cattle. These taxes coming as officials in Washington began to increase the federal presence in the Territory provided city leaders with an excellent opportunity for significant community development.

Public health was the first big challenge for the new city council. Frontier settlers favoring personal independence and expansive private space often found it difficult to live in close proximity with each other. Personal habits were slow to change as well. Human and animal

waste, along with garbage from food preparation and consumption, was typically discarded without regard to community interest. Such attitudes and patterns of behavior often allowed travelers to smell the town before it could be seen. Little Rock was no exception. Putrid vegetables filled filthy gutters, and the stench from slaughtered animals and stagnant water filled the air much of the year. The Council tried to address this problem in an early ordinance that stated:

> All house offal, whether consisting of animal or vegetable substances…shall be safely gathered up, put into convenient barrels, and thrown into the river every forty-eight hours, or oftener if necessary to the health or cleanliness of the city.[23]

In a follow-up ordinance, the Council also ruled that "Every dead horse, cow, or other animal, found lying in the streets or alleys, is declared a nuisance." (The owner must remove the animal within 6 hours or pay a fine of $10 to $50.)[24]

In addition to waste disposal, stagnant water was also a major problem. Although the original town site was on a broad plateau well above the flood plain, it was surrounded by a number of marshes and swamps that served as breeding grounds for mosquitoes while collecting filth and refuse throughout the year. An added problem for Little Rock was a stream, commonly called the "town branch," that originated southwest of town near the present State Capitol building, ran in a northeasterly direction to Main Street, followed on the west side of that street to Cherry (Second) Street, where it then turned east and emptied into a marsh east and south of the little rock. The branch was out of control in the rainy seasons and dried to a dusty stream bed with occasional stagnant pools during the summer. Beginning in the 1820s, it became a dumping ground for people's garbage and only got worse with time. Floodwaters sometimes redistributed the refuse and, what the water did not wash away was often consumed by roving bands of hogs.

Uncontaminated water was another issue the growing city faced. The "abundant" springs used as an early selling point, while attractive

for the few travelers in the early days, were inadequate to sustain an increasing population. Many individuals dug private wells, and for a time some residents took water from the Arkansas River. Neither was satisfactory for public use, particularly when it came to fire protection. To respond to the growing fire danger, the Council moved in 1837 to build a network of thirteen cisterns. Beginning at Markham and Main, the heart of the business district, where two cisterns were built, the network extended every block or so to Holly (Eighth) Street. The cisterns were kept filled either by rainfall or from private wells if rainfall was not adequate. The Council also passed an ordinance making it "…unlawful for any person to take by bucket or pipe any water from the public reservoirs or cisterns of the city used for the extinguishment of fires".[25]

In keeping with being a modern city, the Council purchased a fire engine with a steam operated pump from the city of New York in 1840. It weighed over 5,000 pounds and required 50 people to move it to a fire's location. Firefighters soon adjusted and used horses to pull the engine and Council members "to stimulate interest and assure speed…" voted to pay $20 to the person getting the first horse to the engine after the fire alarm had been sounded.[26] But even with that incentive, volunteer firefighters were no match for fires in a city built primarily from wood. Fires were a regular occurrence, but on February 2, 1854,

✧

The first session of the Arkansas General Assembly chartered a "State Bank." This building to house the institution was constructed on Markham Street opposite the State Capitol Building (Old State House). Completed in 1838, the structure gave added status to Little Rock as a city emerging from the frontier. The above photo was taken in 1911.

COURTESY OF THE BUTLER CENTER, CENTRAL ARKANSAS LIBRARY SYSTEM.

firemen faced the most disastrous fire in the city's history. It began in the early morning at the intersection of Main and Elm Streets. By the time it was brought under control the buildings on three blocks had burned to the ground. Mayor C. C. Danley estimated the cost at more than $100,000. The fire engine proved to be largely useless because its major valves were stuck with mud from using river water at a previous fire. In reality, bucket brigades continued to be the most effective means for fighting fires until after the Civil War.[27]

The infusion of federal dollars that did so much to transform Little Rock in the 1830s also had an impact in the private sector. This could be seen in the "big houses" built by some of the city's leading citizens in the late 1830s and '40s. Little Rock's first elegant house had been built by former Territorial Secretary Robert Crittenden in 1827. Located on the south side of Chestnut (Seventh) Street between Cumberland and Scott Streets, the design was influenced by Thomas Jefferson's style and made of brick. The house was almost 4,000 square feet under roof compared to the typical Little Rock residence of some 400 square feet. Crittenden ran into financial problems after losing his position of territorial secretary in 1828 and began a five-year struggle to save himself from bankruptcy. Failing to reverse his misfortune, he was forced to sell the house to Superior Court Justice Benjamin Johnson, who added two rooms to the structure in the 1830s.

Chester Ashley followed Crittenden in the early 1830s with the first phase of his house in the 200 block of East Markham. Enlarged through the decade, with beautifully landscaped grounds, the "Ashley Mansion" became the landmark for visitors to the city and

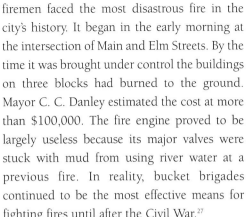

was converted to a hotel in the 1870s, long after the Ashley family had given up ownership.

Ashley was aided a great deal in his efforts to add to his property by a skilled work force of black slaves. When not in use for his personal services, Ashley, as did most of the urban slave holders, "rented" his slaves to other people. By 1860, slaves made up about twenty percent of the city's population. Free Negroes were perhaps another one percent of the population.[28]

From time to time the City Council found it necessary to pass special ordinances limiting contact between slaves and whites who were not the slave's owner. For example, whites were prohibited from buying or selling with a slave without the owner's permission. In another instance slaves were prohibited from "living separately…from the direct supervision of their owners." Slaves were among the city's most skilled craftsmen and also made up a large percentage of the service workers. Among Ashley's slaves were several members of the Warren family who were quite musically talented. Ashley frequently put them on "display" by having them perform at special functions and occasionally giving concerts on the lawn at the Ashley mansion.

The early 1840s saw a wave of "big houses" rise on Little Rock's south side. Albert Pike, lawyer, newspaper editor, poet, and a world leader in the Scottish Rite Free Masonry movement, began the trend in 1840 by building a two-story, Greek Revival, brick structure with six ionic columns. The building and grounds occupied the entire 400 block on Seventh Street. That same year Absalom Fowler, a lawyer and land speculator, built a two-story brick structure at 503 East Sixth Street. Less elegant but a more adaptable structure than Pike's mansion, the building and grounds covered two full blocks.

Above: By the late 1820s, Chester Ashley's real estate investments and law practice proved lucrative enough for him to build an elaborate house on the south side of Markham Street between Scott and Cumberland streets. Known as the Ashley Mansion, it was a prominent landmark for travelers approaching the city on the Arkansas River. Converted to a hotel after the Civil War, the structure remained intact until razed soon after World War I.

COURTESY OF THE ARKANSAS HISTORY COMMISSION.

Below: A former school teacher turned lawyer, writer, and poet, Albert Pike had this house built in 1840 in the 400 block of East Seventh Street. Pike's family lived there until after the Civil War. The house was purchased by Little Rock Mayor John G. Fletcher in the 1880s. Fletcher's daughter Adolphine, married to Congressman David D. Terry, lived in the house until the 1970s before donating it to the city. It remains today one of Little Rock's most treasured structures.

COURTESY OF THE ARKANSAS HISTORY COMMISSION.

War of 1812 veteran Ebenezer Walters followed with another Greek Revival brick house in 1842. Although it was a single story, it and the surrounding grounds also occupied two square blocks at 615 East Capitol. The next year lawyer Frederick Trapnall began construction on a house at 423 Capitol that was larger than Walters' but not as elegant as Pike's, but still "elegant" when compared to typical log structures that dominated the town.[29]

The "crown jewel" of the construction boom was a commercial building, the Anthony House Hotel. This three-story brick structure on East Markham, a block from Ashley's mansion, was rebuilt from a previous hotel destroyed by fire in 1839. It included a "dining room 60 feet long, two parlors, 28 bedrooms, a bar, baggage and store-rooms, kitchen, laundry, meat house, ice house, servants' quarters, a stable, and carriage house."[30]

These "big houses" were not typical, but they did typify something of Little Rock's character in the Antebellum years. They represented a fairly small circle of highly successful individuals, predominantly lawyers by training, but who were also involved in politics and land speculation. Building the territorial capitol illustrated this convergence of political and personal initiatives. At the request of John Pope, the third governor of the territory, Congress donated ten sections of land in 1831 to build a permanent capitol. Governor Pope then appointed Chester Ashley as agent to select and sell the land, but not before Robert Crittenden offered his house in exchange for the ten sections. Moreover, Crittenden persuaded legislators to pass a bill accepting his offer, a bill Pope vetoed; by doing so he sparked a rousing debate as leaders of the legislature threatened to impeach him. Undeterred, the governor continued with his plan. Ashley then selected ten sections east of the little rock, subdivided them and began selling lots in what he called "Pope's Addition"—the first addition to the original town site. Within two years these lots had earned the territory more than $30,000, more than enough money to begin construction on the capitol. Crittenden sold his house in that same year to Judge Johnson for $6,700. The new capitol was built in classical Greek Revival

Style and harmonized well with the great houses built in the next decade.[31]

Little Rock's political leaders entered the 1840s with a high degree of optimism. Improved technology and design in steamboats made it possible for larger boats with smaller drafts to travel on the Arkansas River. National interest in railroads pressured the U.S. Congress to authorize four regional surveys to determine the most feasible route to West Coast. Arkansas and Little Rock leaders were encouraged by reports that the engineers' preferred route followed the Thirty-fifth Parallel—taking it through the state. For most of the decade, immigration remained strong. By the time of the "gold rush" in 1849, Little Rock newspaper editors estimated immigrants were passing through the city at an average of four hundred per week—but most also noted that these travelers did not stay, and, at this stage of their journey, most still had adequate provisions for their trip and were not inclined to make large purchases.

Despite the initial interests in railroads, Congressional leaders could not decide on which of the surveys to choose. Sectional politics caused the question to be put on hold, and steamboat owners and operators continued to shape national transportation policy. Little Rock's business community seemed content to rely on steamboats. The earlier navigation problems on the Arkansas River had diminished considerably, and the newly designed vessels were a much more frequent sight in Little Rock than in earlier days. By the 1850s more boats traveled the river in a year than in the entire decade of the 1820s. The peak year came during the 1858 season when, between November and June 1859, 317 boats docked at the Little Rock wharf. The City Council saw an opportunity for a new tax source in this increasing steamboat traffic and in 1846 passed an ordinance to assess a "wharf fee" on each vessel that docked in Little Rock. Over the next decade the wharf tax became the single greatest source of revenue and kept the city treasury "in the black" until the Civil War.[32]

Over dependence on steamboat traffic had a negative impact on Little Rock in the long term. City leaders became blinded by the short-term revenue and failed to plan for

✧

This house, constructed in 1843 on the south side of East Fifth Street by Frederick Trapnall, a lawyer and Whig political leader who served three terms in the Arkansas General Assembly. Following the Civil War, the house was purchased by physician Charles M. Taylor, who served as chief surgeon for the Confederate Army in the Trans-Mississippi West. In 1929 the Taylor family deeded the property to the Little Rock Junior League. In 1979 the League sold Trapnall Hall to the state of Arkansas, and the site is now administered by the Arkansas Department of Heritage.
COURTESY OF THE ARKANSAS HISTORY COMMISSION.

changes in the national transportation system. With Congress paralyzed by the sectional dispute over slavery expansion, the question of where to build railroads was left to state and local leaders. Railroad construction was expensive and typically beyond the ability of private business to finance. Political leaders in Memphis recognized this in the early stages of development and encouraged Little Rock to join in building a rail system to connect the two cities. Lacking a bank or other source to underwrite the costs, Little Rock's leaders were slow to act. That city revenues were doing quite well from the steamboat traffic no doubt influenced their decision as well. Memphis moved ahead with a plan to use bonds to underwrite the costs and in 1853 approved $350,000 in bonds to build a share of the road. This initiative allowed that city to tap into the cotton agriculture of the Mississippi River's west delta and greatly strengthened the trade ties of eastern Arkansas with western Tennessee. Little Rock did not approve a bond program until 1855 and then only issued $100,000. By the time the bonds were on the market, the early signs of the Panic of 1857 were setting in, sales went poorly, and the Little Rock end of the road extended less than sixty miles east of town.[33]

By the 1850s it was apparent that a national demographic shift was underway. The initial "Oregon Fever" in the early 1840s started a trend that was greatly accelerated by the gold rush to California at the end of the decade. The War Department was the first to acknowledge this new dynamic and in 1852 began a plan to restructure Indian policy. From the "great reservation" that created Indian Country in the Removal period, the new emphasis was on concentrating the tribes into two small reservations north and south of the Missouri River. Federal troops, the vanguard of this new policy, were extended farther and farther west—away from Arkansas. Moreover, the Mexican War ended any international threat near the Arkansas River Valley, and officials in the War Department no longer felt it necessary to maintain a high military presence there. Troops in both Arkansas and Louisiana were, for the most part, redeployed to more active centers in the new west. Fort Smith was all but abandoned, and the Little Rock Arsenal lapsed into disrepair, with fewer than a hundred troops on active duty there.

By the time Little Rock's business leaders recognized the shift in national policy, it was too late to recover. Content to build a community around the business of state government, supplemented with steamboat transportation, and the pass-through traffic of western migrants, they were unable to expand on the promise of 1840. The mix of individualists and civic progressives did not allow for a great deal of planning Even the limited number of manufacturing plants established by 1860—a tanyard, foundry, lead and slate processing, furniture making (specializing in chairs), and shoemaking—were based on responding to a frontier economy rather than supplying a national market.

Little Rock's failure to realize the promise envisioned by its founders and predicted by its boosters prior to the Civil War was painfully evident by its growth. Population numbers tell much of the story. As previously noted, Memphis and Little Rock were essentially the same size in 1840—Memphis having just 268 more people. That comparison had changed significantly by 1850, when Memphis' population increased to 8,841, but Little Rock only had 2,167 residents. By 1860 the numbers were even more dramatic, with Memphis' population at 22,623 and Little Rock showing only 3,727. However, even if there had been an interest in using the census numbers to re-evaluate city policies, the mounting secession crisis would have prevented any serious analysis. Talk of war was pervasive, forcing any other question from the agenda until the issue was resolved.[34]

CITY	1820	1840	1850	1860
San Antonio (1716)			3,488	8,235
New Orleans* (1718)	27,176	102,193	116,375	168,675
St. Louis* (1764)		16,469	77,860	160,773
Memphis (1819)	53	1,799	8,841	22,623
Little Rock (1819)	14	1,531	2,167	3,727
Shreveport (1834)			1,728	2,190
Houston (1836)		1,200	2,396	4,845
Austin (1839)		856	629	3,494
Kansas City (1839)			2,529	4,418
Dallas (1841)			163	775

CHAPTER II ENDNOTES

1. U. M. Rose, "Chester Ashley," *Publications of the Arkansas Historical Association* (Fayetteville: Arkansas Historical Association, 1911), III, 47-73.
2. Vivian Hansbrough, "Little Rock's First Mayor Saw City Emerge From Wilderness," *Arkansas Gazette* September 9, 1951.
3. Margaret Ross, *Arkansas Gazette: The Early Years, 1819-1866* (Little Rock: Arkansas Gazette Foundation, 1969), 3-18.
4. *Arkansas Gazette*, May 27, 1820. 1.
5. S. Charles Bolton, *Remote and Restless: Arkansas 1800-1860* (Fayetteville: University of Arkansas Press, 1998), 18-21.
6. Colonel Charles L. Steel, "Arkansas—Renaissance of a River: Part I," *Arkansas Gazette*, October 26, 1969.
7. Margaret Ross, "Steamboating was a Profitable Trade in the 1800s," *Arkansas Gazette*, December 25, 1966.
8. Ira Don Richards, *Story of a Rivertown; Little Rock in the Nineteenth Century* (Benton, Arkansas: Privately Printed, 1969), 18-19.
9. *Ibid.*, 20.
10. *Ibid.*, 23
11. Hiram Whittington to Granville Whittington, April 21, 1827, quoted in F. Hampton Roy, Sr., and Charles Witsell, Jr. *How We Lived: Little Rock as an American City* (Little Rock: August House, 1984), 29-31.
12. *Ibid.*
13. Bolton, *Remote and Restless*, 89-90.
14. Ross, *Arkansas Gazette: The Early Years*, 124-125.
15. *Arkansas Gazette*, November 20, 1832.
16. Dallas T. Herndon, *Highlights of Arkansas History* (Little Rock: Arkansas History Commission, 1922), 67-68.
17. Steel, "Renaissance of a River," *Arkansas Gazette*, October 26, 1969.
18. Richards, *Story of a Rivertown*, 17.
19. Rita Paschal Wooley, *Sketches of Life in Little Rock, 1836-1850* (Little Rock: Arkansas Commemorative Commission, 1981), 10.
20. Richards, *Story of a Rivertown*, 31.
21. Herndon, *Highlights of Arkansas History*, 64.
22. Richards, *Story of a Rivertown*, 27.
23. George Dodge, and P. C. Dooley, *A Digest of the Laws and Ordinances of the City of Little Rock* (Little Rock: Republican Steam Press, 1871), 261.
24. *Ibid.*
25. *Ibid.*
26. *Ibid.*
27. Ross, *Arkansas Gazette: The Early Years*, 305.
28. Rose, Chester Ashley, 65-70: *U.S. Decennial Census, 1860*, Arkansas.
29. Quapaw Quarter Association, *Quapaw Quarter: A Guide to Little Rock's 19th Century Neighborhoods* (Little Rock: Quapaw Quarter Association, 1976), 1ff.
30. *Arkansas Gazette*, January 10, 1843.
31. Herndon, *Highlights of Arkansas History*, 57-58.
32. Richards, *Story of a Rivertown*, 38.
33. *Ibid.*
34. *Ibid.*, 31.

Church built
Westside Scott St between 3[...]

CHAPTER III

The first outward sign that most Little Rockians had about the approaching Civil War came two weeks after the 1860 presidential election. On a brisk November day a contingent of sixty-five troops from the U.S. Army's Second Artillery Unit disembarked from a steamboat docked at the public wharf and marched the ten blocks to occupy the Little Rock Arsenal. Federal troops returning to a facility largely abandoned after the Mexican War caused some Little Rock residents concern. That the troops were commanded by Captain James Totten who had grown up in Little Rock, the son of William Totten, one of the city's most prominent physicians, was of small consolation. For the next several weeks, rumors swept the city that re-inforcements were coming, and citizens anxiously awaited each arriving steamboat to verify the reports. No additional troops came, but news about the arsenal, carried by a growing network of telegraph lines, spread through the state and prompted anti-union rallies in several communities. At Helena, citizens prepared a petition demanding that Governor Henry Rector seize control of the facility and promised five hundred volunteers to assist him in doing so. The new mood was clearly evident in a new editorial tone in Little Rock newspapers. From a moderate, "wait and see" attitude before the November election, local editors began calling for city and state leaders to prepare for secession from the Union.[1]

By December, Little Rock streets began to get crowded as an increasing number of "outsiders" gathered in the capital city. In addition to the General Assembly, preparing to open its 13th regular session, a growing number of self-styled militia from the anti-Union rally in Helena and also Pine Bluff began to arrive, as did a delegation of commissioners from South Carolina and Georgia to lobby for a new government—the Confederate States of America. But despite the lobbyists, and Governor Rector's repeated calls for secession, the Arkansas lawmakers refused to act and ultimately referred the question to the people. At a special election on February 18, 1861, voters were asked to choose delegates for a convention to consider the secession issue. Ten days before the vote, Rector successfully negotiated control of the arsenal. Captain Totten, realizing his small force was no match for the self-styled militia now numbering close to one thousand men, agreed to surrender the Arsenal to Rector in return for safe passage out of the city.[2]

Voters approved the Convention, and Governor Rector called for it to convene in Little Rock on March 4. After two votes denying secession, delegates agreed to ask the citizens to decide and set the election for August 5. They also agreed to reconvene on August 19, earlier if conditions warranted, to consider the results of that anticipated election. President Abraham Lincoln's decision to call up troops in April, after the clash at Fort Sumter, caused Convention President David Walker to re-convene the Convention on May 6. Without waiting for the delegates' return, Governor Rector took matters into his own hands and sent four companies of the state militia to Fort Smith with orders to capture the federal arsenal there. The hastily assembled and drilled group left Little Rock on April 23 under the command of William Woodruff, Jr. A number of women stayed up all night making "gray jackets" for the troops to wear. However, before they could finish the men marched out of town—many without uniforms, or gray jackets. That detail mattered little, however, because the federals abandoned Fort Smith before the militia arrived. After hastily securing the fort, the troops returned to Little Rock to a heroes' welcome.[3]

The weather was described as "magnificent" on May 6, and, before noon, the House chamber was packed as Little Rock residents gathered at the State Capitol to learn the decision on secession. A committee drew up a resolution in the morning, and, by 3:00 p.m., the issue had been debated, the vote taken, and Arkansas had severed ties with the United States of America.[4]

Following the vote to secede, delegates took steps to prepare for the anticipated conflict by authorizing an "Arkansas Army," divided into eastern and western divisions, each headed by a

❖

First Christian Church in Little Rock. Organized in 1832, the congregation began the first phase of construction on its first house of worship in 1845. The clock tower was completed in 1858 and had the distinction of being the city's first public clock. As one of the larger structures in town, it was used as a hospital in the spring and summer of 1862, when casualties from the Battle of Pea Ridge were brought to Little Rock for treatment and recovery. After the war, the congregation relocated to Tenth and Louisiana Streets.

COURTESY OF THE ARKANSAS HISTORY COMMISSION.

brigadier general. One command was assigned to Fort Smith and the other to Hopewell, across the river from Memphis, Tennessee. Over the next three months, more than twenty thousand volunteers from throughout the state enlisted in one of the two commands. Little Rock was all but a ghost town. In July, after the convention had adjourned and turned over day-to-day administration of the war effort to a three-member military board, an unnamed individual reported that he stood at the corner of Markham and Main Streets and saw "no one walking in any direction for seventeen minutes."[5]

Little Rock's leaders were not overly concerned about defending the city, at least early in the war. Skirted on three sides by slave states, the city was remote from strategic targets, and the Arkansas River's unreliability would no doubt keep any serious attack away. If danger did come, most thought it would come from Indian Territory, and, should that happen, it would be crucial to have the Little Rock to Memphis Railroad in operation. However, beyond expanding the "railyard" across the river in Huntersville, there was little the city could do to prepare an escape route because the state lacked the resources to complete construction on the LRMRR. The section between the White and St. Francis Rivers was still not built. In the early months after the secession vote, when most of the "menfolk" rushed off to war, Little Rock women formed a

"Soldier's Aid Society" and turned their attention to providing support. Volunteers met almost daily at many of the local churches to prepare first aid supplies for the anticipated injuries, others converted the town theatre into a "cloth factory," and some prepared "care packages" to send to troops at the encampments on the eastern and western fronts.[6]

The first direct experience most Little Rockians had of the war came in March 1862 after the Battle of Pea Ridge. As one of the largest battles west of the Mississippi River, the fighting generated a significant number of casualties. Confederate forces alone had over two thousand killed or wounded. Little Rock was the only place in the state to offer even the possibility of caring for that many injured. The first victims were brought to St. John's College, and, when its rooms were filled, doctors and nurses turned to Christ Episcopal Church, but even that was not enough. By early April every public building, church, and many private homes had been pressed into service. At one point more than thirty facilities, housing more than one thousand patients, were in use. To add to the discomfort of all, rumors circulated almost daily that federal troops were coming to attack Little Rock. The early confidence that the city's remote location would be its defense was shattered by the realities of Pea Ridge. Sentinels were posted along the Arkansas River to keep watch for federal gunboats, and the mental

stress of anticipating more conflict weighed on all involved. One physician observed that such anxiety was no doubt a factor in some of the injured dying—the death rate reached as many as eighteen per day at the peak of the convalescent period. In response to the rising death toll, the City Council purchased "a plot of land from William Woodruff on the southeast border of the city" for a cemetery. The heavily forested area was named Oakland, and, before the war was over, had become a burial ground for both Confederate and Union alike.[7]

In June the scare of federal attack seemed real enough that Governor Rector moved his office to Hot Springs, where he remained through the summer. The governor was incensed with Confederate officials for allowing General Earl Van Dorn to take all regular troops out of the state following Pea Ridge. In an angry letter to Confederate headquarters in Richmond, Virginia, Rector threatened that Arkansas may "build a new ark and seek its own safety." CSA officials responded by sending the steamboat *Ponchartrain* and a crew of sixty sailors to protect Little Rock. However, when federal troops moved to capture Vicksburg, Mississippi, the *Ponchartrain* was ordered to Arkansas Post in January 1863, to defend that installation. The boat came under heavy fire from federal gunboats and ultimately surrendered, but not before two of its three eight-inch guns were removed to prevent

them from becoming federal contraband. One of those guns was brought back to Little Rock and placed just downstream from the State House to protect the city.[8]

The military uncertainty, coupled with the hospital/morgue atmosphere that pervaded the city, all but destroyed social conventions in the summer of 1862. Women, old men, children, and African Americans of all ages and both genders were about all that were left to populate the town. The status of African Americans became increasingly confused. Even before the Emancipation Proclamation,

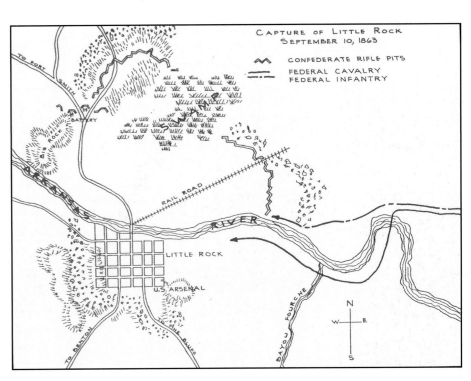

many slaves left their masters and moved around town and the countryside without restraint. The City Council tried to maintain some control by establishing "a curfew on all Negroes within the city's limits," but the ordinance had little impact. Not only had the authority of the male slave master been reduced or removed; the dynamic of slave-owner relationship had been redefined by the uncertainties of war.

After the fall of Arkansas Post, a growing number of deserters, malcontents, and people displaced by the war in general began to drift into Little Rock. A number of "unattached officers" also took refuge here and, by the summer of 1863, the city was facing a housing shortage. The increasing population also created a new set of social problems. The editor of the *True Democrat* complained that "On Markham street, for two or three squares, every third house is a negro brothel." Another local editor, offended by the number of idle former military personnel commented, "It would be a difficult matter for any place, to try to compete with Little Rock in Generals [and] it would be a capital idea to raise a few Regiments of Captains...."[9]

In addition to social concerns, by the summer of 1863, economic problems had also become a major concern. The Union blockade of the Confederate coastline cut off a number of crucial supplies, and prices for the most common goods rapidly inflated. Flour sold in Little Rock for $200 a barrel, leather boots cost $160 a pair, and tea, when it could be found, was $10 per pound. Some goods were not available at any price, and residents had to turn to substitutes. Coffee, one of the most

desired commodities, was most commonly replaced with dried sweet potatoes, ground in a spice mill. As a form of comic relief, one local newspaper ran a column advertising "...beans, soap, turnips, starch, and bacon...not that they are now to be obtained, but to prevent the people from forgetting that such articles theretofore existed."[10]

In late summer 1863, persistent rumors of a federal attack on the city finally turned into reality. In August, Frederick Steele, commander of Union forces at Helena, received orders to capture Little Rock. The city had been made vulnerable in March when Confederate officials decided to re-locate the headquarters of the Trans-Mississippi Department from Little Rock to Shreveport, Louisiana. Steele began his move toward Little Rock on August 17 with fifteen thousand troops. About the same time, General Kirby Smith, appointed in July to head the Confederate Trans-Mississippi Department, arrived in Little Rock to prepare the town's defenses. Using young boys, old men, and a number of slaves, Kirby supervised the digging of a series of rifle pits on the eastern slope of Big Rock Mountain and building a network of breastwork closer to the ferry crossing at the little rock. He also positioned the *Ponchartrain*'s cannon on the south bank of the river to guard the crossing. But with fewer than eight thousand troops, regular and militia units combined, the Confederates offered only minimal defense of the city.[11]

By the last week in August, Steele's forces were on the outskirts of Little Rock. Residents could hear the noise of battle as cavalry units and picket lines skirmished between today's Jacksonville and Rose City. Steele, his troop strength reduced to some twelve thousand, chose not to challenge the defenders in a frontal assault. Instead, he divided his forces into two groups and sent the main body some five miles down stream to cross the river near where the Little Rock Airport is today. With the first column safely across the river, Steele then moved the second group into position to challenge the Confederates' front. However, the much anticipated "Battle of Little Rock" never developed. Rebel leaders, after seeing that they had been outflanked, decided to retreat before Steele's first column could cut off their escape route. Steele, saying he needed to save ammunition, did not pursue. Instead, he entered Little Rock unchallenged late in the afternoon of September 10. A delegation led by Mayor William Ashley and including former newspaper rivals Charles Bertrand and William Woodruff, met with Steele to formally surrender the city and acknowledge Union occupation.[12]

The federal presence revived the city's sagging spirit. Steele placed the city under martial law, and army units occupied the public buildings and the largest private homes as well. Such actions initially angered the townspeople. However, their discontent dissipated when the payroll for twelve thousand troops began finding its way into the local economy. Steele also ordered work crews to build facilities to accommodate the army's multiple needs and to police the town to insure that order and sanitation for a typical army camp was maintained. The town's appearance began to change in a matter of weeks. With the river reopened, steamboats resumed near-normal traffic and the Little Rock and Memphis Railroad was opened to the White River two weeks after the occupation. While military needs had priority, city merchants were also able to get badly needed supplies again. Army construction crews built a number of warehouses near the wharf on Commerce Street and added a fifty-bed hospital unit at St. Johns College. New sanitation procedures also became evident. As previously noted, the City Council had never been very effective in persuading residents to recognize the public

health problems that came with poor garbage disposal. And two years of makeshift operations and uncertainty caused by the war had only added to the problem. But now soldiers modeled the procedures needed for a "healthy camp," and Steele's provost marshal, after first ordering that streets and sidewalks be repaired, placed a notice in the *Arkansas Gazette* that:

> The owners and occupants of all houses and lots of Little Rock will forthwith cause their respective premises to be thoroughly policed; collecting and removing therefrom all filth and garbage, and throwing the same into the river below the steamboat landing.[13]

Steele's conciliatory policy also greatly improved the social atmosphere in town. While order and control were still the prevailing words of the day, by November fraternal orders were again meeting, the

theatre performances were playing to packed houses, and no less than four newspapers were back in circulation.

Little Rock also began to undergo new demographic changes. The former "un-attached" Confederates melted away to be replaced by a growing number of "agents" representing Northern business interests and suppliers for the federal army. A growing number of "Freedmen" also made their way to Little Rock. By the spring of 1864, more than two thousand African Americans were in and around the city, most of whom were destitute. General Steele designated a tract of land on the east side of town near the site where his troops had crossed the river and another place on the southwest side of town, beyond Mount Holly Cemetery, for the Freedmen to settle. On these "home farms" individuals were given a garden plot and allowed to build shelter of their own choosing. Others improvised on their own, including a group who founded "Blissville," a collection of crudely built structures just west of the Statehouse.[14]

Toleration was not a universally favored policy in the Union army, and, by the summer of 1864, Steele was facing mounting criticism for his work in Little Rock. His second in command, General J. W. Davidson, wrote a letter to a Missouri newspaper complaining of low morale among the officers and troops because of Steele's lenient treatment of Confederates. Newspaper editors and some political leaders added their complaints and asked that he be removed from command. To add to his difficulties, Steele had made some key mistakes that did not help his cause. His "banishing" the venerable William Woodruff from the city for not being loyal enough to the Union, his execution of teenage spy David O. Dodd, and the near disastrous Red River Campaign in the spring of 1864 were enough for his critics to win. Steele was reassigned to California.[15]

General J. J. Reynolds, who replaced Frederick Steele, was also a moderate, but four years of war had taken a toll, and he faced a new set of circumstances. Guerrilla activity from both Union and Confederate units destroyed or confiscated most of the food supplies for miles around Little Rock. Civilians, white and black, destitute and with nowhere

else to turn, made their way to Little Rock, and the number of deserters from the Confederate army continued to grow. Reynolds spent much of his time in "relief work," but there were not enough resources to go around. The nationally funded Freedman's Bureau began operation in the summer of 1865. It provided limited support but was often a wedge between black and white citizens. The early gains under federal occupation also began to slip away. As one resident remembered the last year of the war: "Fences were broken and prostrate—trees were broken and peeled—sidewalks were torn up and worn out—grogshops and gambling houses, and worse, lined the ways ... the streets were full of swaggering soldiers and more swaggering women."[16] In some respects the atmosphere was similar to the first year under Confederate rule—with a different clientele. News that Richmond had been captured was greeted with relief and some excitement as residents realized that the end of the war was near. The editor of a local newspaper observed the change in attitude and wrote: "It was agreed by common consent that it [fall of Richmond] should be a jubilee...not a difficulty was

known, or angry word heard.... All were merry with thankfulness that the great Babylon of rebellion had fallen."[17]

While it still took several weeks for the war to wind down in the west, the end was in sight. Politicians now took over from the military leaders—at least partially. Even though Kirby Smith officially surrendered Confederate claims to Arkansas and the Trans-Mississippi Department on May 26, 1865, General Reynolds kept the town under

martial law and supervised state and city officials until municipal government was restored in Little Rock on January 1, 1866. Elections for the City Council were held that day, and just over six hundred voters elected Dr. J. J. McAlmont, mayor, along with eight aldermen, two justices of the peace, a city recorder, and a constable.[18]

For a brief two years Little Rock had a degree of self-government. However, in March 1867, the U.S. Congress enacted the "First Reconstruction Act," which returned military rule to former Confederate states. Arkansas and Little Rock were placed under the command of General Edward C. Ord, and, while most of the focus was on state government, Little Rock felt the impact of this new central authority when city elections were canceled in 1868, and General Ord appointed eight new council members—four white, four black. The new Council served while a new voter registration system was put into place. The new procedures registered 823 whites and 1,319 blacks and set a pattern of integrated city government for the next twenty years. When new elections were held in 1869, a different set of leaders emerged to govern the city. Old line Democrats could only produce 310 votes, while a coalition between blacks and newly enfranchised Republicans polled over 1,000 votes. Democrats complained about the results, as one noted: "Boys voted, non-residents voted, the same parties voted repeatedly, the law was disregarded, and there is conclusive evidence of attempted ballot-box stuffing of the grossest character." Even so, the results stood, and the "old" residents were replaced by a group of

immigrants, most new to the city and many who came from out of state. As one of its first actions, the Council established a free public education system and voted to increase the tax rate to support the schools. They also re-named the east-west running streets from trees to numerals beginning with Second Street (formerly Cherry Street). The changes went into effect in 1870.[19]

The new Council presided over a very different city than did its predecessors. Most noticeable was the increase in the black population. In 1860 the city's 853 black residents represented 23 percent of the 3,727 population; however, ten years later, blacks made up 43 percent (5,274) of the city's 12,380 residents. There were also significant influences from Irish and German settlers—not so much in numbers as in cultural distinctiveness. Both groups established Catholic churches, and the Germans were diverse enough to have a Lutheran Church as well. While the Irish soon merged into the Anglo society, the Germans maintained an identity east of Cumberland Street between the river and arsenal grounds. For almost a quarter century, they maintained a German language newspaper, a German National Bank, and a scattering of beer gardens that were favorites of all the city's residents.[20]

The dramatic increase in population reflected the dynamic changes throughout the city. After a brief lull in 1866, construction boomed after the infusion of northern capital. The city's three brick yards ran at full capacity to meet building demands. In May 1869, a visitor observed that there were 100 buildings, 25 of them brick, then under construction; they joined 70 others that had been built "since the fall." The peak years of growth came in 1871 and 1872, when twelve hundred new houses were added to the landscape. Financing the construction was aided by a group of northern capitalists who formed a building association to provide low interest loans, and the chartering of three additional banks to join the German Bank previously mentioned.[21]

New developments, particularly residential housing, continued to expand south away from the river between Main and Rock Streets. Expansion to the west was limited by the

"town branch" and to the east by a mosquito-infested marshy area that served as a catch basin for Fourche Creek. This compact settlement pattern caused the commercial and residential districts to overlap, and there was limited class distinction in housing patterns. Few residents could afford to purchase, nor did they have the space to maintain, a horse and carriage, and Little Rock was of necessity a "walking city."[22]

Little Rock's composition was perhaps best illustrated in the city's first directory, published in 1871. In addition to individuals being listed by street address, occupation, and race, the directory also listed schools, churches, and business establishments. A close check of school addresses illustrates how the city was integrated. For example, there were three "white" schools: Sherman (Seventh and Sherman Streets), Peabody (Gaines and Fourth and Fifth Streets), and Kramer (Second between Bird and McLean Streets); and four "colored" schools: Union (Sixth between Gaines and State Streets), Howard (Broadway between Ninth and Tenth), Battery (Second between Bird and McLean Streets), and Capitol Hill (Wolfe between Tenth and Eleventh Streets).[23]

Railroads also played an important part in the Little Rock's postwar boom. The Memphis and Little Rock Railroad Company finally completed its missing link between the White

and St. Francis Rivers in 1869, giving merchants their first viable alternative to the steamboat since the city was founded. By 1870, the Little Rock segment of the Little Rock and Fort Smith Railroad had been completed, while the Cairo and Fulton Railroad Company, following the old Southwest Trail from St. Louis, reached the north bank of the Arkansas opposite Little Rock in 1872. The Choctaw and Oklahoma Railroad Company south of the river, coming from Indian Territory, added to the congestion of freight and passengers at the

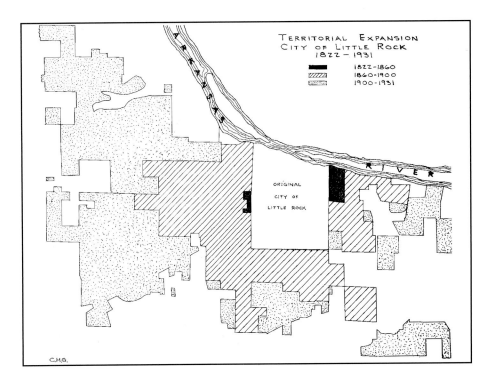

river's edge. For a time the railroad companies cooperated to run a steam ferry, the *Nellie Thomas*, across the river from two locations. One originated at the foot of Arch Street and the other from Broadway Street. Railroad workers considered unloading and reloading freight and passengers on either side of the river inefficient and inconvenient. However, inconvenience turned to economic liability in 1872 when the Cairo and Fulton Company lost a switch engine and two box cars after a sudden shift in the ferry's load caused the equipment to tumble into the river. Officials began pursuing plans to build a bridge across the river in earnest.[24]

Railroad owners were not alone in wanting a bridge across the Arkansas River. Since 1867 the state of Arkansas and city council members in Little Rock had agreed to charter companies to build such a bridge. Several investments groups were granted license, and Little Rock citizens approved a bond issue of $200,000 to assist in building a bridge. When none of the companies would act, Cairo and Fulton officials bought the charter, signed a contract with the American Bridge Company of Chicago, Illinois and began seeking additional investors to build a bridge. A British firm, Baring and Company, agreed to help finance the costs and purchased the charter from the Cairo and Fulton while agreeing that the railroad would be the principal user. With charter in hand, Baring formed a subsidiary, the Baring Cross Bridge Company, and subcontracted with the American Bridge Company to do the structural work.[25]

Construction began in March 1873, but less than a month later flood waters washed away the piers and form work. Work had barely resumed in May when the Department of War issued an injunction to stop the project. Citing federal law that required any inland waterway receiving public funds to be kept free of "navigational obstructions," the Department's Corps of Engineers argued that the bridge must have federal approval. Railroad and bridge officials countered by saying that state authorization was all they needed. After weeks of wrangling, the Chicago firm agreed to build according to Corps specifications, and work

OLD NAMES.	NEW NAMES.
First Street	Commerce Street
Second Street	Sherman Street
Cherry Street	Second Street
Mulberry Street	Third Street
Walnut Street	Fourth Street
Orange Street	Fifth Street
Elizabeth Street	Sixth Street
Chestnut Street	Seventh Street
Holly Street	Eighth Street
Hazel Street	Ninth Street
Caroline Street	Tenth Street
Sevier Street	Eleventh Street
Fulton Street	Twelfth Street
Arsenal Street	Thirteenth Street
Watkins Street	Fourteenth Street
Woodruff Street	Fifteenth Street
Pope Street	Sixteenth Street
Russell Street	Seventeenth Street

resumed in September. Using a fifty-man crew, working three shifts a day, the American Bridge Company completed the project in three months and seven days at a cost of just under $350,000.[26]

On the afternoon of December 20, the Chicago firm turned the bridge over to the Baring Cross Bridge Company. As Little Rock townspeople gathered to watch the ceremony transferring responsibilities from construction to operations, an unidentified woman walked across the newly completed structure—thus becoming the first person to cross the Arkansas River on a bridge. Ironically, none of the local newspapers covering the event recorded her name. Two days later the Cairo and Fulton ran a test train, engine No. 20, the *Jesse Lyon*, and several freight cars over the bridge and declared it officially opened for business. A few weeks later the Baring Cross Company placed wooden planks between the rails and designated it both a "highway" and railroad bridge. The Company also established toll fees as follows:

The policemen, besides maintaining the peace and serving warrants, are expected to report defective sidewalks, unemptied garbage boxes, leaking water pipes, flooded sewers, broken pavements, and dangerous buildings. They are also to prevent fast or immoderate riding of horses; restrain the running at large of cattle, horses, swine,, sheep, and prevent the running at large of dogs; ... and see that no horse, cow, or other cattle within the city limits be permitted to wear a bell after the hour of 9 o'clock pm.

George Dodge and P.C. Dooley, <u>A Digest of the Laws and Ordinances of the City of Little Rock</u>, (1871), pp 71-73

❖

Left: A key part of Little Rock's growth extended along the River to the West. Northern investors, many associated with the new Reconstruction government, began to arrive in the city the first decade after the War. Some chose to move west and build a series of large houses along a new street appropriately named Lincoln Avenue west of the newly constructed Baring Cross Bridge. Since so many of the houses were built during the "era of good stealings" when graft and corruption ran rampant at all levels of government, thoughout the nation, local residents referred to the new development as "robbers' row."

COURTESY OF THE ARKANSAS HISTORY COMMISSION.

Locomotive Engines	$2
Loaded box cars	$2
Passenger Coaches	$2
Double teams and wagons	90 cents
Horse buggies	35 cents
Pedestrians	5 cents

Having a monopoly on the bridge traffic, at least for a while, was quite profitable. The Company earned over $300 a day during peak seasons.[27]

Ironically, success in bridging the Arkansas River coincided with a collapse in the local economy. Signs of trouble began in 1870 with an internal political dispute in the Republican Party. Beginning as a state issue, it quickly spilled over into the capital city. The conflict began over money—how it was collected and where it was spent. Office holders, commonly referred to as Regular Republicans, at both state and local levels significantly raised taxes and debt upon gaining power in 1868. For example, the Little Rock City Council raised taxes seven fold between 1868 and 1874, and the tax rate reached 45 mills by the latter year. In the same period, the city budget grew to $125,000 annually—compared to just over $10,000 in 1865. The city's indebtedness exceeded $400,000. Outsiders charged office holders with fraud and corruption in the wake of high taxes and expenditures.[28]

At the state level, the outsiders were known as Liberal Republicans, and the split in the Party that first appeared in 1870 spilled into open revolt in 1872. The Liberal challenge, led by Joseph Brooks, was rebuffed at the ballot box by the Regulars, led by Elisha Baxter, who controlled the election personnel. Brooks challenged the election results in court after initially being denied. Eighteen months later he was awarded a court order making him governor. For almost a month in April and May 1874, the state and Little Rock resembled two armed camps as supporters of each governor took up arms. After Brooks took over the governor's office, Baxter

Below: The McDonald-Wait-Newton House, c. 1872. The house was representative of the new structures along Lincoln Avenue. The house was built in 1870-71 by Pennsylvania born Alexander McDonald, who moved to Little Rock in 1868 to invest in banking. In the twentieth century the structure was commonly referred to as the "Packet House" in reference to Packet Boats that traveled along the Arkansas River.

COURTESY OF HARRY WORLEY.

established his office at the Anthony House Hotel, and the three-block strip of Markham Street between the two buildings became a war zone as militia units faced each other. For about three weeks violence flared throughout the state and over two hundred individuals were killed in this "Brooks-Baxter War." Both sides appealed to the federal government for assistance, and, after first sending regular army troops to take up positions between the two groups, President U.S. Grant asked Attorney General William Butler to review the case. Butler ruled in favor of Baxter, and President Grant ordered the two groups to disband. Faced with an attorney general's opinion, supporters of both men reluctantly complied with the order. The streets of Little Rock were again quiet.[29]

The rift between Regular and Liberal Republicans could not be mended in the short term, and Democrats, who had largely stayed out of politics since 1868, now returned in force. Governor Baxter, recognizing the new dynamic, responded to the Democrats' call for a new constitutional convention. The new document, which was drafted and approved in the summer of 1874, returned the Democrats to power and reduced Republican influence to almost nothing. It also led to a new government in Little Rock. The old Councilmen were replaced by a new group of "Redeemer Democrats" who pledged to redeem the city from its debt and the charges of fraud and corruption. A new era in city life had begun.

CHAPTER III ENDNOTES

1. Ira Don Richards, *Story of a Rivertown: Little Rock in the Nineteenth Century* (Benton: Privately Printed, 1969), 58-63; Margaret Ross, *Arkansas Gazette: The Early Years, 1819-1866* (Little Rock: Arkansas Gazette Foundation, 1969), 357-60; John Gould Fletcher, Arkansas (Chapel Hill: University of North Carolina Press, 1947), 144-147; Tom DeBlack, *With Fire and Sword: Arkansas in Civil War and Reconstruction, 1861-1874* (Fayetteville: University of Arkansas Press, 2003), 18-22 and Carl Moneyhon and Bobby Roberts, *Portraits of Conflict: A Photographic History of the Civil War in Arkansas* (Fayetteville: University of Arkansas Press, 1987), 120-125.
2. DeBlack, *With Fire and Sword*, 22-24.
3. Fletcher, *Arkansas*, 147-48.
4. Ross, *Arkansas Gazette*, 356.
5. Fletcher, *Arkansas*, 149.
6. *Ibid.*, 63-65.
7. *Ibid.*
8. Fletcher, *Arkansas*, 156.
9. Richards, *Story of a Rivertown*, 65-67.
10. *Ibid.*, 67.
11. DeBlack, *With Fire and Sword*, 96-99.
12. *Ibid.*, and Fletcher, *Arkansas*, 178-79.
13. *Arkansas Gazette*, May 13, 1865.
14. Richards, *Story of a Rivertown*, 67-68.
15. DeBlack, *With Fire and Sword*, 114-15 and Ross, *Arkansas Gazette*, 388-89.
16. Richards, *Story of a Rivertown*, 78.
17. *Ibid.*, 79.
18. Ross, *Arkansas Gazette*, 400.
19. Richards, *Story of a Rivertown*, 86.
20. *Ibid.*
21. *Ibid.*, 81.
22. Margaret Ross, *The Building of the Quapaw Quarter: Guide to Little Rock's Nineteenth Century Neighborhoods* (Little Rock: Quapaw Quarter Association, 1976), 3-4.
23. City Directory, 1871.
24. Bryan D. McDade, "The Six Bridges at Little Rock: Understanding the Historical Significance and Relevance of the Six Bridges that Span the Arkansas River at Little Rock," unpublished master's thesis, University of Arkansas at Little Rock, 2000, pp 48-53.
25. *Ibid.*
26. *Ibid.*
27. *Ibid.*
28. Richards, *Story of a Rivertown*, 89-90.
29. DeBlack, *With Fire and Sword*, 216-23.

MAIN ST. NORTH FROM FIFTH ST.

CHAPTER IV

THE CITY OF ROSES:
LITTLE ROCK IN THE NEW SOUTH, 1874-1916

The optimism that accompanied the new political regime in 1874 did not extend to the economy. Conservative Democrats, calling themselves "Redeemers," moved to refocus the Republican agenda of the previous decade. Rather than the liberal spending policies of the "radicals," Redeemers at city hall drastically cut expenditures. Nowhere was the change in philosophy better illustrated than in public works. In their last year in office, the "Reconstruction" city council budgeted $38,578 for street construction and maintenance, but the new council cut spending in that area to $437 its first year in office. The latter figure was less than that spent on the street department in 1860. The public school system, created in 1868, and enrolling more than 1,000 students with 80 teachers and principals in its second year of operation, was reduced to fewer than 30 teachers a decade later, even though enrollment had more than doubled. The Redeemers' stringency, coupled with a national depression that lasted for over five years (1873-1878), brought "hard times" to the capital city.[1]

Fear of yellow fever and cholera epidemics added to the "gloom" of the mid- and late 1870s. The first signs of trouble came in 1873, when a "yellowjack" epidemic broke out in Memphis. When news about the outbreak reached Little Rock in early September, a hastily organized city Board of Health began plans to quarantine travelers coming from the east. However, while they were discussing plans for implementation, others among the city's leadership expressed concern about the economic impact travel restrictions might have on the city's merchants. It was early October before the Board imposed a "partial" ban on traffic from Memphis. Fortunately an early frost greatly reduced the mosquito population, and Little Rock only recorded 13 cases of yellow fever that year.[2]

In 1878 a "yellowjack" scare again spread through the city. Memphis was again the origin for concern in Little Rock. The first case was reported on August 13, and ,three days later, the local Board of Health organized for action. This time there was no debate as health officials seized full control. After setting up a five-mile perimeter around the city, they sent agents to Hopefield on the west bank of the Mississippi River opposite Memphis with orders to stop all traffic by boat or rail leaving Memphis for Little Rock. Similar action was taken at the mouth of the Arkansas River to intercept boats coming up from New Orleans. Traffic coming from St. Louis, Missouri, was also screened, and no one was allowed to enter Little Rock from points east unless he or she could document they had not been in an infected area for at least the past forty days. One train already inbound from Memphis when the orders went into effect was stopped in Forrest City, and more than 100 passengers were stranded. The quarantine was kept in place for 74 days and not lifted until October 28. Health officials were frequently criticized for their "autocratic methods," but the city again escaped a major epidemic. Memphis reported over 17,000 cases and 5,000 deaths but Little Rock did not have a single case. The ironclad policy was not without economic side effects, however, and city merchants all but exhausted their inventories during the two-and-a-half month embargo, and smaller towns along the Arkansas River and the Memphis and Little Rock Railroad suffered even more.[3]

The end of the decade brought with it an end to yellow fever scares and an easing of the economic depression as well. In 1879, the city's Board of Health prepared early for an epidemic and issued an order in July to screen traffic from Memphis. However, Memphis did not report any cases, and Little Rock avoided the disease as well. A combination of immunity and improved public health practices kept the lower Mississippi River Valley free from epidemic diseases for the balance of the century. By 1880 a restructured railroad industry that eliminated all-out competition in favor of regional dominance, and market share allowed a limited number of companies to jumpstart the economy

✧

Chartered in 1886, the electric company quickly lured customers from the gas company, which had begun offering service in 1860. The first street lights were installed in 1886utiliIng four 125-foot towers, and, by the turn of the century, most of the principal business district had electrical service.

COURTESY OF THE ARKANSAS HISTORY COMMISSION.

again. The railroads operating through Little Rock came under the control of financier Jay Gould, based in St. Louis.

The 1880s saw the river city return to prosperity and brought a new surge in population. The decade began with a visit from former President Ulysses S. Grant. Arkansans in general and Little Rockians in particular had developed a new appreciation for the former Commander of the Union forces

since his intervention in the Brooks-Baxter War. With the Civil War now fifteen years in the past, most area citizens were willing to forgive and move on. The city's merchants were anxious for the potential business such a visit would bring, and Grant's arrival on April 14, 1880, did not disappoint. Newspaper sources estimated that between 15,000 and 20,000 turned out (the 1880 census listed Little Rock's population as 21,280) to see and hear the President address the group at "Ringo Square" and watch a parade that followed. Grant then held a two hour reception and concluded the evening with a dinner for 250 invited guests at the Concordia Hotel.[4]

The last twenty years of the nineteenth century also saw Little Rock experience a growth spurt similar to that during the decade following the Civil War. The changes were evident in both buildings and aesthetics. An increasing number of the city's more affluent residents made special efforts to landscape their yards with a variety of flowers and shrubs. Union soldiers had frequently commented on the number of variety of flowers, as did northern journalists who visited in the post-war period. Local residents took particular pride in growing roses, and, a decade after the war, the city had earned the sobriquet "City of Roses."[5]

As the city physically expanded and its population more than doubled, transportation became an increasing priority. As was true of most cities in the late nineteenth century, most people did not own horses or carriages for personal transportation and walked to all their destinations. Obviously distance became an increasing problem, and the city council began to spend more time on improving the public transportation system. As previously noted, street construction and improvements were major expenditures beginning in 1870, when the council authorized the Little Rock Street

Rail Company to construct the first "railway" in the city. Street cars were added on Main Street in 1877, and a mile of track was laid down from Main to Glenwood Park at Seventeenth Street. Known to locals as the "South Main Line," the street car proved immensely popular. Cars, called "bob tails" because of their short, squat appearance, pulled by mules ran on an "as needed" schedule. Their popularity led the rail company to expand service in the early 1880s down Rock Street to the city's largest residential district south of Ninth Street, and west along Markham beyond Broadway. The Markham route required the company to build a "magnificent wooden trestle" to cross a deep ravine between Broadway and the river, near where Robinson Auditorium is today. The line was profitable from the beginning, and, in 1888, the company began replacing the bob tails with new cars. A writer for the *Arkansas Gazette* commented on the changes and noted:

Yesterday two or three elegant new street cars were placed on the Little Rock Street Railroad. They are nice looking cars much handsomer and more commodious than the others, but the prettiest part about them is they are built by the company right

Main Street business buildings began to change in the late nineteenth century. The First National Bank was representative of those changes. Although not of the "skyscraper" variety seen in the larger cities, these multiple story buildings made of brick and concrete construction largely replaced the wood structures of the pre-Civil War era and greatly expanded the square footage open to retail.

here in Little Rock. Everybody should feel proud of such nice work being done right here at home.[6]

That same year, a new company, the City Electric Railway Company, introduced a rail system that used steam engines to power the cars. Quickly dubbed the "dummy line" because the cars were built to look like those used by the railroads, the steam engines could be heard all over town and became an increasing annoyance after the novelty wore off. These heavy cars also required new construction techniques for the roadbed, and the company used granite rock quarried from Granite Mountain south of town in the construction.[7]

The noise factor from the steam trolley began to be solved in 1891, when City Electric Railway added electric powered cars to their lines. Electric service was first introduced in 1886, when power lines were hung from poles placed along Markham and Main Streets. Within two years electric lights began replacing gas street lights when the city council authorized four "light towers 125 feet high with five lights at the top" to be placed in the Markham-Main corridor. Over the next decade shorter "electric light poles" were added throughout the business district to replace the gas system that had been in place since the Civil War. The Electric Railway Company used this expanded electric network to increase its service, and, by the time company officials were ready to launch the new electric rail car, the city had more than twenty miles of electric wires in place. Called a "magnificent rapid transit" service, the new rail system operated with 28 new cars painted bright yellow, illuminated inside with electric lights, at a cost of $3,300 each.[8]

While city officials were concentrating on providing transportation to area residents, railroad officials were exploring additional ways to bridge the Arkansas River. A breakthrough came in 1883 when representatives from the Little Rock and Fort Smith and the Little Rock, Mississippi River, and Texas Railroad companies met to discuss an alternative to the Baring Cross Bridge. Although the St. Louis and Iron Mountain company had been accommodating in allowing other trains to use their bridge, the growing volume of traffic and a desire to avoid paying fees to a competing firm prompted interest in a new bridge. Officials of the two companies signed an agreement on December 8 to form the Little Rock Junction Railway and Bridge Company and selected a site on the Arkansas River at the historic little rock to build a new bridge.[9]

After a brief delay while seeking approval from the Department of War to build another structure over a "navigable river," officials began construction in March 1884. To securely anchor the footing on the south bank, engineers removed a large section of the little rock and sank concrete piers at its base in the river channel. The city's most historic site was all but eliminated by this construction. Work was completed on December 8, a year to the day that the plans were first formulated. As with the Baring Cross Bridge, railroad officials laid wooden planks between the rails and made it a toll bridge for pedestrian traffic. Complaints from farmers claiming the tolls were excessive prompted Little Rock and Pulaski County officials to build a "Free Bridge" just upstream from the Junction Bridge in 1897. This hastily constructed structure ran from the foot of Main Street to Maple Street on the north side of the river and also serviced military personnel from Fort Roots. However it could not withstand the heavy volume of traffic and was closed in 1917, when city leaders could not guarantee the bridge's safety. It was replaced by the Main Street and Broadway bridges to be discussed later.[10]

By the turn of the century, Little Rock's transportation systems were a major asset in the city's growth. Street cars, initially introduced in response to rapid population growth, now became a key factor in expanding the city's territorial growth. Up to that point most of Little Rock's "fashionable" residences were close to the center of town, and neighborhoods generally deteriorated the farther one moved away from Markham and Main Streets. The City Council repeatedly passed ordinances to protect the "inner city" but paid less attention to the periphery, and, as a result, the city became encircled with slaughterhouses, brothels, foundries, and other types of less desirable enterprises.

Improved transportation now made it possible for the "fashion and socially conscious" individuals to move out of the city, with its race and class integrated neighborhoods, to new locations beyond the periphery. That there were those desiring to "get away from the city" became increasingly apparent after the state adopted "Jim Crow" laws in the early 1890s. Ironically, prior to the segregation laws, Little Rock had a national reputation for racial toleration and was a magnet for some of the South's most successful African-American business and professional men.

The Electric Railway Company's construction techniques in building the wooden trestle across the ravine between Broadway and the river attracted attention from other construction teams. In 1903, city leaders decided to build a similar structure over a much deeper ravine that had stopped Third Street's extension just west of the new state capitol building then under construction. The project was complicated in that it had to span the Iron Mountain and Choctaw Railroad tracks and required cooperation from railroad officials. But, expanding settlement in the area around Union Depot and the area near the new state capitol construction on Capitol Hill, along with lobbying from a group of real estate developers, pushed the City Council to act.

The developers were key players in the decision. In 1891 a group of investors, led by Michigan businessman Henry Franklin Auten, purchased eight hundred acres west of the Third Street ravine and began plans to develop a residential area outside the city limits. Auten called the area Pulaski Heights and organized the Pulaski Heights Land Company to promote sales and settlement. The company sold its first lot in 1892, but a decade later only eight families had moved into the subdivision. Efforts at promotion had been largely unsuccessful due to the distance and inconvenience of commuting to Little Rock. Completing the Third Street viaduct changed all that. The Electric Railway Company quickly extended streetcar service to the area, and, in 1905, the new development incorporated, as the city of Pulaski Heights with a population of 683.[11]

Success of the Heights developers caused members of the Little Rock City Council to re-think the city's growth plan. Since 1890, when the Council annexed the Huntersville area on the north side of the Arkansas River and made it the "eighth ward," growth had been north-south perpendicular to the river. Annexing such a large area to the west would not only change the city's "footprint" but strain its ability to deliver resources. A move by developers north

✧

Little Rock created its first publicly funded school system in 1868, and interest in education grew rapidly in the late nineteenth century. The city's first high school, named in honor of Civil War general William Tecumseh Sherman, (above) burned in the 1880s and was replaced, along with the name, by a more substantial building (below) now designated Little Rock High.

of the River to reorganize the various communities there gave Little Rock an opportunity to restructure. When Argenta voters agreed in 1904 to take the lead in forming an independent city, eventually to become North Little Rock, the Little Rock City Council decided to concentrate its attention south of the river and specifically began to look at Pulaski Heights. The annexation did not come until 1916 when the "Heights" became the city's Ninth Ward. However, with an increasing number of Little Rock's business and professional class moving into the area in the decade before the First World War, the identities of the two areas were merged long before the formal union.[12]

In the decade before the First World War, Little Rock changed rapidly. The new look was best expressed in the growing number of automobiles. The entire state of Arkansas did not register one hundred automobiles until 1907. However, five years later, Little Rock alone had over three hundred vehicles, and traffic control became a necessity. After adopting its first traffic ordinance in 1911 to control speed, turns, and parking, city councilmen discovered that issues involving automobiles were never ending problems. The volume of pedestrian and vehicular traffic prompted council members to have stop signs

installed at the city's three busiest intersections, Main and Markham, Main and Capitol, and Fifteenth and High Streets. Motorists were required to "come to a full stop" and, reminiscent of the steam trolley days, the council moved to control noise by prohibiting "muffler cut outs" on the automobiles.

Regulation increasingly became the norm for the decade and a half before the First World War. Responding to national trends for "progressive reforms," the City Council extended the Board of Health's responsibilities to inspect meat, milk, ice cream, fruits and vegetables sold to the public and to provide more control over garbage disposal. Concern in these areas was sparked by a growing fear of typhoid, a new endemic disease that had replaced yellow fever as the new public health problem. By 1911 the fear had become so great that city officials asked Governor George Donaghey to seek help from the U. S. Surgeon General's office. At the governor's request, federal officials sent Assistant Surgeon General Dr. W. H. Frost to investigate conditions in Little Rock.[13]

While waiting for Frost to finish his investigation, newly elected Mayor Charles E. Taylor led the Council to establish the city's first garbage collection service. A $10,000 appropriation provided funding to build a stable and buy the mules and wagons necessary to collect the garbage. Residents were charged ten cents a can to have their garbage

✦

Above: Little Rock received its first public transportation in 1877 when the Little Rock Street Railway company completed installation of its first track. The original cars were pulled by horses and mules along steel rails before being replaced by steam and later electric cars.

COURTESY OF THE ARKANSAS HISTORY COMMISSION.

Below: By the 1890s steamboats had largely been replaced by railroads for freight and passenger service. The new "railroad era" was symbolic of other societal changes, as horses (and the need for livery stables) were gradually phased out, and new businesses, symbolized by this Arkansas Carpet and Furniture store, gained a foothold in the new industrial economy.

COURTESY OF THE ARKANSAS HISTORY COMMISSION.

removed and were prohibited from disposing it in the Arkansas River—thus ending a century-long practice. Joining with the mayor and Council in stepping up regulations, the Board of Health required all meat sold to the public to be inspected in a slaughterhouse at Seventh and Gaines Street and set up a schedule to inspect dairies, restaurants, soda fountains, bakeries, and food stores.

Frost spent more than six weeks doing his investigation. He found no central source for typhoid but recommended that city officials pay particular attention to several areas, beginning

with milk dairies, water coming from the Arkansas River, and an expanded sewer system. He also encouraged the city to expand the Board of Health into a full Department of Public Health with broad regulatory powers. The Council readily agreed with the recommendations and quickly passed ordinances to establish the new department and expand its regulatory powers.[14]

Not everyone was pleased with the City Council's new found interest in regulation. The butchers' and dairymen's associations, claiming economic hardship, jointly filed suit in the Pulaski County Chancery Court to block the new ordinances. When the lower court ruled against the associations, the butchers worked out a compromise that allowed them to have five inspection stations, rather than a central location, where inspectors would be available on specific days. The dairymen appealed to the state Supreme Court, and the higher court ruled in favor of the city. Systematic meat and milk inspections began in the fall of 1911. With those challenges behind, the new Department of Public Health extended its "inspections" to health care and general sanitary conditions as well.[15]

Improving the water and sewer systems were also critical steps in fighting typhoid fever and providing for better sanitation in the city. With the Town Branch now "walled up and covered over," and with the prohibition against dumping garbage in the Arkansas River in place, extending the capability for household and industrial waste became a priority. As a follow-up to the Frost report, specific areas of the city, such as the foul-smelling, polluted farmer's market along West Capitol Street between Louisiana and Spring Streets, became targets for special clean up. Members of city hall and a group of volunteers organized a City Beautiful Commission, moved block by block through each ward to identify and eliminate all "unsightly and unsanitary" conditions. While progress was uneven, by the end of 1911, citizens in all sections of town noticed a considerable difference in the city's appearance which offered a more suitable image for the "city of roses." At the turn of the century, the city had fewer than 60 miles of sewer lines but by World War I, the system had been extended to a 183 mile sewer network reaching

✧

Little Rock had a small African American population before the Civil War—a mixture of "urban slaves" and "free colored." However, in the last quarter of the nineteenth century, the city became a magnet to a large number of Black citizens. By the early twentieth century most of the business and professional activities had been concentrated to a few blocks along Ninth Street west of Broadway. Black males, in a segregated setting, were involved in all aspects of business and professional life. In addition to almost 100 businesses, African Americans administered and staffed two colleges (Arkansas Baptist and Philander Smith) and the national headquarters of the Mosaic Templar fraternal organization. Shown here (clockwise from top, left) are: John E. Bush, Jefferson Ish, Joseph Booker, and Mifflin W. Gibbs.

most portions of the city.[16] Perhaps most significant of all, the number of deaths attributed to typhoid declined to seven in 1912 after averaging thirty per year for the three previous years.[17]

The water system had been a source of contention since the city contracted with a private company, the Little Rock Water Works Company, in 1877 to provide water to city residents. The company pumped water directly from the Arkansas River without filtering it, and users complained frequently about the foul odor and muddy appearance. City officials canceled the contract with the company in 1879. The next year the Home Water Company was organized and awarded a contract to supply city water. Company officials agreed to build two sedimentation basins and a new pump station in an attempt to provide better service. The basins were built in Pulaski Heights at Ozark Point and the pump station was on Lincoln Avenue just west of the Baring Cross Bridge. This limited "treatment" improved the appearance and smell, but distribution continued to be a

problem. In 1889, Home Water was sold to the Arkansas Water Works, a company owned by investors in Pittsburgh and New York. The new company agreed to add a filtration system; however, during the spring and fall flood seasons, the river water was frequently so muddy even the filters failed to work satisfactorily. Just before World War I, city officials tried to buy the facilities, but company leaders put them off with a pledge to improve service by using an alternative water supply. The War interrupted plans to make the improvements. However, in 1919, the company purchased six hundred acres of land along the Arkansas River below Ozark Point and drilled a series of water wells. For the next twenty years, the company mixed well and river water in its distribution system. Not until 1936 was the city able to take over the water works and make it a public utility.[18]

Issues related to the city's water system were closely related to fire protection. Expansion caused firefighters trouble not only because it took longer to reach a site, but also because

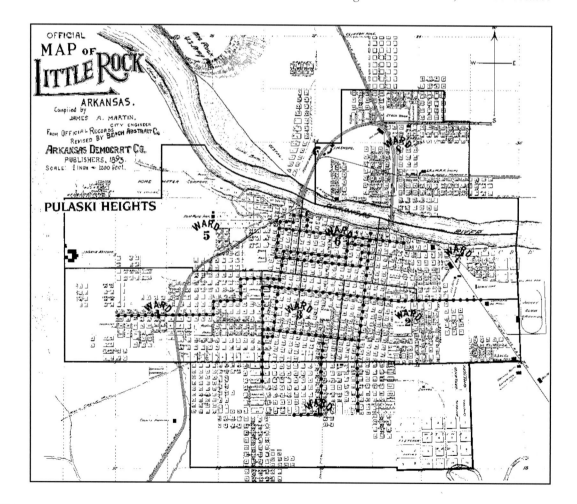

✧

A project of northern investors in the 1890s, the Pulaski Heights region got off to a slow start due to limited access and inadequate social services. However, when the Third Street Viaduct opened in 1903, settlement and services followed quickly. For a time the area functioned as an independent community before being annexed to Little Rock in 1916, shown here as Ward 5 on a city map.

COURTESY OF THE ARKANSAS HISTORY COMMISSION.

expansion typically extended beyond city services. Also, the density of people and structures that continued to increase along the waterfront in the downtown business district increased the possibility of fire. City councilmen discussed the potential for trouble at numerous city council meetings, but it took a disastrous series of fires in 1911 to push the council to act. Armed with a report from the

National Board of Fire Underwriters, which sent a team to investigate the devastating fire, the Council designated a "fire district" from the river on the north to Ninth Street on the south, and between Cumberland and Arch, east to west. Council members also committed to building a "central fire station" in the heart of the district and to purchase a "motorized, aerial, fire truck." The fire station was completed in 1913, and, by the time of the First World War, the city had added three additional stations and equipped them with motorized vehicles. These additions made Little Rock the "first fully motorized Fire Department" in the South. The ordinance established a building code requiring owners of existing structures to add more "fire proof protection" and designated strict guidelines for new construction. The law also authorized a "fire inspector" with authority to enforce the code. There was some opposition, but the threat from the Underwriters that higher rates would follow unless the new standards were adopted caused most opponents to drop their complaints.[19]

Reform and improvements in Little Rock's physical appearance and infrastructure also extended to social reform as well. Throughout its history, the city had experienced periods of unregulated vice, particularly gambling, prostitution, and illegal consumption of alcohol. In a predictable cycle, the "forces of vice" would become emboldened only to be "restrained" for a time by a "good citizens council" that worked to reclaim the streets for the "decent people." Beginning in the 1890s and continuing for almost two decades, vice claimed a strong hold on several sections of the city. Symptoms of these periods of "wide-open behaviors" were best illustrated by "drinking intoxicants" in public spaces and transporting "buckets of beer" from the neighborhood saloon to private homes. This practice was particularly popular in the eastern section of the city where former German immigrants still practiced traditional social customs. However, as the temperance movement turned increasingly to prohibition, such wide-open behavior was increasingly criticized. The prohibitionists also tied drinking

to gambling and prostitution and, by the first decade of the twentieth century had a broad based coalition to either limit or stop all three.

Advocates for reform received a major boost in 1911 when voters elected Charles E. Taylor as mayor. Taylor had campaigned on a platform to clean up the "wide-open town," and, as Sunday School superintendent of Little Rock's influential Second Baptist Church, he had an established base to push for change. Taylor addressed the alcohol issue first and led the City Council to pass an ordinance that prohibited transporting beer in open containers and made drinking "intoxicants on streets, sidewalks, or public parks" illegal. The Council also raised the annual license fee for saloons by 20 percent—from $1,000 to $1,200. [20]

Taylor also pledged strict enforcement of existing vice laws and took steps to do that by replacing the chief of police with an individual more committed to enforcement. The new mayor complained that the city's problems stemmed from police officers who "enforce the laws that suit them and wink at violation of the laws they or their friends personally do not favor." [21] The city had a long standing ordinance that prohibited "dice

games, raffles and games of chance in saloons, drug stores and cigar stands." [22]

But for more than a decade the law had been largely ignored, and "the gamblers knock—three short and one long"—typically gained one entrance to "backroom" or "upstairs" gaming activities. Taylor joined the new police chief to personally lead raids against such establishments, and, according to the local newspapers, "confiscated…wagons-loads of gambling paraphernalia" and arrested various individuals for violating city ordinances. [23] The Mayor's "get tough" policy drove the "gamblers" deeper underground and, at least in public perception, was successful in eliminating the casual attitude toward such activities.

The issue of prostitution presented a challenge to the new mayor. In his first year in office, Taylor appointed a twenty-six member, bi-racial (21 white, 5 black) Vice Commission and charged it to investigate "ways by which the evil [prostitution] may be curbed, handled or suppressed…." [24] This was a huge problem. The decades of lax enforcement had allowed a large "red light district" to develop, encompassing much of the original town site of Arkopolis. Beginning at the Arkansas River to the north, extending south to Third Street between Rock and Main Streets, there were nineteen "known houses of prostitution" and three other commonly known sites outside the district. The identified "houses" employed an estimated 75 workers with another 200 to 600 prostitutes working independently in local hotels, public parks, and assignation houses. The penalty for operating a brothel was a fine of $25 if no beer was served, $50 if beer was involved, and $3 for each prostitute. In the decades prior to Taylor's administration, police officers typically issued arrest warrants to the proprietors who ran the "houses." However, the "madams" could post bond for the amount of the fine, continue operating their brothels, and forfeit the fine for failure to appear in court. The sequence was repeated every month or so, or "as the city needed money," as some madams complained. It was variously estimated that the city received an average of $800 a month from such an arrangement. [25]

The Commission failed to identify similar practices in the predominately black

communities but did note that "pool halls and rooming houses" were suspected hangouts for prostitutes and should be regulated. With respect to the other areas, the Commission recommended that the bawdy houses be closed, that the police and courts stop their "de facto licensing prostitutes," that three new police officers be hired to specifically monitor the problems associated with vice, and that the city improve the lighting system in public parks "to end clandestine prostitution." Taylor moved to implement the recommendations even though the "loss" of revenue was significant in the city's operating budget.

The recommendation for better lighting in the city's parks focused attention on another area for social reform. In addition to the Vice Commission's report, the City Beautiful Association's recommendations, growing out of efforts to improve sanitation during the typhoid epidemic, caused many to see the need for public parks. Not only could parks improve the beauty of the landscape, but by providing opportunity for recreation, and leisure time activities they improved the quality of life as well. To promote the idea, a group of citizens organized the Little Rock Parkways Association in 1911 and invited noted landscape architect John Nolen of Cambridge, Massachusetts to develop a comprehensive plan for a city parks system. Nolan visited Little Rock in 1913 and prepared a master plan that was finally adopted by the City Council in 1916. The total cost was estimated at $500,000. This delayed implementation, but it did serve as a planning document for future growth. The Parkways Association purchased some of the sites Nolen recommended and donations by private citizens also added to the ability to expand its parks system. By the First World War the city had added West End Park, now the campus of Central High School, Southside Park at the end of High Street and three unnamed parcels, one between Fourche Bayou and Granite Mountain, now a part of Gilliam Park, a second seventy-five-acre tract along Rock Creek west of the city, and an additional forty acres just north of that tract. The land donations and purchases coupled with Nolen's planning gave Little Rock one of the most advanced park systems in the nation.[26]

The inability to acquire property to expand the parks system identified the major issue facing Little Rock before World War I—lack of funding for public works projects. The Arkansas Constitution prohibited cities from adopting bond programs, nor could they impose the power of eminent domain. In short, cities did not have home rule, and, as Little Rock expanded its boundaries, the costs of delivering police and fire protection, in addition to street and sewer improvements, brought the city under serious financial strain. This problem was well illustrated by the aging Third Street viaduct connecting Little Rock with the emerging area of Pulaski Heights. Its hasty construction in 1903, while liberating at the time, had become almost too dangerous to cross ten years later. City officials wanted to replace the wooden structure with a new concrete design that would not only be safer, but would also harmonize with the newly constructed state Capitol building. Cost was prohibitive, given the city's financial

✧

Few changes illustrated how much Little Rock had grown in the nineteenth century than construction of two new government buildings. Progressive reformers placed confidence in public policy as a way to improve the quality of life for all citizens. These two buildings, a new city hall (below) and a new state capitol (above) symbolically stood for a new era in politics and social policy. They also illustrated a transition in Little Rock's development. The new city hall was situated on Markham Street, just off the River, and symbolized the city's ties to the nineteenth century. However, when commissioners responsible for building the new state capitol selected a site miles west of downtown and away from the river, it ushered in a century-long expansion away from the river.

constraints, but delay would only add to the problem. Mayor Charles Taylor decided to resolve the issue by borrowing enough money to get the project started and then persuading the city's trolley company, Pulaski County officials, and the presidents of the St. Louis, Iron Mountain, and Southern as well as the Chicago, Rock Island & Pacific Railroads to share the remaining costs. The new viaduct was completed in 1914 and became the major avenue for the city's westward expansion.[27]

Mayor Taylor's plan of borrowing, while meeting immediate needs, also had long term consequences. Repeated attempts to amend the state constitution to allow cities to issue bonds failed and if not borrowing, the only other avenues the city had for revenue was the various user taxes, taxes generated from improvement districts, and warrants that were sometimes discounted as much as thirty percent. Even the improvement districts carried a liability. On a positive note, the districts allowed property holders to add improvements to their property by agreeing to a special tax dedicated specifically for those improvements. But the downside of that was the city had to cover at least fifteen percent of the costs, which only added to the debt.

The city's borrowing practices came to a head after 1912, when Mayor Taylor began his "clean up campaign" to stop vice in the city. As has been mentioned, the new policies toward prostitution caused city revenues to decline by over $800 per month and, when the state passed a prohibition law in 1916, the city's revenues declined by over 30%. The results were that Little Rock in the "progressive era" sank progressively into debt. By the time of the First World War, the city was over $1 million in debt.[28] Paying interest on the debt strained the city's limited budget and challenged the abilities of city leaders to keep the city functioning. However, the War brought changes, and, for a period of almost two years, refocused attention on national and world events. City priorities had to wait until the Great War was over.

CHAPTER IV ENDNOTES

1. Ira Don Richards, *Story of a Rivertown: Little Rock in the Nineteenth Century* (Benton, Arkansas: Privately Printed, 1969), 91-93.
2. *Ibid.*, 96-97.
3. *Ibid.*
4. "Ex-President Grant at Little Rock," *New York Graphic*, April 15, 1880. Reprinted in the *Arkansas Gazette*, April 14, 1957.
5. Richards, *Story of a Rivertown*, 97.
6. *Arkansas Gazette*, January 14, 1888.
7. Mrs. Dan W. Colton, "Streetcars and Society," *Pulaski County Historical Society* (Spring, 1981), 4.
8. *Ibid.*
9. Bryan D. McDade, "The Six Bridges at Little Rock: Understanding the Historical Significance and Relevance of the Six Bridges that Span the Arkansas River at Little Rock," unpublished master's thesis, (Little Rock: University of Arkansas at Little Rock, 2000), 81.
10. *Ibid.*, 83-86.
11. Cheryl Griffith Nichols, "Pulaski Heights: Early Suburban Development in Little Rock, Arkansas," *Arkansas Historical Quarterly*, XLI (Summer, 1982), 138.
12. *Ibid.*, 144.
13. Martha Williamson Rimmer, "Charles E. Taylor and His Administrations, 1911-1919: Progressivism in Little Rock," unpublished master's thesis (Fayetteville: University of Arkansas, 1977), 27.
14. *Ibid.*, 27-29.
15. *Ibid.*
16. *Ibid.*, 57.
17. *Ibid.*, 32.
18. James W. Bell, *Little Rock Handbook*, (Little Rock: Privately Printed, 1980), 39.
19. Rimmer, "Charles E. Taylor," 37, 53-55.
20. *Ibid.*, 24-25.
21. *Ibid.*, 21.
22. *Arkansas Gazette*, April 11, 1911.
23. *Ibid.*, February 4, 1912.
24. Rimmer, "Charles E. Taylor," 67.
25. *Ibid.*, 68.
26. *Ibid.*
27. *Ibid.*, 58-60.
28. *Ibid.*, 89-94.

CHAPTER V

LITTLE ROCK BETWEEN THE WARS, 1916-1946

America's entry into World War I drew attention away from the city's financial dilemma—at least in the short term. Eager to support the war effort, a group of Little Rock businessmen formed the Army Post Development Commission and joined with colleagues in Argenta to subscribe $500,000 and purchased 13,000 acres of land northwest of the city. They then donated the site to U.S. government for use as a military training camp. The U.S. Army Corps of Engineers prepared the site, and named it Camp Pike in honor of Zebulon Montgomery Pike, an Army officer who led numerous expeditions to explore the Trans-Mississippi West. The new military base and other support services became the training ground for more than fifty thousand recruits, most of whom came through Little Rock or used the city's services while on leave. As an indication of how constrained the city's resources had become, it could not initially provide bus service to transport soldiers, averaging more than one hundred arrivals a day in 1917, to and from the Union Depot to Camp Pike. This gap in service caused a group of Little Rock women to hastily organize a private taxi service until the city could establish a regular bus route. Also, as previously noted, the Free Bridge across the Arkansas River could not withstand the increased military traffic and city officials were forced to close it for the duration of the war.[1]

The military presence in Central Arkansas also played a major role in expanding one of the state's, and nation's, greatest natural disasters, the Spanish Influenza epidemic of 1918. Beginning with soldiers at Fort Riley, Kansas in late summer of 1918, the disease rapidly spread throughout the nation. Before running its course in the spring of 1919, the "flu" had killed over six hundred thousand Americans—more than fifteen times the number killed in the Great War. Reports about the epidemic nature of this flu first appeared on September 7 in eastern news reports. However, Arkansans were slow to respond to the dire warnings. In its September 20 edition, the *Arkansas Gazette* ran a headline "Spanish Influenza is plain la grippe." The paper went on to report that the flu was "the same old fever and chills" previously associated with the flu season. The Federal Public Health Service officer for Arkansas, James C. Geiger, similarly downplayed the severity by calling it "simple, plain old-fashioned la grippe."[2] He and other public health officials were in a bit of a dilemma, caught between taking necessary precautions to prevent a pandemic while also trying to avoid causing a panic among the general population.

During the two week period following the public announcements, Little Rock and North Little Rock reported 506 cases of the flu. However, Geiger issued another statement on October 4 that read: "Situation still well in hand."[3] When an additional 296 cases were reported the next day, health officials again responded by reporting "The disease has reached its highest point…and will begin to decline from now on."[4] In reality, the epidemic was just underway. On October 6, state health officials reported eighteen hundred cases and issued a statewide quarantine. All schools, churches, and civic meetings were closed, and retail business had to operate with greatly reduced hours.

For Little Rock the quarantine initially seemed little more than an inconvenience. The *Gazette's* society editor reported that the order had canceled the traditional parties and receptions and reduced the city's elite to "reading and playing solitaire."[5] However, as the epidemic continued through the month, children staying at home from school and the lack of normal social activities began to weigh on the citizens. Beyond isolating the victims, there was little public health officials could do to stop the spread of the disease. The city council passed an ordinance prohibiting "spitting in public places," Dr. Geiger coined a phrase "cover up each cough and sneeze; if you don't you'll spread disease," and volunteer "street police" sometimes patrolled neighborhoods empowered to report anyone "spitting in public," but enforcement was lax and irregular.

✧

In the nineteenth century, most railroad companies followed a "goes it alone" strategy, which led to a duplication of services. By the twentieth century consumers were pressing for more accommodations, and the Arkansas General Assembly required railroad companies to build depots to assist passengers. This Union Depot, first built on this site in 1873, replaced in 1911, and then rebuilt in 1920 after a destructive fire, was one response to being more consumer friendly.

COURTESY OF THE ARKANSAS HISTORY COMMISSION.

October proved to be the most difficult month. Almost 10,000 flu cases were reported in Little Rock, out of a total population of just over 58,000. More than three hundred died. The quarantine continued for six weeks and was not lifted until November 11, coinciding with the formal end of the War. While outbreaks continued well into the new year, the epidemic was over. Statewide some 7,000 Arkansans died, compared to just over 500 casualties in the Great War.[6]

But even the excitement caused by World War I and the Spanish Flu epidemic could not long delay attention to Little Rock's financial troubles. Unable to persuade Arkansas voters to amend the state constitution and allow the city to issue bonds, city officials were stuck with borrowing more money to meet short term capital needs. After the state's prohibition law took effect in 1917, town leaders persuaded the General Assembly to allow the city to collect an "occupation tax" to replace the revenue lost to liquor sales and saloon franchise taxes.

Lawmakers agreed, provided local citizens would approve such a tax, but the measure failed to pass in May 1917. This forced the city to continue its policy of borrowing to meet basic needs. To compound the problem, with the war came steadily increasing interest rates, reaching an all-time high of ten percent in March 1918. Despite the wartime prosperity, the city could not keep pace with providing new services for the military and covering the interest payments on its various loans. By the end of the war, the treasury was running a deficit in excess of $5,000 a month.[7]

A climax to the city's plight came in July 1919. Interest rates still hovered near ten percent, the debt had grown to $750,000, and note holders were demanding to be paid in cash. Lacking a solution at city hall, a small group of businessmen took matters into their own hands by initiating a petition to force the city council to submit the occupation tax proposal to the voters again. The election was scheduled for September 15, and, with the prospect of a new source of income, local bankers agreed to extend the city's line of credit to cover the interest due on the note and hold off the creditors. Voters approved the new tax by a four to one margin and, for the first time in almost two decades, the city had a sufficient cash flow to meet its monthly obligations.[8]

With the War over and a new source of income, Little Rockians entered the 1920s with a burst of enthusiasm. One indication of this new confidence was reflected in the number of new buildings built during the decade. First to be noticed was the Fones Brothers Hardware Store that opened at Second and Cumberland Streets in 1920. Noted for its simple, functional design with an emphasis on efficiency, the building set

the tone for the new style of architecture that dominated the era. The next year a new train station was completed to replace the Union Depot that burned the previous year after only a decade of use. In May 1922, Scottish Rite Masons laid the cornerstone to their new building on Scott Street between Seventh and Eighth Streets, named to honor Albert Pike. Former Governor

George Donaghey, returning to his building trade after retiring from politics, began plans at mid-decade to build the city's tallest structure at the corner of Seventh and Main Streets. Completed in 1926, the fourteen-story Donaghey Building dominated the city's skyline until it was overshadowed by the Tower Building at Second and Center in 1960. The ten-story Rector Building (now the 300 Spring Building), also completed in 1926, at Third and Spring Streets added aesthetic balance to the downtown business district.

One of the city's largest buildings, in square footage, came in 1927, when a new facility for Little Rock High School was completed at the former West End Park on Park Street between Fourteenth and Fifteenth Streets. Called by some architects "the most beautiful school building in the nation," it was a fitting tribute to a city that was rapidly expanding its physical boundaries as well as its skyline.[9]

Built with less grandeur, but equally significant in its own right, was a second school building, this one for "negroes," located nine blocks east of Little Rock High at Seventeenth and Chester Streets. Named for famed poet Paul Laurence Dunbar, the building was completed in 1929 and quickly became a landmark for academic excellence. Dunbar High symbolized a temporary end to the building boom that had almost spanned the decade. The major structures built in the depression years of the 1930s were constructed primarily with public monies.[10]

✧

The decade following World War I saw another major change in the Little Rock skyline. Unlike the wave of business development in the late nineteenth century, the new "tall buildings" were bona fide "sky scrapers" with the fourteen-story Donaghey Building, completed in 1926, leading the way. The nineteenth century development had focused on public service and retail, whereas these new buildings offered thousands of square feet for office space.

The new technology reflected in the
buildings was an indication that a new era had
come to Little Rock. The automobile became
the new symbol for the age, and, just as the
railroad signaled an end to the steamboat era,
so the "gas buggies" began to replace steam
locomotives as the vehicles of choice for
personal transportation. The challenge the
automobile presented to city officials before the
Great War became increasingly complex as the
number of vehicles increased and forced the
city police to spend more and more of their
time with traffic related issues. The relatively
simple technology in building an automobile
spawned over two hundred manufacturing
companies nationwide, including the Climber
Motor Corporation on East Seventeenth Street
in Little Rock. Over a five-year period between
1919 and 1924 the company built some two
hundred vehicles before problems in obtaining
parts and increasing competition forced the
company into bankruptcy.[11]

The growing volume of automobiles put
added pressure for crossing the Arkansas River.
With the Free Bridge unsafe for heavy traffic,

Little Rock officials faced growing demands for
a new structure. Having a new source of income
from the Occupation Tax, the city issued
warrants in 1921 to begin construction on a
new bridge extending Broadway across the
river. The structure, completed in 1922, was
followed two years later by the Main Street
Bridge and the Free Bridge was torn down. The
two new bridges did more to extend Little
Rock's influence in Central Arkansas than did
the railroad bridges in the Nineteenth Century.[12]

The 1920s also saw city leaders finally
subdue the Town Branch, a nemesis that had
plagued residents since before the Civil War.
The Branch was a frequent topic for comment
by local newspapers, but in 1926, the *Arkansas
Gazette* began a determined campaign to find a
permanent solution to the problem. Noting
that the waterway had degenerated into "a
'crazy quilt' system" of sewer pipes of various
sizes and grades, the editor urged policy
makers to put an end to the perpetual flooding.
Using legislation originally passed to stimulate
road construction, the Council, in 1926,
organized over fifteen hundred residents into
"Sewer Improvement District 104" and began a
final push to convert the Branch into a
permanent sewer. A sense of urgency was
added to the project in late December when
almost six inches of rain fell in a single day. The
overtaxed Branch responded not only by
flooding downtown businesses, but also
caused a cave-in near Collins Street that was
more than thirty feet deep. Before work on the
project could be completed, the great Flood of
1927 caused additional local flooding when
the sewer run-off could not empty into the
Arkansas River. However, by the end of the
year the Branch had been walled in, covered
over with concrete, and converted into a bona
fide, gravity flow storm sewer.[13]

The decade following World War I also
saw a new focus in politics. As the state
capital, political activity always played a
significant role in Little Rock's development.
However, a new force in the form of a revived
Ku Klux Klan made its appearance in 1921
and took the city by storm. Ironically, the Klan
organization had been slow to come to central
Arkansas. Nationally organized in 1915 in
Atlanta, Georgia, the "new Klan" was initially a

social organization built on preserving "one hundred percent Americanism."

Reacting to the rapid increase in immigration from eastern and southern Europe in the decade before World War I that included a high percentage of Roman Catholic and Jewish immigrants, Klansmen of the new order were more concerned with defending Protestantism, prohibition, and "traditional values" than the racial issues which had defined the nineteenth century Klan. The new group quickly spread to neighboring states in the South and Southwest,

CLIMBER MOTOR CORPORATION

but it took more than five years for the first "Klavern" to be organized in Little Rock.[14]

Meeting in September 1921 at the Marion Hotel, representatives of the national Klan recruited the requisite "hundred native-born white Protestants" for a local chapter. They also chose James A. Comer, a Little Rock attorney and former leader in the local Republican Party, to be the "Exalted Cyclops of Klan Number 1"—the first in the state. Over the next six months the Little Rock chapter focused on helping local law enforcement officers combat crimes of "bootlegging" and prostitution, while disciplining men for "drunkenness" and for failing to provide adequate financial aid to their families. However, in April 1922 the Little Rock Klan followed the lead of the national group and became involved in politics. By that time, Comer reported that he represented over four thousand members and despite being late to organize, Klan Number 1 was successful in "winning a spot on the city board of directors" by electing Charles M. Snodgrass, a candidate in the Fifth Ward.[15]

The taste of victory led to a shift in orientation and, over the summer of 1922, the Klan, both local and national, turned increasingly to politics and placed less emphasis on social reform. By the time the next citywide elections came in December, Klan Number 1 boasted of having seventy-eight members and endorsed a full slate of candidates for all city and county offices. When Klan-backed politicians won seven out of nine alderman seats on the city council and most of the county offices as well, state leaders for both Democratic and Republican Parties took notice. The Klan

✧

Little Rock was not immune from the "automobile craze" that hit the country shortly after World War I and for a decade or so had its own automobile manufacturing company. The Climber Automobile was assembled in a plant at 1800 East Seventeenth Street. Between 1919 and 1925 the company produced two hundred vehicles before being forced into bankruptcy. After the automobile company declared bankruptcy, company officials retooled and manufactured airplanes for the balance of the decade before market conditions and the pressures of the Great Depression forced the aircraft company to close as well.

COURTESY OF THE ARKANSAS HISTORY COMMISSION.

continued to have success, particularly at the local level, through 1924. However, the fruits of victory also brought the seeds of defeat. As Klan backed candidates became more successful, state Democrats began to call for Party discipline and charged Klan members with being Republicans in disguise. The Klan also experienced a growing internal dispute over whether to continue its political agenda or to return to the social reforms that had initially energized the organization. The combination of a more united Democrat Party and internal divisiveness caused the Klan to decline almost as quickly as it had burst into prominence. By 1926 the Klan could not even control the Little

Rock City Council and, while it continued to maintain a presence in the state until modern times, both its political and social effectiveness were largely over.[16]

A key factor in the Klan's rise to national prominence was directly related to the motion picture *Birth of a Nation*. This new form of communication also signaled the changing times, as did radio, another new medium that made its appearance in 1920 in Pittsburgh, Pennsylvania. A short six years later, Little Rock had its first permanent radio station, WLBN, which began broadcasting in December 1926. Two years later the station changed its call letters to KLRA and currently remains on air with the

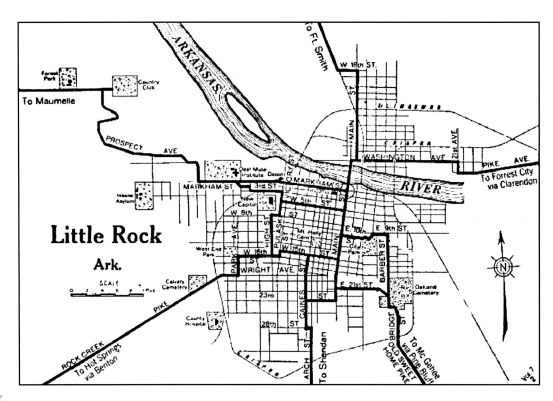

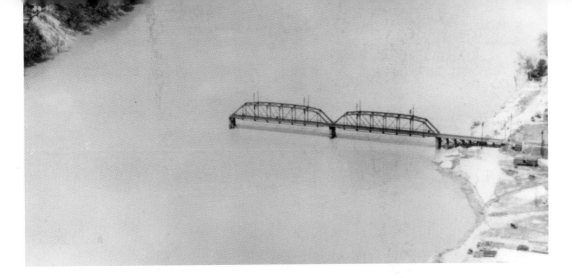

same identification. The new sound was also reflected in the motion picture industry, and "talkies" began to replace the silent movie. By the early 1930s all the downtown theaters had changed to the new format. Vaudeville and variety shows almost disappeared as the new "picture show" took over.[17]

Education was also in the spotlight during the 1920s. The two new high school buildings already discussed had academic programs that matched their architecture in professional excellence. In 1926 the University of Arkansas began offering night classes in Little Rock for freshman and sophomore students using vacant classrooms in the Little Rock public schools. For unexplained reasons University of Arkansas officials discontinued the program after one year, and John A. Larson, principal at Little Rock Senior High, persuaded the school board to approve opening a junior college on the second floor in the north wing of the new building. Little Rock Junior College (LRJC) was accredited by the North Central Association in 1929 and, in the same year, former governor George Donaghey established an endowment for the new college. In 1931 the college moved to a vacant elementary school building at Thirteenth and State Streets, where it remained until 1949.[18]

While LRJC prepared to graduate its first class, officials at Dunbar High were preparing to admit the first class into Dunbar Junior College. Accredited by the North Central Association in 1932, DJC became the first public college for African Americans in Central Arkansas and only the second industrial arts junior college in the South. The school attracted students from throughout the state, and by offering classes from junior high through junior college it became a major influence in shaping the attitudes of Black Little Rockians.[19]

In national history, the 1930s are typically characterized as a decade-long economic depression that symbolically began with the stock market crash in October 1929. For Arkansas and Little Rock, however, the economic crisis began more than two years earlier. The Wall Street crisis may have ushered in the "the Great Depression," but in Arkansas the Great Flood of 1927 was a more fitting indication that hard times were ahead. Cresting at 43 feet above flood stage, the Arkansas River washed away a portion of the historic Baring Cross railroad bridge but otherwise the city itself largely missed the high water. Such was not the case in North Little Rock, where the downtown area stayed under flood waters for weeks. Nor was rural Arkansas spared, as thousands of acres of farmland were flooded and hundreds of roads, bridges, and structures destroyed. Property losses approached $15 million. Much of Little Rock's trade area south and east of town was devastated. Ironically, the flood waters had hardly subsided before another natural disaster, a drought, hit with almost as much devastation. Beginning in the spring of 1930 and continuing for over a year, Little Rock and the surrounding state experienced a prolonged dry spell with rainfall totals less than half the historic averages. The most extreme conditions came in the summer of 1930 when, from June through much of August, Little Rock recorded seventy-one consecutive days with no rainfall. By the winter of 1932 over a third of the residents in Pulaski County were totally dependent on charity for food and clothing.

As previously mentioned, hard times began to affect the building trades in 1927. However, a more immediate and visible problem developed in the farm economy two years later. The weather problems started a ripple that became a "tidal wave" by the end of the decade. Not only

❖

While North Little Rock and other communities downstream suffered greater damage, the historic Flood of 1927 remains the index to measure the high water mark on the Arkansas River. Flood waters washed out this span on the Baring Cross Bridge.
COURTESY OF THE ARKANSAS HISTORY COMMISSION.

did farmers face foreclosure for failure to repay loans, but many businessmen could not sustain their operations without the farm trade. The final straw to the faltering economy came in November 1930 with the collapse of Little Rock's American Exchange Trust Company. Organized by A. B. Banks and based at Third and Main Streets, the AETC rapidly expanded its operations in the decade following World War I to include sixty-six branches throughout the state. However the depressed local economy coupled with a crisis in the national banking industry brought a sudden halt to Banks' expansive operations, and he declared bankruptcy in 1930. The AETC's collapse had a corresponding ripple effect through Little Rock's business community. Before the year was out over one-third of the residents in Pulaski County were unemployed and in dire need of immediate financial help.[20]

Responding to the crisis in the job market, the Little Rock Chamber of Commerce opened an "Emergency Employment Bureau" in December 1930, with a $10,000 budget and a plan to provide support for one month. Bureau officials began by encouraging private citizens to do maintenance work on their homes; it also appealed to store and plant owners to "stagger their shifts of workers" to retain as many jobs as possible. The Chamber also called for city officials to provide work for "jobless men" on streets, parks, and alleys.

The campaign worked. Business owners temporarily stabilized their work forces and retained three hundred workers who otherwise were scheduled to be laid off. The restructuring provided for three shifts and three days work per worker per week at a rate of $1.50 per day. Response to the Employment Bureau's plea was so successful that the program was extended for an additional six weeks. By the time all finances for work relief had been exhausted in mid February, the Chamber had spent more than $14,000 and created more than 8,500 hours of work for individuals who would otherwise have been unemployed.[21]

The Chamber's program was an obvious benefit for those involved; however, it had only a limited impact on a mounting problem. Every day brought news about problems in the national economy and the gaunt, hungry look of unemployed workers became an increasingly familiar sight in the streets of Little Rock. Responding to what many considered an alarming situation, city officials created the Citizens Emergency Relief Committee and authorized that group to find ways to keep as many Little Rockians employed as possible. The committee began with a sense of urgency, met with all the city's employers, and gained permission to contact each employee. The committee's message was simple, each worker who could afford to do so, was asked to give up one day's pay ($1.50) each month for three months to create a "relief fund" for the unemployed. In addition, the committee also organized a number of benefit dances, shows, and raffles to raise money for the fund. Despite the gloom and anxiety caused by an economy reeling from recession toward depression, citizens rallied with a show of unity that belied the hard times. The funds raised allowed an additional three hundred individuals to be employed, admittedly part-time and temporarily, through April. By that time the seasonal work required in the farm economy eased some of the unemployment pressure in the city.

Little Rock parks were the chief beneficiaries of the new work opportunities. Existing facilities were given a face lift with trash picked up, landscaped entrances, new walk and driveways, and picnic areas either

FOR GOD AND HOME AND NATIVE LAND

KU KLUX KLAN
KOMMEMORATION
AT LITTLE ROCK

Under Auspices of the
Realm of Arkansas, Little Rock Klan No. 1, Rose
City Klan No. 1 and Junior Klan

SEE GREATEST ROBED PARADE IN HISTORY OF STATE
LARGEST CLASS EVER NATURALIZED IN ARKANSAS
STATE'S MOST STUPENDOUS FIREWORKS DISPLAY

renovated or built. The new labor force also allowed the city to begin work on Allsopp Park. This 140-acre tract west of town had gone undeveloped since 1913, when Fred Allsopp, manager of a local newspaper, donated the land to the city for public use. Now, with surplus labor available and long term capital projects in short supply, the city could afford to implement the ambitious plans noted landscape architect John Nolen had originally proposed for the site.[22]

The Allsopp land was situated in two ravines with a varied topography, filled with trees and dense underbrush. Nolen designed, and workers now constructed, a series of pedestrian walkways, and bike and bridle paths to connect the two areas while still maintaining the natural character of the woodlands. Workers also built a central recreation area with tennis courts, an outdoor theater, playground, and flower gardens. Few could have anticipated at the time the role the park would play in providing a respite for individuals and families increasingly stressed by the decade long Great Depression.[23]

South and west of Allsopp Park, the city inherited another large, green space when local businessman John F. Boyle donated 231 acres of land along Rock Creek south of Twelfth Street for a public park. Boyle made the donation in 1926, but the area had gone undeveloped until the new work relief program was put in place. While Allsopp Park had priority, city officials were able to commit enough funding to the new area to build a pavilion with a fireplace and a small picnic area.[24]

Efforts by city officials to employ individuals forced out of work by the faltering economy had only a temporary impact. The problem was national in scope, and federal officials were slow to realize its magnitude. Led by President Herbert Hoover, the official response was that the "economy was fundamentally sound" and after a "correction" in the market cycle, the prosperity of the past ten years would resume. But while Little Rock's leaders became increasingly skeptical about the rosy predictions, they had few options. On one occasion, by joining with the governor and the state's congressional delegation, they were able to persuade federal officials to move up the construction schedule for a new Federal Building to meet some of the unemployment problems. This multi-million dollar project, originally scheduled to begin in 1932, was moved to the summer of 1931. However, there were few other public works projects of this type.[25]

By the end of 1932 almost a third of the city's workforce was either unemployed or working a limited number of hours at reduced pay. Concern for the unemployed became an increasing issue in

✧

Above: The economic hard times of the 1930s were reflected in the sparse setting of Main Street. But movie theaters were one of the areas that still did a thriving business as millions of Americans turned to the "silver screen" to escape the harsh realities of the Depression. The Rialto was among those providing Little Rockians with inexpensive entertainment.

COURTESY OF THE ARKANSAS HISTORY COMMISSION.

Left: Initially supplied by a private company in the last quarter of the nineteenth century, the City of Little Rock was finally able to take over the water supply with loans and labor made possible by the federal government. Beginning in 1936, the Centennial year of state history, Little Rock was able to launch its municipal water system.

COURTESY OF THE ARKANSAS HISTORY COMMISSION.

decision-making. Then-governor J. M. Futrell began staying at the capitol until after dark to avoid being confronted by individuals seeking work. Even so, he reported that both sides of the street from the State House to his rented quarters on Third Street were lined with men in dilapidated jalopies seeking an opportunity to talk about their need for a job. Sections of east and south Little Rock began to take on the appearance of a shanty town as the city, county, state, and private charities ran out of relief funds.[26]

It took a change in national politics before any major improvement came at the local level. Franklin D. Roosevelt's election as President brought a "new deal" in economic philosophy that had some benefit to Little Rock. Initially, the New Deal work projects were largely of the temporary, "make work" variety that city officials had tried when unemployment first became a problem. However, by the mid-1930s the President's "brain trust" had been able to formulate more significant, capital work projects that had long term benefits. Under the umbrella of the Works Progress Administration, federal funds were made available to local contractors and service providers for capital projects that left a legacy for the agency. Chief beneficiaries of the funding included the Little Rock Zoo, where new landscaping and several new buildings made a former caretaker operation into a modern facility. Downtown Little Rock

also received a major new building when WPA administrators approved plans for a new city auditorium. Named in honor of Arkansas Senator Joseph T. Robinson, the structure was built at the northeast corner of Markham and Broadway under the supervision of former Governor George Donaghey. WPA funds were also essential in building a new "terminal building" at the Little Rock Airport (named Adams Field in 1942), and in extending the runways first built in World War I. The improvements allowed the city to service the major aircraft of the day and to offer opportunities to the nation's emerging airline industry. City leaders were also pleased to get Boyle Park included in the Civilian Conservation Corps list of projects; and, with that agency's funds, the young men of the CCC built additional pavilions, playgrounds, and picnic areas that greatly enhanced the park's natural beauty.[27]

Little Rock's water system was the most enduring legacy of the depression decade. In 1936, city officials were finally able to purchase the privately held water works and, with the help of several New Deal agencies, were also able to gain an alternative to water from the Arkansas River. Using 4 percent revenue bonds, the city paid approximately $3.8 million for the water facilities and then persuaded New Deal officials in the Public Works Administration to put up another $3.5 million to construct a lake and pipe line that replaced river water.[28]

The impoundment dam on the Alum Fork of the Saline River was approximately thirty-five miles west of Little Rock. Named Lake Winona, the completed reservoir was

Above: The Great Depression slowed private construction to a trickle, and the only substantial new buildings were built with federal dollars. Two examples of that construction can be seen in the New Federal Building and Robinson Auditorium.
COURTESY OF THE ARKANSAS HISTORY COMMISSION.

Below: Another federal project that aided Little Rock's development was the Little Rock Zoo. City officials began providing limited care for a variety of abandoned circus animals in the 1920s, but it was over a decade before federal funds from the Works Progress Administration allowed the city to build more adequate facilities.
COURTESY OF THE ARKANSAS HISTORY COMMISSION.

ENTRANCE TO ZOO, LITTLE ROCK, ARK.—15

supplied by a drainage basin of more than forty miles that provided more than 10 billion gallons of water a year. The water was transported by a "39-inch steel cylinder, reinforced concrete pipe," manufactured in Little Rock, to a 20-acre "emergency reservoir," named Lake Jackson, 1½ miles outside the city limits (in what is now Reservoir Park) adjacent to State Highway 10. From Lake Jackson the water was piped to a new filtration plant on "Water Works Hill" at Ozark Point in Pulaski Heights. There, an automated central processing system mixed the appropriate chemicals and distributed the "purified" water to users. The pipeline was completed in 1937, and the new system was operational in 1938. One indication as to the differences in the new and old water supplies can be seen in a category of "total dissolved solids." The Arkansas River water had an index of 327 parts per million while the new supply had an index of 29.6 ppm.[29]

While planning the new water system, city leaders also moved to improve the area's sewage disposal. As noted with efforts to control the Town Branch, the city traditionally dumped its sewage directly into the Arkansas River adjacent to the central business district. Aided again with federal funds, city engineers selected a site downstream from the city to build a new "sewage relift station," laid some twenty-seven miles of new concrete-clay sewer pipe, and rehabilitated most of the existing sewers. The project cost more than $1.6 million and was an appropriate complement to the new water system.[30]

Federal funds were a vital part of Little Rock's development in the 1930s. However, by late 1938 the clouds of another European war began to gather. President Roosevelt called the activity "storm signals from across the sea" and began shifting domestic spending into funding for defense related industries. In many respects wartime spending was an even greater stimulus to the local economy than the programs of the New Deal. The first sign that changes were in order came in early 1939 when the World War I military base, renamed Camp Joseph T. Robinson after Senator Robinson's death in 1937, began to show activity. Army officials began to negotiate leases from area farmers that ultimately increased the original base to over seventy thousand acres. The U.S. Army's II Corps region, which included Arkansas, began a series of "war games" in the summer of 1940, and, before the year was out, more than twenty-five thousand new residents had moved into Little Rock and the surrounding area.[31]

A decline in the construction industry which foreshadowed the economic depression

✧

Left: The death of U.S. Senator Joseph T. Robinson in 1937 led the U.S. Army to expand Camp Pike into a larger facility which was named Camp Robinson. With the outbreak of World War II, the Camp became a national site for basic training, and thousands of raw recruits went through their first military experience at the base. The base's importance is illustrated by this visit by President Franklin D. Roosevelt in 1944.
COURTESY OF THE ARKANSAS HISTORY COMMISSION.

Below: The large number of soldiers training at Camp Robinson contributed to an economic boom for Central Arkansas and greatly influenced social customs. The USO club in downtown Little Rock drew thousands of soldiers with weekend passes into the city. Their purchasing power caused many local merchants to ignore local "blue laws" by keeping stores open on Sunday.
COURTESY OF THE ARKANSAS HISTORY COMMISSION.

✧

Above: John Marshall Robinson was another individual who built his career between World Wars I and II. A physician by training with an office on West Ninth Street, Robinson devoted his life to getting the "all white primary" rule adopted by the state Democratic Party repealed. To aid in his efforts, Robinson organized the Arkansas Negro Democratic Association (ANDA) and devoted more than thirty years of his life trying to increase the political opportunities for African Americans.
COURTESY OF THE BUTLER CENTER,
CENTRAL ARKANSAS LIBRARY SYSTEM.

Right: Composer William Grant Still. Growing up on West Fourteenth Street and graduating valedictorian of his class in 1912, he began his musical career in Memphis and had risen to national prominence by the end of World War II.
COURTESY OF THE BUTLER CENTER,
CENTRAL ARKANSAS LIBRARY SYSTEM.

of the 1930s now led to a new wave of prosperity in the 1940s. In addition to expanded housing at Camp Robinson, military officials also contracted with the city of Little Rock to build three new housing projects to house personnel involved in the war effort. Two of the projects, Sunset Terrace and Highland Park, were in southern and western sections of the city for white personnel, while Tuxedo Courts on the city's east side was for African Americans. Another major project of over one hundred houses was developed by entrepreneur Dan Cammack on the northwest edge of Pulaski Heights just outside the city limits.[32]

Opportunities to work in the construction industry and, beginning in 1942, in a variety of other war-related industries eliminated the unemployment lines as if by magic. Most of the defense plants were outside the city at Jacksonville, Marche, and Bryant, but were an easy commute for Little Rock residents. There were exceptions. The United States Time Inc., armed with a contract to produce a "delicate military timing device" and aware of the labor surplus in the capital city, opened a manufacturing plant that became one of the city and state's most successful companies. Even without a defense contract, the Waterbury, Connecticut based company remained in Little Rock after the War as Timex Incorporated before finally closing in the 1990s.[33]

Despite the gravity of the War effort, it was still not enough to break down the color barrier, and Little Rock remained a divided city. Even the defense plants maintained segregated shifts or job assignments. In keeping with the segregation theme, Little Rock's "City Recreation Council" organized a downtown center for white soldiers that featured game rooms, reading and classrooms, as well as weekly dances for the troops. Black soldiers were limited to Taborian Hall on West Ninth Street. This segregation was a primary cause for a crisis in March 1942. An African-American soldier, Sergeant Thomas P. Foster, was shot by white Little Rock policeman Abner Hay after the two scuffled. Two military police officers were attempting to arrest a

resistive Foster when Hay came to their assistance. During the melee Foster was knocked unconscious and while he was lying on the ground Hay shot him four times. Foster died hours later during surgery at a local hospital. Hay was not charged with a crime despite investigations by the city police, a board of inquiry from Camp Robinson, and a grand jury from the Eastern District of Arkansas. However, Black community leaders, particularly L. C. Bates, editor of the *State Press* newspaper, would not let the matter drop, and, after more than six months of agitation, the City Council yielded to what had become national pressure for change and appointed eight African Americans to the city police force. The new policemen were limited in their authority and assignments, but as public policy they represented the first of the city's agencies to be integrated since Reconstruction.[34]

The racial conflict notwithstanding, World War II was a positive development and transformed Little Rock's history. By the time the 1950 census was taken, the city had surpassed one hundred thousand residents and with improvements in infrastructure, largely made possible by federal expenditures, the capital city was in position to become one of the top cities in the nation.

CHAPTER V ENDNOTES

1. Jim Lester and Judy Lester, *Greater Little Rock* (Norfolk, Virginia: The Donning Company, 1986), 152 and Bryan D. McDade, "The Six Bridges at Little Rock: Understanding the Historical Significance and Relevance of the Six Bridges That Span the Arkansas River at Little Rock," unpublished master's thesis, (Little Rock: University of Arkansas at Little Rock, 2000), 105-116.
2. Kim Allen Scott, "Plague on the Homefront: Arkansas and the Great Influenza Epidemic of 1918," *Arkansas Historical Quarterly*, 47 (Winter,1988), 320-329.
3. *Ibid.*, 323.
4. *Ibid.*
5. *Ibid.*, 331.
6. Scott, "Plague on the Homefront," 336-337.
7. Martha Williamson Rimmer, "Charles E. Taylor and His Administration. 1911-1919: Progressivism in Little Rock," unpublished master's thesis, (Fayetteville: University of Arkansas, 1977), 101.
8. *Ibid.*, 104-105.
9. F. Hampton Roy, Sr. and Charles Witsell, Jr. *How We Lived: Little Rock as an American City* (Little Rock: August House, 1984), 188-191.
10. http://www.aia.org/nwsltr_Print.cfm_dunbarhigh.
11. Lester and Lester, *Greater Little Rock*, 163.
12. James W. Bell, *The Little Rock Handbook* (Little Rock: James W. Bell Publisher, 1980), 34 and McDade, "The Six Bridges at Little Rock," 110-114.
13. William B. Worthen, "Municipal Improvement in Little Rock—A Case History," *Arkansas Historical Quarterly*, 46 (Winter, 1987), 345-347.
14. Charles C. Alexander, "White-Robed Reformers: The Ku Klux Klan Comes to Arkansas, 1921-1922," *Arkansas Historical Quarterly*, 22 (Spring, 1963), 15.
15. *Ibid.*, 198.
16. *Ibid.*, 323-325.
17. Bell, *Little Rock Handbook*, 34.
18. James E. Lester, Jr. *The People's College: Little Rock Junior College and Little Rock University, 1927-1969*, (Little Rock: August House Publishers, 1987), 37ff.
19. http://www.aia.org/nwsltr_Print.cfm_dunbarhigh
20. Ben F. Johnson, III, *Arkansas in Modern America*, 1930-1999 (Fayetteville: University of Arkansas Press, 2000) 13-14.
21. D. Hodson Lewis, "Unemployment Relief," *American City*, 44 (May, 1931) 143.
22. "Unemployment Relief Work Creates Permanent Improvement," *American City*, 46 (February, 1932), 110.
23. *Ibid.*
24. Lester and Lester, *Greater Little Rock*, 183.
25. Lewis, "Unemployment Relief," 143.
26. Johnson, *Arkansas in Modern America*, 60.
27. Lester and Lester, *Greater Little Rock*, 183.
28. "Sewage Relift Station at Little Rock, Arkansas," *American City*, 52 (December, 1937), 64.
29. L. A. Jackson, "Little Rock, Ark., Extends Water Distribution System," *American City* (September, 1946), 121.
30. *Ibid.*
31. Johnson, *Arkansas in Modern America*, 60.
32. *Ibid.*, 61.
33. George Sessions Perry, "Little Rock," *Saturday Evening Post*, 220 (April 24, 1948), 20-21.
34. Berna J. Love, *End of the Line: A History of Little Rock's West Ninth Street* (Little Rock: UALR Ledbetter Monograph Series, 2003), 21-22 and John A. Kirk, *Redefining the Color Line: Black Activism in Little Rock, Arkansas, 1940-1970*, (Gainesville: University Press of Florida, 2002), 44-52.

CHAPTER VI

WHY IT HAPPENED HERE:
THE LITTLE ROCK SCHOOL CRISIS, 1945-1965

The decade following World War II was a boom time for Little Rock. Stimulated by wartime production, the city and its surrounding metropolitan area grew rapidly in population and job opportunities. Local business leaders did not want to lose the massive infusion of federal dollars. To maximize the opportunities for replacing military spending, one hundred of the city's leading businessmen formed an alliance to promote the area's economic development. Calling themselves "The Committee of 100," these men pooled their resources and contacts, purchased a six-hundred-acre tract of land on the southwestern edge of the city, and began an all-out effort to persuade business firms to locate there. They also lobbied the state's congressional leaders and members of the state General Assembly for assistance in replacing the federal dollars.[1]

State leaders were quite anxious to assist Little Rock with economic development. By the end of the War anecdotal information was showing an out-migration of people from the state—an impression confirmed by the 1950 federal census. The population loss was not a problem in Little Rock, but it was a near crisis situation in many communities and prompted the state Chamber of Commerce, based in the capital city, to launch its own aggressive plan for industrial development.[2]

Armed with the slogan "Arkansas: The Land of Opportunity," Chamber officials worked with Little Rock's political and business leaders to recruit clients for the city's new industrial park. The Arkansas General Assembly joined the campaign as well. Beginning in the early 1950s, the Assembly passed a series of bills that created an "industrial development commission;" authorized the University of Arkansas to expand its graduate offerings in Little Rock (including forming an "Institute of Technology"); established a modern Public Service Commission; and endorsed the Chamber's advertising slogan touting the state as "The Land of Opportunity."[3]

While state and local businessmen were still getting organized, federal officials privatized the multi-million dollar bauxite processing operations some fifteen miles southwest of Little Rock. Reynolds Metal Company and the Aluminum Company of America bought the plants for a fraction of the original costs and retained much of the existing work force. The aluminum industry became a key factor in the Committee of 100's plan for economic growth. Officials with the United States Air Force made another major contribution to the city's economic future with their decision to build a major base for the Strategic Air Command just outside Jacksonville. As was the case with previous military decisions, Little Rock's business community secured the site for the air base then donated it to Air Force officials. The Committee of 100 also used the bauxite and air base decisions as incentives to attract other firms. Over a two-year period from 1954 to 1956, the city's industrial recruiters persuaded thirty-four new firms to relocate to the Little Rock area and prior to 1957 there were excellent prospects for getting more.[4]

Little Rock school officials watched efforts by their Main Street colleagues with anticipation. By the early 1950s the demographic effects of the Post-War "baby boom" were becoming evident, and the increase in new job opportunities brought additional residents to the city. Little Rock added more than twenty thousand people to its population base between World War II and 1957. Between 1950 and 1957, an average of one thousand new students enrolled in the public schools annually. This rapid increase in enrollment required that school officials move quickly to build enough buildings to stay ahead of the burgeoning enrollments. Well before the 1954 *Brown* decision by the U.S. Supreme Court, the school district's Board of Directors began acquiring property, and making plans to promote bond programs in order to add more buildings. Included in this planning was a commitment to build two new high schools, one on the city's east side and another on the west side. Plans also included converting the existing high school for Blacks into a junior high school and changing the name of Little Rock High

✧

Although economic issues dominated much of post World War II Little Rock, politics was never far behind. In response to Governor Sid McMath's strong support, and Arkansas being the only Southern state to give him a majority in the 1948 presidential election, Harry S Truman made a ceremonial visit to the city to thank voters for their support.

COURTESY OF THE ARKANSAS HISTORY COMMISSION.

School to Central High School. Residents of Little Rock supported the school district's efforts by approving a major bond program in 1953. These additional monies allowed school officials to begin the new school construction program.[5]

The *Brown* decision served to accelerate the District's new school initiative. But implementing the decision proved difficult. For a year after voting to obey the ruling to integrate, school officials did little. Following the Court's May 1955 clarification that school integration must begin "with all deliberate speed," Superintendent Virgil Blossom and his staff began work in earnest to develop a plan. After considering several options, the Superintendent presented the Board with a proposal to begin integration with the high schools followed by the junior highs, then the elementary schools. Blossom noted that the plan could not be realistically implemented before the 1957-1958 school year and decisions about how rapidly to integrate the lower grades would be made on a year to year basis. The Board unanimously adopted the "Little Rock Phase-in Plan," more commonly known as the "Blossom Plan."[6]

A key factor in the Board's attitude toward the Blossom Plan was its earlier decision to build two new buildings for high school students. In preparing for two new schools, district staff members became increasingly aware of the city's demographic data, as well as its natural

and adapted terrain that could be factors in attendance zones. The recent industrial development efforts had added to and exacerbated the city's historic housing patterns. For example, since the end of the Civil War, African Americans had settled predominately on the city's east side. East of today's Bond Street, and south of Twenty-eighth Street, the plateau on which the original town-site was platted slopes down into the Fourche Creek bottom lands. As previously noted, it was in this lowland region that Union Army officials established a "home farm" that extended some five miles from downtown and settled several hundred Freedmen there after 1863. Additional Freedmen were settled in an area west of Mount Holly Cemetery between Ninth and Twelfth Streets. Over the years this population extended south and west of its original sites and formed the nucleus for the city's black neighborhoods in the twentieth century. A four block section along West Ninth Street between Broadway and Chester became the center of the black business district from the late Nineteenth Century until after World War II.[7]

Following World War II, new housing developments began in the southwest to accommodate the Committee of 100's industrial park and the bauxite processing plants farther south. Many of the workers recruited for these jobs were new to the city and wanted to live in close proximity to their place of work. Building contractors responded to the situation and developed a number of low-cost units in the area. Many working class families also began to occupy houses in the central part of town being

vacated by those moving to the northwest neighborhoods of Pulaski Heights, Cammack Village, and beyond.[8]

Changes in residential housing patterns also reflected, perhaps precipitated, new directions in the city's retail activities. The Markham-Main Street axis that had symbolized the core business district since the town was founded began to yield to the new pattern. The rapid influx of people, coupled with the boom in automobile sales, fundamentally changed downtown Little Rock. By 1950, the volume of traffic was too great to be adequately serviced by the Broadway and Main Street bridges and delays approaching gridlock were common during the morning and afternoon rush hours. City planners responded by restricting certain streets to one-way traffic and extending Water Street west until it intersected with Highway 10 and changed the name to La Harpe Boulevard. But the move was only a stop-gap measure to a long-term problem. An increasingly impatient public became weary of the inconvenience and congestion, an impatience that was increased by city officials' decision to install parking meters along the major thoroughfares.[9]

Developers responded to the growing dissatisfaction with downtown by bringing a new retail concept, the shopping center, to Little Rock. The city's, and state's, first "center" opened on the southwestern edge of town at the intersection of Asher Avenue and Hayes Street. Appropriately named Town and Country Shopping Center, the new retail concept opened in 1957 and was followed a few months later by University Shopping Center which opened across the street, immediately south of the new campus of Little Rock Junior College. LRJC relocated from its Fourteenth Street campus to a new eighty-acre site along Hayes Street in 1949. In recognition of the new developments Hayes Street was renamed University Avenue.[10]

The new shopping centers were strategically placed to accommodate residents in the Broadmoor Subdivision, a middle-class housing area designed for seven hundred homes that followed the Levittown model begun on Long Island, New York in the late 1940s. The first Broadmoor residents moved in in 1953. These new residents, coupled with the growing working class neighborhoods on the city's south

side, further complicated the Little Rock school board's decisions on school building construction and attendance zones.

Ironically, while one section of the city was expanding into new territory, another, older part of town, was undergoing re-development. The change was prompted by a 1950 survey done by the city Health Department which revealed that "one out of every four houses" in the city were substandard. A high percentage of those houses were concentrated south of Seventh Street to Wright Avenue and west of Broadway to High Street. This was the same area that many of the "post-war immigrants" were attracted to because of low rent. Most of the houses also lacked indoor bathroom facilities. Using data from the Health Department survey, the Little Rock Housing Authority prepared a comprehensive plan to build 1,000 new, low-rent, housing units— 750 of which were reserved for minorities.[11]

A forty-acre site near Dunbar High School was selected for the first project. Using federal funds provided by the recently created Urban Renewal Program, Housing Authority officials razed over two hundred structures and replaced them with a 240-unit, multi-story apartment complex. The project also included a community center and an elementary school. Over the next decade ten more projects were included in the Urban Renewal program. The concept was based on replacing single family,

❖

Another aspect of protecting the economic gains made during World War II was maintaining ties to the U. S. military. The Committee of 100 scouted several sites before choosing property north of Jacksonville to purchase and donate to the U. S. Air Force. Construction on the Little Rock Air Base began in 1952 and was sufficiently completed in 1955 to allow planes from the Strategic Air Command to establish a presence. Following the Vietnam War the base was transferred to the Tactical Air Command and became a home base for C-130 cargo planes.

COURTESY OF THE LITTLE ROCK AIR FORCE BASE.

✧

*A "bump in the road" to Little Rock's
economic development came in 1957, when
efforts to desegregate the city's school system
became the object of international attention.
First National Guard troops were stationed
at the school, followed by troops from the
101st Airborne division of the U. S. Army.
For the balance of the 1957-1958 school
year, Guardsmen under the supervision of
Army officials remained at the school until
Ernest Green, one of the original "nine"
students admitted to Central, became the
first African American to graduate from the
newly integrated Little Rock School District
in May 1958.*

COURTESY OF THE ARKANSAS HISTORY COMMISSION.

sub-standard housing with modern multi-family apartment complexes and represented the most advanced thinking by professionals in urban design. Over the twenty year period the Urban Renewal program was in operation more than five thousand families were relocated. Most gave up their substandard houses for modern apartments in high-density housing projects.[12]

By the mid 1950s, Little Rock had become a city of three dominant regions identifiable by race and/or class differences. The eastside was predominately African-American, the southwest was blue-collar white, and the northwest was essentially upper-middle class white. There were the usual transition zones, such as mixed-race neighborhoods in the central city, but in general Little Rock residents identified with one of these three areas. City government, public services,

and the school system were all organized to reflect this arrangement.[13]

The above housing patterns had been almost a century in the making. However, changes brought on by World War II and the post-War industrial development activities added new race and class pressures to the city. For one thing, most of the new immigrants to the city were from rural areas in the state. Attracted by defense jobs during the War and the new manufacturing jobs after the War, thousands of former farm workers and small town residents flocked to the capital city. The increase came rapidly, and it was difficult for many Little Rockians, old and new, to make the social and economic adjustments required by the relocations.[14]

The strain on personal relationships posed by the new immigration was quite evident in the city's political alignments. Traditionally, Little Rock politics had been dominated by a coalition among white businessmen along Main Street, a contingent of black businessmen along West Ninth Street, and ministers of the city's Black churches. The rural and small town newcomers came in such time and numbers that they were hard to assimilate quickly. Moreover, there was another dynamic at work in the African American community. A number of black veterans were not content to accept the status quo, and, in the decade following the war, they either challenged existing leaders for positions in the black community or formed new groups. After 1950 it became increasingly difficult for the traditional coalition to hold together.[15]

To a large extent Little Rock had become a divided city in the decade following the War. Business leaders focused on maintaining the momentum of war-time prosperity; city politicians tried to enlarge public policies to include the new clientele; and school officials faced the same issues while trying to implement the *Brown* decision. Most businessmen gave passive support to the Blossom Plan, but they were more concerned with how the school situation might affect business conditions.

In an effort to respond to the changing needs presented by the "new city," a group of businessmen formed a Good Government Committee (GGC) to study community concerns. Most Committee members were from "old line" Little Rock families and were well

established in the business community. From their meetings, the GGC came to the conclusion that a new form of government was the best way to respond to the city's changing demographics. The existing mayor-alderman system was all but paralyzed in its decision-making, as aldermen representing the central city and east side were often at odds with councilmen from the Wards on the city's west side. Council meetings frequently continued for hours and often adjourned without resolving questions of how and where city services should be provided.[16]

The GGC recommended that the existing mayor-alderman form of government be replaced by a city manager system. Their recommendation was placed on the ballot and approved by voters in the 1956 general election. Under the new plan, the ward system for electing the city's political leaders was replaced by a seven-member board of directors elected at large. These elections were scheduled for November 1957.

Superintendent Blossom's desegregation plan ran headlong into the restructuring of city government. While most of the downtown businessmen were lukewarm at best toward school integration, the support they could offer the school district was diluted by their involvement in city politics. At a crucial juncture in school desegregation planning when Blossom and the school board needed strong support, the business community was embroiled in political debate. A strong minority wanted to retain the old mayor-alderman system, and with the new demographic make-up of the city, no one could be certain how the new voting alliances would shape up. Trying to figure out how the fall elections would go became a favorite "coffee-shop" game along Main Street. In the weeks and months leading up to the school crisis, when District officials might reasonably expect to rely on the strong civic mindedness of the business community, their potential allies were distracted.[17]

To further complicate the local picture, the city's African American community was more divided than it had been since the 1920s. Some of the disagreement had to do with strategy, some with style, and some was along generational lines. Since the *Brown* decision, leaders of the National Association for the Advancement of Colored People (NAACP) had emerged as the most visible spokespersons on education issues. However, the local NAACP chapter had sometimes been at odds with the national organization, and support for its strategy was uneven in the Little Rock community. The group of black church ministers had been moved out of the spotlight, but they still commanded strong political allegiance in some quarters. The generational fracture centered on several World War II veterans who were impatient with traditional policies and anxious to organize their own following. On the one hand these G.I.'s could not tolerate the "gradualism" favored by most church leaders. But at the same time, while the NAACP's aggressiveness was appealing, most

✧

Soon after World War II, city planners began to develop ideas for dealing with an increasing number of vacant and/or substandard buildings that did not meet city code. The plan was to raze many of those buildings, replace some with high rise structures, both residential and commercial, keep some vacant lots for "green space, and build neighborhood community centers." Little Rock's urban renewal began in earnest in the 1960s.

COURTESY OF THE ARKANSAS HISTORY COMMISSION.

veterans wanted a broader agenda than education. This intramural squabbling among the city's Eastside residents, while more style than substance, was frustrating to the white leadership at both city hall and the school district's central office.[18]

Ironically, despite growing complexity in the Little Rock community, city leaders moved to implement the spirit of the *Brown* decision in areas other than education. For a time there was an effort to re-establish the "separate and equal" provisions of the original *Plessy* decision, but ultimately even the appearance of separation was given up, and the city yielded to full integration. The Little Rock Public Library was the first to react to the new era. Responding to faculty and student requests from Philander Smith College, the Library's Board of Directors first identified a "separate" section in the building for blacks to use, but, with limited staff, it was difficult for librarians to meet all patrons' needs, and the separation was gradually abandoned. Similar changes came in the city parks, where initially only parks on the east side were open to blacks, and the zoo, which was initially opened to blacks only on Thursdays. The service that received the most attention was integrating the city bus system which came in 1956. This was symbolically significant, not only because it was

the U.S. Supreme Court's ruling on a transportation issue, (*Plessy vs Ferguson*) rather than education, that launched the nation on the road of segregation in the 1890s, but also with Little Rock's post War expansion, a reliable, inexpensive public transportation system was essential for future growth.[19]

Between 1954 and 1957 school integration issues were largely confined to the local community. Then the calendar forced the issue to another level. Three years of maneuvering came down to September 3, 1957—the day after Labor Day and the day the eighty-ninth public school year was to open in Little Rock. Up to that time, school officials had taken most of the initiative for implementing the *Brown* decision. State officials, particularly Governor Orval Faubus, had stayed in the background. For example, Faubus had two opponents in the 1956 Democratic Party primary election, and both tried to make the *Brown* decision an issue. However, Faubus largely avoided the integration question and campaigned on his record of increased support for education, welfare reform, and improving highways. Other than to say, "no school board would be forced to integrate against the will of the community," he tried to ignore his opponents and the "race-mixing" issue.[20]

Faubus easily won the primary and had only token opposition in the November general election. However, while elated over his reelection, the governor could not help but notice that voters had also approved an amendment to the state constitution in the

November elections. That amendment declared the *Brown* decision unconstitutional and required state officials to "interpose" the state's sovereignty between the federal government and the state's citizens. Failure to defend the state from federal intervention could result in officials being arrested, fined, imprisoned and/or removed from office. He also noted that Little Rock residents approved the new form of city government and that six of the seven members elected to the new board of directors lived in the Pulaski Heights neighborhood. Four of six LRSD school board members also lived there.[21]

In January 1957, Faubus went before the Arkansas General Assembly for a second time and quickly learned that he could not get his own program approved without supporting the segregationists' agenda. That he agreed to go along with that group was due in part to his decision to run for a third term. In surveying election results from other Southern states in the preceding year, he noticed that every candidate taking a "moderate position" on the *Brown* decision was either defeated or had his margin of victory dangerously reduced. His own polling showed that public opinion had shifted from grudging compliance to outright defiance of the court's ruling on *Brown*. He was convinced that he could not win a third term without taking a more conservative approach on the school integration issue.[22]

Political circumstances placed Governor Faubus in an increasingly uncomfortable position as the last week of August 1957 played out. Segregationists, led by Jim Johnson and

Amis Guthridge, conducted a telephone and letter writing campaign threatening violence if the Little Rock school board went ahead with its plans. Supposedly they had organized a caravan of people from all parts of the state who were preparing to descend on the capital city the day school opened to prevent Central High School from being integrated. In reality the segregationists were not so well-organized, but the volume of communication caused Faubus to believe their words were true. He was caught in a dilemma. His political future was in jeopardy if he opposed the segregationists, and, more immediately, there was the real possibility that people would be physically hurt, perhaps killed. Moreover, his previous requests to the Justice Department to send federal Marshals to assist with implementing the court decision had produced only a token response.[23]

Believing that he had been left in a political "no man's land," caught between a deeply divided state citizenry and intransigent federal officials, Faubus made a decision. On Friday before the Little Rock schools were to open, he contacted the state National Guard commander, and asked him to have guardsmen at Central High School early on Tuesday morning September 3. He instructed the commander to prevent violence with the tacit understanding that the anticipated crowd would resort to violence if the school was integrated. When the nine black students appeared, guardsmen blocked their entrance to the school grounds.[24]

The results of Faubus' decision were soon heard and seen around the world. President

❖

Above: One reason for the new shopping centers' success was their ability to attract national chain stores, including grocery stores. These "name brand" stores, such as Safeway above, were increasingly strong competition to the traditional family owned stores that dominated Main Street.

COURTESY OF THE ARKANSAS HISTORY COMMISSION.

Below: Organized in 1879 as a department of the University of Arkansas, the medical school was first located on Second Street between Main and Louisiana before re-locating to Second and Sherman Streets in 1890. In 1912 the school moved to the "Old State House" when the General Assembly moved to the "New State Capitol." In 1935 the school was moved to McAlmont Street on the east side of City (MacArthur) Park and in 1957 relocated to a large campus along West Markham Street near University Avenue.

PHOTO COURTESY OF DR. FRED HENKER.

Above: Originally housed in the north wing of Little Rock High School as Little Rock Junior College, the college out grew its space following World War II and in 1949 moved to its own campus in west Little Rock along an emerging corridor then known as Hayes Street, but soon to become University Avenue. In 1957 LRJC became Little Rock University, a four-year liberal arts school, and in 1969 the institution merged with the University of Arkansas to become the University of Arkansas at Little Rock.

Below: Part of the reason for the mass exodus of "old town" residents to the new suburbs in the west was the popularity of the automobile. Pent up demand and financial savings during World War II were unleashed, in part, on the "personal freedom machine" the automobile. The auto rapidly reduced the role of the city's public transit lines in transporting individuals.

COURTESY OF THE ARKANSAS HISTORY COMMISSION.

Dwight Eisenhower, who had made no secret of his disagreement with the speed at which the Courts were pushing school integration, was now forced to act. From his perspective, the situation involved more than enforcing a court order. It was an ideological and public relations problem of international magnitude and had to be handled with utmost care. It also became clear that he must act decisively. On September 20, the President federalized the Arkansas National Guard and ordered the 101st Army Airborne Division to proceed to Little Rock to assist the nine black students in attending classes.[25]

Federal troops changed the "chemistry" of the crisis in a significant way. The core issue of racial integration remained but it now became overshadowed in a "David vs. Goliath" struggle between state and federal governments while Little Rock became a kind of pawn in the conflict. Faubus not only won his third term, but, before the year was out, had been recognized as one of ten most admired individuals in the nation by a national magazine. He also went on to win three more gubernatorial elections. In the process, the capital city became the symbol for resisting racial integration. Moreover, the year following the school crisis, Faubus, safely on his way to

winning a record vote and a third term as governor, used segregationist sponsored legislation to temporarily close all four Little Rock high schools rather than continue with court ordered integration. Citizens of Little Rock approved the Governor's decision by voting overwhelmingly to keep the schools closed for the 1958-1959 academic year.

The "lost year," as the 1958-1959 school year came to be called, deeply divided Little Rock. The economic momentum generated by the Committee of 100 came to a sudden halt when not a single new industry opened in the city for a full year following the school crisis. A regional newspaper reported that five prospective companies, representing more than 300 jobs and a $1 million payroll had chosen to locate elsewhere to avoid the turmoil in the schools. In the meantime, thousands of families scrambled to find ways to continue their young people's education. While over ninety percent of the white students found ways to continue their education, less than half of the black students attended school that year and many dropped out permanently. The long-term impact on the city and state has been hard to calculate.[26]

While parents worried about their children's future, political activists became embroiled in a contest that first centered on the school board and later extended to city government. Segregationists and moderates clashed over keeping the schools closed while the board of directors deadlocked with three members for segregation and three for integration. Board meetings became increasingly acrimonious, and, at one point in May 1959, while the Board was in recess, the three members supporting segregation voted to fire more than forty teachers and administrators who had expressed support for integration. This action led a group of women and downtown businessmen to initiate a petition campaign to recall the board members. Calling themselves the committee to "Stop this Outrageous Purge" (STOP), many in the group had initially organized as the Women's Emergency Committee the previous September in an attempt to defeat the referendum supporting Governor Faubus' order to close the schools. Segregationists rallied to support the school board's action by forming the "Committee to Retain Our Segregated Schools"

(CROSS). In a heated campaign, the STOP forces won by a narrow vote on May 25. The new Board members moved almost immediately to rehire the fired staff members and agreed to begin the new school year on August 12. In a follow-up meeting the new Board also voted to desegregate Hall High School by assigning three black students to attend there beginning with the new school year. Three black students were also assigned to Central but no white students were assigned to Horace Mann.[27]

With schools reopened and the national spotlight shifted elsewhere, Little Rockians tried to reclaim their community as the decade ended. But such was not possible. The school crisis had fundamentally altered personal relationships in the city, and while selected buildings had been desegregated, the district was far from being integrated. A decade following 1957 fewer than 20% of Little Rock's black students attended integrated schools. The school board adopted a "freedom of choice" policy that allowed students to choose where they wanted to attend, and most continued to go to neighborhood schools.[28]

Little Rock's downtown business district also remained segregated almost two decades following World War II. However, in the early 1960s, students from Philander Smith College organized "sit-in" demonstrations in selected stores along Main Street. The students' first efforts failed. In March 1960, fifty Philander students sought service at F. W. Woolworth's lunch counter only to be refused, and the counter closed. The store manager then called the police, and the students were arrested under Act 226, passed by the 1959 Arkansas General Assembly, which made sit-in demonstrations illegal. Similar demonstrations at Pfeiffer and Blass department stores also ended in arrests. In

each instance the students were fined from $300 to $500 in Municipal Court, and, even though their cases were appealed, the amount of the fines caused many students to have second thoughts about the strategy.[29]

The sit-in appeals were still in process in the summer of 1961 when Civil Rights advocates adopted a new strategy to call attention to segregation issues. Called "freedom rides," groups of activists boarded buses and toured key cities in the South. When Freedom Riders arrived in Little Rock on July 10 on a bus from St. Louis, Missouri, they too were arrested for sitting in a "whites only, intra-state waiting room" at the bus terminal. Under Act 226 they were fined $500 each and sentenced to six months in jail. As planned by the Freedom Riders, the case attracted considerable media attention, and Little Rock's business leaders were in no mood for a new round of national publicity. An ad hoc group, calling itself the Civic Progress Association (CPA), prevailed on the local court to release the Riders under federal interstate commerce rules, with the agreement that they would not return to Little Rock.[30]

Recognizing that it was only a matter of time until another incident provoked more unfavorable publicity, the CPA began a behind the scenes campaign to end all forms of segregation in the city. Working patiently and visiting one on one with the city's leading merchants, the

✧

Above: With Little Rock rapidly expanding to the west and south, public transportation became more a necessity than convenience for those who could not afford an automobile. Following the Birmingham, Alabama, controversy in 1955, Little Rock quietly integrated its bus lines in 1956 without incident.
COURTESY OF THE ARKANSAS HISTORY COMMISSION.

Below: Beginning in 1960, civil rights activists broadened their integration efforts to include retail stores in the central business district in major Southern towns. In Little Rock students from Philander Smith College and other volunteers targeted a number of stores, including the lunch counter at F. W. Woolworth. Store officials reversed policy in 1963 and began to serve African Americans. Other retail establishments quickly followed suit.
COURTESY OF THE ARKANSAS HISTORY COMMISSION.

Association had success. On January 2, 1963, Woolworth, McClellan, Walgreen, and Blass opened their lunch counters to all customers. The action was without fanfare or publicity and done so quietly that merchants in Pine Bluff only learned about it three weeks after it happened. However, other Little Rock merchants knew about the major stores' efforts, and they followed suit. By the end of January most of the city's retail establishments, hotels, motels and a downtown bowling alley were desegregated. Two weeks later federal district judge J. Smith Henley ruled on a lawsuit, filed the previous March by a group of black professionals, that desegregated all public facilities in the city, except swimming pools. The transformation in the city's race relations that came during the early 1960s attracted national attention, including a feature article in *Jet* magazine. Black and white leaders commended the city for integrating in such a peaceful fashion.[31]

Success with integration allowed Little Rock's developers to return to their plans for expanding the city's western boundaries. Ironically, even as the school crisis focused attention on the central city, significant developments were happening on the western edge of town. A new campus for the University of Arkansas for Medical Sciences was completed on Markham Street, approximately a mile east of Hayes Street. St. Vincent Infirmary completed its new campus at the intersection of Markham and Hayes Streets, and Little Rock Junior College expanded its curriculum to a four-year program and became Little Rock University. All of these changes came in 1957. The shopping centers at the intersection of Hayes Street and Asher Avenue were soon joined by two even larger shopping malls two miles to the North. The first, Park

Plaza Shopping Center, opened in 1960 on the Northwest corner of Hayes Street, now renamed University Avenue, and Markham Street. Then University Mall, the new star for retail stores, opened in 1966 on the southwest corner of University and Markham Street. These shopping centers, coupled with a separate Sears Roebuck store, also on University Avenue, and the new Southwest City Mall that opened some five miles south of the Asher and University intersection gave "western Little Rock" more shopping options than were available downtown. Perhaps as a portent of future developments, the new centers were anchored by major chain stores that promised stiff competition to the downtown merchants. Gus Blass opened a store at Park Plaza but kept the original business on Main Street open, too.[32]

A further indication that change was coming to old Little Rock occurred in 1961, when a third automobile bridge was completed across the Arkansas River. Located just downstream from the Main Street bridge, the new structure was the beginning link in the new Interstate Highway System authorized by Congress in 1956. The bridge was part of the Interstate 30 highway, which began in Little Rock and extended to Dallas, Texas. I-30 connected to another Interstate, Highway 40, that ran east-west through North Little Rock. The addition of these four-lane roads improved access to and through Little Rock similar to the way the first railroad bridge did in 1873.[33]

In the 1960s, Congress extended the urban renewal program to include business districts. City officials responded by consolidating the neighborhood projects with a plan to redevelop downtown and applied for additional aid in 1962. Called the "Central Little Rock Urban Renewal Project," the proposal included slightly more than five hundred acres and represented a mix of residential and commercial structures. It was the first project of this type to be approved under the expanded definition of urban renewal.[34]

The enlarged renewal project included plans to redevelop downtown by demolishing a number of older commercial structures and replacing them with parking lots and modern high-rise buildings. Plans also included an East-West Expressway to replace Tenth Street and

connect Interstate 30 on the east while extending to the western edge of town. Under this new plan, the character and appearance of downtown began to change rapidly. Joining the eighteen-story Tower Building, already completed (1960) at Fourth and Louisiana Streets, two new bank buildings, the 24-story Worthen Bank and the 21-story Union Bank, were completed in 1969. A third, the 30-story First National Bank building, opened in 1975. All three structures were along Capitol Avenue west of Main Street.[35]

The addition of these tall buildings transformed the original town site from a predominately retail center to a district dominated by financial services and office space. Rather than being the sole center of attention, downtown quickly became a commuter's haven where workers drove in for the work day and retreated to their suburban neighborhoods for evenings and weekends.

The changes that came with downtown redevelopment made it increasingly difficult for traditional "Main Street" businessmen to turn a profit. In a further effort to "revive" the area, merchants formed "Little Rock Unlimited Progress" (Little Rock UP) in 1970, and created the Metrocentre Improvement District. This allowed the group to increase property assessments and borrow money to redesign the area. Assisted by a $4.5 million federally insured loan, Little Rock UP closed Main Street to automobile traffic and made a four-block strip between Fourth and Eighth Streets into a mixed-use mall.[36]

Leaders in Little Rock UP also had hope that a revitalization of the Arkansas River would be an ally in their movement. Soon after World War II, Senators Robert Kerr of Oklahoma and Arkansas's John McClellan sponsored legislation to make the River a navigable waterway. The Army Corps of Engineers began work on the project in the early 1950s, and, by 1959, Little Rock leaders were encouraged enough by the progress to create the Little Rock Port Authority to receive and send anticipated trade goods. A decade later the Corps declared the River open for navigation to Little Rock, and, for the first time in one hundred years, the Arkansas again became an important part of city life.[37]

In addition to revitalizing the River, Little Rock UP also promoted the city's cultural opportunities. The Little Rock Art Center, with major financial support from Winthrop and Jeannette Rockefeller, opened in 1962 and within a decade was recognized as one of the outstanding arts centers in the Southwest. Complementing the fine arts, performing arts at the Arkansas Repertory Theatre and the Arkansas Symphony Orchestra also played a vital role in Little Rock UP's plans. The "Rep," organized in 1976 in a local church, was given a permanent home on Main Street in the Metrocenter Mall when the latter opened in 1978. The Symphony, organized in 1966, included musicians from throughout the state and performed at Robinson Auditorium.[38]

Outside the Main Street area neighborhood renewal continued. Congress had expanded the original "urban renewal" to include a new concept of "Model Cities" that emphasized redevelopment of entire neighborhoods rather than focusing on specific structures.[39]

The rapid disappearance of some of the city's oldest structures under the Urban Renewal

✧

Beginning in 1960 a new round of "tall buildings" began to appear in downtown Little Rock. For over thirty years the fourteen story Donaghey Building was the city's tallest building. However, it was superseded by the eighteen-story Tower Building in 1960, which in turn was trumped by the Union Bank Building (21 stories) and the Worthen Bank Building (24 stories), both completed in 1969. The First Commercial Bank Building (30 stories) was completed in 1976.

COURTESY OF THE ARKANSAS HISTORY COMMISSION.

program was a concern to some. In 1961 a group of these "concerned citizens" came together to form a Technical Advisory Committee on Significant Structures to advise Urban Renewal officials on buildings that had historical significance. Two years later the group reorganized as the Quapaw Quarter Association named in honor of the original claimants to the area. Armed with federal tax policies that encouraged redevelopment of historically significant structures, the QQA led a mini revival for re-investment in "old town." Initially focused on preserving and restoring single structures, the Association expanded its mission in the 1970s to include preservation of entire neighborhoods.[40]

Urban renewal was finally replaced by the Housing and Community Development Act of 1974. This new program was based on block grants and designed to produce "model cities" by redeveloping entire neighborhoods and properties, rather than demolishing substandard housing. It also placed emphasis on developing the infrastructure of streets, sewers, and drainage in depressed areas. Funding for this program was never adequate and the block grant projects were so widely distributed that most residents in the city were unaware of the program. Renewal plans continued but on a reduced scale and with the focus being primarily on neighborhoods rather than single structures.

Few Little Rockians anticipated how quickly development along the University Avenue corridor, coupled with redevelopment efforts downtown, would change the city. Until the 1960s most expansion had been residential and downtown merchants were still able to draw shoppers back to Main Street. However, the combination of inconvenience in getting around downtown and the convenience of shopping in West Little Rock caused a dramatic shift in consumer habits. The 1970s saw the beginning of even more spectacular demographic and economic changes. For one thing, the cross-town expressway was completed after Congressman Wilbur Mills got it included in the nation's Interstate Highway system. Initially designated Interstate 630, it was renamed the Wilbur D. Mills Expressway after the Congressman secured the funding. With the east-west corridor established, planners began work on a north-south connection linking

Interstate 40 with Interstate 30 on the city's West side. Designated Interstate 430, the first step in the construction, a bridge over the Arkansas River, was completed in 1974.[41]

Decisions by the federal courts brought the other "spectacular" change in the decade. In 1970, Judge J. Smith Henley ruled that student assignments and attendance zones did not comply with federally mandated desegregation guidelines and ordered school officials to prepare assignments that would insure that the district was fully integrated. Moreover, the Court maintained jurisdiction over the district in order to ensure compliance with the ruling. The plan that Little Rock school officials developed required that students be transported from one neighborhood to a school in another part of town. This policy of "busing to achieve racial balance" destroyed the concept of neighborhood schools and became increasingly unpopular. Thousands of white parents responded by taking their children out of public schools.

By the time Little Rock celebrated its 150th birthday as an incorporated city in 1981, it had lost its cohesion as a unified city. For over a hundred years, generations of city leaders had been able to expand the boundaries of the original town-site but still retain the vitality of the core community. However, rapid changes in technology, public policy decisions, and a changing economy allowed suburbs to become the dominant force in defining the city's identity.

CHAPTER VI ENDNOTES

1. Elizabeth Jacoway and David Colburn eds., *Southern Businessmen and Desegregation* (Baton Rouge: Louisiana State University Press, 1982), 15-41; C. Calvin Smith, *War and Wartime Changes: The Transformation of Arkansas, 1940-1945*, (Fayetteville: University of Arkansas Press, 1986), 36-55 and Jim Lester, *A Man for Arkansas: Sid McMath and the Southern Reform Traditon* (Little Rock: Rose Publishing Company, 1976), 128-155.
2. Ben F. Johnson III, *Arkansas in Modern America, 1930-1999* (Fayetteville: University of Arkansas Press, 2000). 111-117.
3. *Ibid.* and James C. Cobb, "The Lesson of Little Rock: Stability, Growth, and Change in the American South," in Elizabeth Jacoway and C. Fred Williams, *Understanding the Little Rock Crisis: An Exercise in Remembrance and Reconciliation* (Fayetteville: University of Arkansas Press, 1999), 107-122.
4. M. A. Lamberson, "An Analysis of the Financing Experiences of New and Expanding Manufacturing Firms in Arkansas," unpublished doctoral dissertation (Fayetteville: University of Arkansas, 1972), 11ff.
5. Little Rock Planning Commission, "Growth Pattern and Proposed Annexation: A Report," (September, 1956), 2-5.
6. Virgil Blossom, *It Has Happened Here* (New York: Harper & Collins, 1959), 9-97.
7. Carl H. Moneyhon, "From Slave to Free Labor: The Federal Plantation Experiment in Arkansas," Arkansas Historical Quarterly, 53 (Summer, 1994), 137-160 and Berna J. Love, *End of the Line: A History of Little Rock's West Ninth Street* (Little Rock: UALR Ledbetter Monograph Series, 2003), 2-7.
8. Planning Commission, "Growth Pattern and Proposed Annexation," 6ff.
9. James W. Bell, *Little Rock Handbook* (Little Rock: Publishers Bookshop, Inc., 1980), 31-48.
10. *Ibid.*
11. Irving Spitzberg, "A History of the Little Rock Housing Authority," unpublished manuscript, 1-5.
12. Knox Banner, "Relocation: Heart and Soul of Urban Renewal," *The American City*, 73 (October, 1958), 163-165.
13. "Cleared Two Years Ago and Still No Housing," *Arkansas Gazette*, November 11, 1957
14. B. Finley Vinson, "Little Rock's Low-Rent Housing Program," *The American City*, 67 (February, 1952), 86-87.
15. Love, *West Ninth Street*, 13-17 and John A. Kirk, *Redefining the Color Line: Black Activism in Little Rock, Arkansas, 1940-1970* (Gainesville: University Press of Florida, 2002), 34-53.
16. "Six GGC Candidates Win Close Vote," *Arkansas Democrat*, November 6, 1957.
17. Blossom, *It Has Happened Here*, 85-97.
18. John A. Kirk, "The Little Rock Crisis and Postwar Black Activism in Arkansas," *Arkansas Historical Quarterly*, 56 (Autumn, 1997), 273-293.
19. Interview with Georg G. Iggers, December 7, 2005, notes in possession of author and Kirk, *Redefining the Color Line*, 92-102.
20. Roy Reed, *Faubus: The Life and Times of an American Prodigal* (Fayetteville: University of Arkansas Press, 1997), 117126,
21. *Arkansas Gazette*, November 6, 1957 and Orval Faubus, *Down From the Hills* (Little Rock: The Pioneer Press, 1980), 32-51.
22. Author interview with Orval Faubus, May 14, 1992, Conway, Arkansas. Recording in possession of author.
23. Faubus, *Down From the Hills*, 198-203.
24. Faubus Interview, May 14, 1992.
25. Reed, Faubus: *The Life and Times*, 169-204.
26. Sondra Gordy, "Empty Class Rooms, Empty Hearts: Little Rock's Public School Teachers, 1958-1959," *Arkansas Historical Quarterly*, 56 (Winter, 1998), 427-442.
27. Kirk, *Redefining the Color Line*, 127.
28. Johnson, *Arkansas in Modern America*, 151-154.
29. Kirk, *Redefining the Color Line*, 149.
30. *Ibid.*
31. *Ibid.*
32. Bell, *Little Rock Handbook*, 48-50.
33. *Ibid.*
34. Johnson, *Arkansas in Modern America*, 152-153.
35. Jim Lester and Judy Lester, *Greater Little Rock: A Pictorial History* (Norfolk, VA: Donning, 1986), 212.
36. *Ibid.* 217.
37. *Ibid.*
38. Bell, *Little Rock Handbook*, 49 and Lester and Lester, Greater Little Rock, 214.
39. Johnson, *Modern Arkansas*, 158.
40. Quapaw Quarter Association, *The Quapaw Quarter: A Guide to Little Rock's 19th Century Neighborhoods*, (Little Rock: Quapaw Quarter Association, Incorporated, 1976), 1ff.
41. Love, *West Ninth Street*, 82-85 and Bell.

CHAPTER VII

LITTLE ROCK IN MODERN TIMES: SINCE 1980

Little Rock in the last quarter of the twentieth century posed a serious challenge to a generation of city leaders. Admittedly the capital city had always presented unique problems and opportunities unlike any other community in the state. However, after 1980, Little Rockians faced a choice of being one community or a series of suburbs in search of a city.

Population density was the key factor in shaping the city's development. It took almost a hundred years for Little Rock to grow to a population of fifty thousand. However, it gained its next 50,000 residents in approximately forty years and an additional 50,000 people were added in the next thirty years. But this healthy population growth was not equally distributed. Between 1980 and 1996 "old town" neighborhoods lost twenty-one percent of their population as people moved farther and farther west. In the next decade the imbalance became even greater due primarily to improvements in transportation and new opportunities for investment.[1] A north-south expressway (Interstate 430) connecting Interstates 30 and 40 had been in the planning stages since 1962 and was finally opened in late 1975. Two years later, Interstate 630 (Wilbur D. Mills Expressway) was extended west to join I-430 and together the two systems gave access to the city from all parts of the state.[2]

National events, including high interest rates, runaway inflation, and uncertainty about availability and costs for oil and gasoline, prevented immediate development at the junction of the two expressways. However, by the mid-1980s, inflation and interest rates were in decline, and developers became active at the I-430/I-630 intersection. The economic boom of the 1990s greatly accelerated construction in the area, and some urban planners began talking about the junction as the "second downtown."[3]

The Deltic Timber Company also stimulated growth in the region west of the I-430 expressway. The company owned more than thirty thousand acres in that region and for decades had kept it off the real estate market. However, in 1989 Deltic officials decided to develop forty-eight hundred acres into an upscale, residential subdivision called Chenal Valley. Just as the Broadmoor subdivision served as the catalyst for development along University Avenue, so Chenal Valley became the economic engine for growth beyond the beltway. The impact of that action was also reflected in population density.[4] In 1960 the Little Rock had roughly forty-five hundred people per square mile. However, by 2000 the density had dropped to fifteen hundred per square mile.[5] Moreover, the once prosperous University Avenue merchants now felt the pinch of competition as their Main Street colleagues had two decades earlier. Both Park Plaza and University Mall underwent major remodeling in the late 1980s but with limited success. By the turn of the century, the Mall was struggling to avoid bankruptcy and Park Plaza was trying to persuade its major tenants to reject temptations to move farther west. Down the avenue, Town and Country Shopping Center lost all of its original tenants except a bank and remained viable only by limiting its market primarily to service activities. University Shopping Center was purchased by the University of Arkansas at Little Rock and converted to academic space. Farther to the south, the Southwest City Mall closed and sold its property to the Arkansas State Police. Meanwhile, in the last two decades of the twentieth century, population west of University Avenue increased by sixty-seven percent. The composition of the city's population changed also. In 1960 the city's 107,793 residents were 82,461 white and 25,352 African American. By 1990, the white population had increased to 113,707, (an increase of 37.9 percent). However, in that same period the number of African-Americans increased to 59,742 (an increase of 135.7 percent).[6]

Little Rock's rapid expansion westward had a profound effect on the school district. The 1970 court order mandated that district officials establish a racial balance that approximated the city's racial make-

✧

While the last quarter of the twentieth century was known as a time of new directions for Little Rock, the Arkansas State Fair held in October of each year was one "tradition" that survived changes. The fairgrounds, with Barton Coliseum as its centerpiece, became a melting pot for citizens from throughout the state.

COURTESY OF THE ARKANSAS HISTORY COMMISSION.

up while also providing equal opportunity for each student. As previously noted, since the 1957 School Crisis, the district had been using a "controlled choice" plan for assigning students to specific buildings. Such a policy allowed students to stay in neighborhood schools; a decade later, in 1966, fewer than twenty percent of the city's African American students attended integrated schools.[7] The historic housing patterns that had kept blacks on the east and south side of the City and whites in the west were reflected in neighborhood schools. A majority of those schools were still racially identified—five were all black, eleven were all white. In 1966 Little Rock was approximately 67 percent white and 33 percent black.[8]

Responding to the Court, school officials developed a plan that transported black children in grades 1-3 to schools in predominantly white neighborhoods, while white students in grades 4-6 were transported to schools in black neighborhoods. Junior high and high schools also had attendance zones that required busing to maintain racial

balance. That part of the court order requiring equal opportunity was complicated by the school board's decision made in the 1950s to build new buildings in the areas experiencing the most rapid growth. Now there was a disparity between newer buildings in white neighborhoods and older buildings in black and mixed neighborhoods.[9]

Providing "racial balance" in a city so culturally divided presented a difficult challenge for public officials and it did not take white patrons long to express their displeasure with the policy. By 1976 the racial make-up district-wide was essentially 50-50, white and black. That percentage was achieved, however, not so much by increasing the number of black students but because so many white students left the district. By 1986 all the schools were integrated, and the district was 71.4 percent black. The year before the 1970 court order, there were 15,211 white students enrolled in the Little Rock public schools. In 1986 the number had fallen to 5,564. Overall enrollment in the district also declined for a decade, reaching its lowest mark in 1979-1980 at 18,971. In 1971 the district had had 23,227 students.[10]

To counter the "white flight" from the district, school officials first tried to make random attendance assignments for all students without respect to neighborhoods or school buildings. The results caused students on the same block to be assigned to different buildings. The plan was a public relations nightmare and accelerated white flight from the district. Scrapping that plan, the district then turned to "magnet schools" and placed a major emphasis on academic content and variety of course offerings. Patrons were initially offered a choice of programs that included: basic skills, international studies, fine and performing arts, and math and science. Attendance zones were still maintained, but the district also allowed "minority to majority" transfer and with African Americans in the majority, white students typically had their choice of schools after 1980. However, it soon became apparent that choice and "quality education" were not the only things influencing white parents to keep their children in the Little Rock public

schools. In another attempt to achieve racial balance, the magnet schools opened enrollment to students in both the North Little Rock and Pulaski County school districts. This approach was largely successful, and most magnet schools maintained an approximate 50-50 black-white ratio after 1990.[11]

District officials also returned to the courts in 1982 to find a way to stabilize the white out-migration. Many white families moved to communities just outside the city limits, and school officials filed suit in federal district court to consolidate with the North Little Rock and Pulaski County Special Districts. Attorneys for the district argued that Little Rock suffered by the failure of state officials to aggressively pursue desegregation on a state-wide basis and from real estate interests who failed to actively support the federal open housing law adopted in 1965. In 1984 lower court judge Henry Woods ruled in favor of Little Rock, but his decision was overturned by the Eighth Circuit Court of Appeals. The Appeals Court then issued its own remedy for the problem by ordering the Pulaski County Special School District to transfer approximately thirty-eight square miles to the Little Rock district in order to make the latter essentially coterminous with the City of Little Rock's boundaries. At the same time, the Court ordered Little Rock to transfer the Granite Mountain community to the Pulaski County district.[12]

As a result of the Eighth Judicial Circuit's decision, the Little Rock district gained 14 schools and almost 7,000 students. More importantly at the time, the decision changed the black/white ratio from 70/30 to 60/40 in the LRSD. Seizing on the idea that the district's boundaries should correspond with the city limits, school officials asked, and the lower court agreed, that such should continue to be the case—that when the city's boundaries changed, the LRSD would automatically change to coincide with them. However, the Eighth Circuit again reversed the district court order, on the basis that such a practice was "too intrusive." To date the Little Rock School District boundaries remain as they were on June 19, 1986, as established by the court.[13]

While waiting for the court ruling on consolidation, Little Rock school officials also moved to reestablish neighborhood schools on a limited basis. Called the "partial K-6 plan" the decision allowed four elementary schools in historically "all black" communities to return to segregated status. There was one caveat: per pupil funding for these schools was doubled and the district committed to closely monitoring how the schools were administered. Opponents filed a lawsuit against the decision; however, the plan was upheld by the district court and sustained by the Eighth Circuit. These schools and others that followed were called "incentive schools" and allowed to remain neighborhood schools. But this did not change the trend line in the Little Rock district. White students continued to leave, and the number of black students increased. By the year 2000, the ratio had returned to almost what it was in 1986; blacks made up 68.3 percent of the district's 25,323 students.[14]

While trying to respond to federal court mandates, Little Rock school officials faced a growing number of issues that ran counter to the court orders. Clearly the loss of neighborhood schools caused many white parents to abandon the district. But there were other reasons for the decline in white enrollment. The creation of Pulaski Academy, a private, K-12 school "beyond the beltway" in

✧

In 1981 Little Rock celebrated its sesquicentennial of being an incorporated community. Activities to celebrate the 150th birthday included a parade featuring floats for various decades in the city's history.
COURTESY OF THE ARKANSAS HISTORY COMMISSION.

western Little Rock also drew white students from the district. In other instances some parents turned to parochial education. Catholic and Lutheran schools, which had existed for over a century in the city for children of their membership, began to accept a larger percentage of non-Catholic or non-Lutheran students. Other denominations also opened schools, and home schooling, all but forgotten since the plantation days of the Nineteenth Century, became an increasingly popular choice after 1980.[15] Enrollment in non-public schools has been difficult to determine. However, U. S. Census data offer some clues to the dramatic shift in the Little Rock school district. The 1990 Population Census identified 14,693 non-African-American children, between ages 5 and 17, within the district's boundaries. Only 9,193 were enrolled in the public schools, an almost 40 percent discrepancy. Since state law requires children of these ages to be enrolled in school, it seems evident that they had chosen private over public education.[16]

In the late 1980s and early 1990s both the school district and the city were hit by a growing amount of violence perpetrated by street gangs. While it was not historically unusual for juveniles in urban settings to form "social clubs," few could have been compared to the gangs that organized in the closing years of the twentieth century. Local law enforcement officials reported

that new types of neighborhood groups began organizing as early as 1984 in the Highland Court housing project. As previously noted, this area developed as one of the public work projects in the 1930s on West Twelfth Street. While not as visceral as the later gangs, the self-named "Highland Court Crew" began to show evidence of more formal structure in 1987, using graffiti to mark boundaries and engaging in more and more street crime. By the end of the decade the Crew was associated with the California-based "Bloods." A number of other area gangs formed in the late 1980s and early '90s, with the biggest growth year being 1990. These groups were extremely violent, engaged in drug trafficking, and were driven by revenge and a determination to protect their self-identified boundaries. Drive-by shootings became their method of choice for defending territory and retaliating against violators. By 1993, Pulaski County Coroner Steve Nawojczyk, a nationally recognized expert on street gangs, reported that there were approximately forty gangs in the greater Little Rock area with an estimated membership approaching one thousand. Nawojczyk also noted that most of the local groups were affiliated with major gangs from major cities in other states and that the reason for the exponential growth was due primarily to crack cocaine, which came into common use in the late 1980s.[16]

The crime situation became so bad that the *New York Times* featured Little Rock in a front page story in 1993, stating that the city's per capita homicide rate was equal to New York City and Los Angeles. The *Times* article also reported that not all gang members were black and not all were male, but that young African-American males were the age and ethnic cohort most commonly involved with gang activity. The *Times* report attracted the attention of Marc Levin, who produced a film for the Home Box Office network entitled *Gang War: Bangin' In Little Rock*. Using a documentary format, Levin chronicled the lives of rival gang members in the capital city, used extensive interviews, and "on site" filming that provided an in-depth look into the intimate dealings in the dark underworld of gangs and their leaders.[18]

The gang documentary was the city's most significant public image problem since the school crisis from 1957 to 1959. It also

✧

Demolition of the Grady Manning and the Marion Hotels in 1980, and their replacement with the a new hotel and convention center signaled a renewed interest in "old town" as Little Rock returned to its roots along the Arkansas River. Led by a $160-million investment of the Clinton Library and School for Public Service, downtown developers expanded a strip from Broadway to Ferry Street along Markham Street as the River Market District. Beginning with a Farmers' Market, gourmet restaurants, office, and specialty shops, this "mixed-use" zone again became an address of distinction, as it had been in the days of Chester Ashley.

COURTESY OF ARKANSAS DEMOCRAT-GAZETTE.

spurred city officials and private developers to redouble their efforts to restore the vitality of the old city. One problem particularly vexing to political leaders came from individuals who expressed feelings of being disconnected and not being a part of the city. Many people in the old town area did not participate in city-wide elections and complained that City Hall did not represent their interest. These complaints came despite Charles Bussey, an activist in the Black Veterans' movement in the immediate post World War II years, being elected to the city board of directors in 1968. A decade later he was joined by Lottie Shackleford, the first black female elected to the board. In 1980 Bussey was chosen mayor by his fellow directors, and that same year the board chose Mahlon Martin as city manager. He was the first African American to hold that position in the city's history.[19]

Other critics attributed the disconnect between old town residents and city hall to what they believed to be a disproportional share of city resources and services going to affluent neighborhoods in West Little Rock. The new neighborhoods were being developed to the detriment of maintaining and re-developing the central city. When out-of-state developers presented a plan to the City Planning Commission for a new upscale mall on the West Belt Freeway (I-430), a multiracial coalition, claiming to represent low- income and working-class neighborhoods, organized to resist the plan. Affiliating with the Wisconsin-based New Party, the local group demanded that the mall question be put to a popular vote. How significant the Little Rock New Party's protest was in shaping policy has not been determined, but developers did put their plans on hold.[20]

The New Party also became active in local politics. Before the end of the decade, it had been successful in electing four of the ten members on the Little Rock Board of Directors. Part of the reason for the New Party's success was due to the changes made in city board elections. In 1994 voters approved a long discussed plan for returning to a partial ward system in city government with an elected mayor. In the years following the city manager system being put in place in 1957, directors were elected in city-wide races, and were chosen

for at-large positions. The intent, at least in the old Progressive Movement argument, was to emphasize professionalism in policy decision making and reduce parochial and special interests. In reality, the at-large elections allowed a relatively small group of white males from a small number of precincts in West Little Rock to dominate the Board. Between 1957 and 1994, eighty-five percent of the directors were male, eighty-two percent were white, and sixty-eight percent lived west of University Avenue. The reforms approved by city voters and in effect in time for the 1994 elections designated seven of the eleven board positions to be chosen from wards, three were at-large positions, and one was the office of Mayor, elected city-wide. The New Party was able to concentrate on the newly created Wards and win four of the ten seats.[21]

While the political reforms were playing out, developers were also moving forward with new plans for redeveloping the downtown area. Planning for the new look actually began in 1980, and, while much of the attention focused on the Main-Markham Street axis, there were some key developments elsewhere in Old Town. Chief among these was the city's tallest building, the forty-story TCBY Tower, which opened in

✧

Included in the city's sesquicentennial celebration was a project to refurbish the plaque marking the 'little rock.'

Above: Riverfest was one of the first attempts to revive the downtown area, when city leaders organized a three day celebration in May each year preceding Memorial Day featuring arts and crafts, entertainment and food, and a giant fireworks display.

COURTESY OF ARKANSAS DEMOCRAT-GAZETTE.

Below: The end of the Cold War brought major changes in the United States Air Force's mission in world affairs that was accompanied by many bases being closed. The Little Rock Air Force Base benefited from the re-organization as personnel and equipment were transferred to Arkansas. The first and second Iraq wars increased the base's strategic importance, as did the relief efforts for victims of hurricanes Katrina and Rita in 2005, when LRAFB became the collection point for air cargo sent from all over the world.

COURTESY OF ARKANSAS DEMOCRAT-GAZETTE.

1986 at Capitol and Broadway. The building, purchased by Metropolitan Bank in 2004, became the city's signature structure and extended the initial urban renewal plan of concentrating more people in vertical rather than horizontal spaces.[22]

The Tower also reflected new thinking about urban development that began in the late 1970s. In reviewing the old Urban Renewal and Model Cities programs, developers saw two crucial problems. One had to do with the "critical mass" of people living downtown, and a second concern was to find a consistent "economic engine" to replace the lost retail market. The key for any enterprise was to rebuild the population density in the old core city to a level that would sustain enterprise and justify providing traditional city services. Many experienced observers of Little Rock's history came to believe that the convention and tourist business might well replace retail sales and was an underdeveloped opportunity. Traditionally, Chamber of Commerce and convention staff members saw Hot Springs and other regional communities within the state as being their major competition. However, in reexamining Little Rock's potential, recruiters made plans to compete with regional cities outside the state. A critical factor in this decision was where to locate a "convention center" followed by whether to build new facilities or upgrade existing buildings. The location decisionand, which was to keep the focus downtown, was decided fairly quickly . But

a more extended discussion followed on renovating the Marion Hotel, the city's leading hotel and unofficial headquarters for convention activity, which had been built in 1907. Those wanting to raze the Marion and surrounding area won the debate, and in 1980 the political landmark was imploded. Construction on new facilities began quickly and by 1982 a new hotel, the Excelsior, and the new "Statehouse Convention Center" were ready for business.[23]

The wisdom of expanding the city's convention business as a way for revitalizing downtown was not immediately evident. The economic hard times of the 1980s made it difficult for quick growth, and the Excelsior struggled as did the convention business. However, an improving economy, a dedicated group of planners and developers, and the Presidency of Bill Clinton served to launch major new development in the 1990s. In an ironic twist of events, the new developers turned to the Arkansas River as the gateway for reviving "old town." Beginning in 1991, two Fortune 500 companies, Dillard's Department Stores, Inc., and Alltel Communications built multi-million dollar headquarters buildings in a five mile strip along the Arkansas River between the original "little rock" and "big, or French rock." Both companies were helped greatly in their relocation by financing from Stephens, Inc. Headed by Witt, and after 1973, Jack Stephens, this investment banking company provided the capital for much of the economic growth in the last quarter of the twentieth century. In addition to Dillard's and Alltel, Stephens also provided start-up funds for Systematics, Inc., a bank software company that began operation in the

late 1960s and became a national success story by the 1980s. Stephens, Inc. played a central role in providing the investment capital to launch the redevelopment, not only in Little Rock but throughout the state.[24]

The area around the original "point of rocks" also became the center of attention in the early 1990s. Beginning with landscaping, the little rock was the star attraction in a new Riverfront Park developed by the city Parks Department. Private developers followed with a $3.5 million plan to create a "River Market District," of restaurants, up-scale retail shops, and loft apartments. The district was designed to extended eight blocks from Broadway to Ferry Street.[25]

While private developers were at work, city residents approved a new bond program that more than doubled the size of the Convention Center. The Excelsior Hotel also underwent change, first being purchased by a Japanese company, which then sold it to the Peabody Hotel chain of Memphis, Tennessee. The Peabody group put their stamp on the hotel with a multi-million dollar renovation. A decision by the Board of Directors for both the Little Rock Public Library and the Museum of Discovery to relocate to the River Market District proved to be major assets for the area as well. The refocus on the Arkansas River allowed urban designers to incorporate the north side of the river into the revitalization efforts. Calling attention to the six bridges that spanned the

River, planners pointed out that the residential and commercial areas on the north side could play an important role in providing the population density necessary to rebuild downtown. They chose the Junction Bridge as the unifying link between the twin cities and developed plans to convert it into a pedestrian walkway that served as an icon for the project. While local politics prevented Little Rock from extending its boundaries back across the River as they had done in the nineteenth century, re-development along both sides of the waterway was mutually beneficial.[26]

Of all the plans for downtown Little Rock, however, the single most important factor in stimulating revival to the area came from Governor Bill Clinton's two campaigns, and subsequent elections, as President of the United States (1993-2001). Making downtown Little Rock the headquarters for both campaigns, coupled with the multitude of news stories, generated by his eight years in office, kept a steady flow of people into the downtown area. But perhaps of even more long-term importance to the city was Clinton's decision to build his Presidential Library on the eastern edge of the River Market district. That anchor ensured the economic viability of the downtown region. Almost 500,000 people visited the library during its first year of operation (2004-2005). The town that started on a plateau overlooking the Arkansas River returned to the river and rediscovered its spirit.

✧

Little Rockians rediscovered the river after one hundred years of moving away from its shore line. However, the steamboat, once the proud symbol of the city's contact with the outside world returned only as a tourist attraction in the new era.

COURTESY OF *ARKANSAS DEMOCRAT-GAZETTE.*

CHAPTER VII ENDNOTES

1   "Arkansas Population Per Square Mile by City," IEA Census State Data Center, 2000. Little Rock reached approximately 50,000 population in 1915, in 1950 the population was 102,213, and in 1980 the population was 158,461.
2   Seth Blomeley, "Report offers solutions for traffic snarls at I-630/I-430," *Arkansas Democrat Gazette*, July 18, 2005. Completion of Interstate 440 connecting Interstate 30 with Interstate 40 on the east side of town via the Little Rock Airport.
3   Ben F. Johnson III, *Arkansas in Modern America*, 1930-1999 (Fayetteville: University of Arkansas Press, 2000), 160.
4   Deltic Timber Company, "Press Release," December 30, 2005.
5   Johnson, *Arkansas in Modern America*, 160.
6   Arkansas Quick Facts. http://quickfacts.gov/states.
7   Johnson, *Arkansas in Modern America*,154.
8   *Ibid.*
9   Joel E. Anderson, et al, *Plain Talk: The Future of Little Rock's Public Schools* (Little Rock: University of Arkansas at Little Rock, 1997), 11-16.
10 Office of Student Assignment (LRSD), "Historical Census of Black-White Enrollment, 1968-2004."
11 Anderson, *Plain Talk*, 17-27.
12 *Ibid.*
13 *Ibid.*
14 Office of Student Assignment (LRSD), "Historical Census".
15 Johnson, *Arkansas in Modern America*, 156-157.
16 Anderson, *Plain Talk*, 29-47.
17 Steve Nawojczyk, "Coroner's Report: Information and Resources on Gang Intervention and Prevention," available at http://www.gangwar.com.
18 Marc Levin, *Gang War: Bangin' in Little Rock*, Home Box Office Network, 1994.
19 *Arkansas Gazette*, July 8, 1980.
20 *Arkansas Democrat Gazette*, September 22, 1999.
21 *Ibid.* and Johnson, *Arkansas in Modern America*, 156-157.
22 http://www.downtownlr.com
23 Jim Lester and Judy Lester, *Greater Little Rock* (Norfolk, Virginia: The Donning Company, 1986), 216.
24 George Waldon, "Witt & Jack Stephens: Rural Charm, Urban Money," *Arkansas Business* (January, 2006).
25 Bill Hornaday, "Downtown Revival," *Arkansas Democrat Gazette*, May 2, 2005.
26 *Ibid.*

BIBLIOGRAPHY

Books

Arnold, Morris S. *Colonial Arkansas, 1686-1803*. Fayetteville: University of Arkansas Press, 1991.

Bell, James W. *Little Rock Handbook*. Little Rock: Publishers Bookshop Inc., 1980.

Bolton, S. Charles. *Remote and Restless: Arkansas 1800-1860*. Fayetteville: University of Arkansas Press, 1998.

De Black, Thomas A. *With Fire and Sword: Arkansas in Civil War and Reconstruction, 1861-1874*. Fayetteville: University of Arkansas Press, 2003.

Fletcher, John Gould. *Arkansas*. Chapel Hill: University of North Carolina Press, 1947.

Foti, Thomas and Gerald Hanson. *Arkansas and the Land*. Fayetteville: University of Arkansas Press, 1993.

Graves, John William. *Town and Country: Race Relations in an Urban Context, Arkansas, 1865-1905*. Fayetteville: University of Arkansas Press, 1990.

Herndon, Dallas T. *Annals of Arkansas, 1947*, 4 volumes. Little Rock: The Historical Record Association, 1948.

Johnson, Ben F. III. *Arkansas in Modern America, 1930-1999*. Fayetteville: University of Arkansas Press, 2000.

Kirk, John A. *Redefining the Color Line: Black Activism in Little Rock Arkansas, 1940-1970*. Gainesville: University Press of Florida, 2002.

Love, Berna J. *End of the Line: A History of Little Rock's West Ninth Street*. Little Rock: Center for Arkansas Studies, Ledbetter Monograph Series, 2003.

Lester, Jim and Judy Lester. *Greater Little Rock*. Norfolk, Virginia: The Donning Company, 1986.

Moneyhon, Carl H. *Arkansas and the New South, 1874-1929*. Fayetteville: University of Arkansas Press, 1997.

Quapaw Quarter Association. *Quapaw Quarter: A Guide to Little Rock's 19th Century Neighborhoods*. Little Rock: Quapaw Quarter Association, 1976.

Richards, Ira Don. *Story of a River Town: Little Rock in the Nineteenth Century*. Benton: Privately Printed, 1969.

Ross, Margaret. *Arkansas Gazette: The Early Years, 1819-1866*. Little Rock: *Arkansas Gazette* Foundation, 1969.

Roy, F. Hampton, Sr., and Charles Witsell, Jr. *How We Lived: Little Rock as an American City*. Little Rock: August House, 1984.

Thomas, David Yancy. *Arkansas and its People, A History 1541-1930*. New York: American Historical Association, Inc., 1930.

Articles

Alexander, Charles C. "White Robed Reformers: The Ku Klux Klan comes to Arkansas, 1921-1922." 22 *Arkansas Historical Quarterly* (Spring, 1963), 8-23.

Dickinson, Samuel Dorris. "Colonial Arkansas Place Names," Arkansas Historical Quarterly, 48 (Summer 1989), 137-168.

Gordy, Sondra. "Empty Class Rooms, Empty Hearts: Little Rock's Public School Teachers, 1958-1959," *Arkansas Historical Quarterly 56* (Winter 1998), 427-442.

Nichols, Cheryl Griffith. "Pulaski Heights: Early Suburban Development on Little Rock," *Arkansas Historical Quarterly 41* (Summer 1982) 138-142.

Ross, Margaret Smith. "Squatters Rights: Some Pulaski County Setters Prior to 1814," *Pulaski County Historical Review 47* (Fall 1999), 60-63.

Scott, Kim Allen. "Plague on the Homefront: Arkansas and the Great Influenza Epidemic of 1918," 47 *Arkansas Historical Quarterly* (Winter 1988), 320-329.

Worthern, William B. "Municipal Improvement in Little Rock—A Case History," *Arkansas Historical Quarterly* 46 (Winter 1987), 317-347.

Newspapers

Arkansas Gazette, 1819-2005.

Master's Theses

McDade, Bryan E. "The Six Bridges at Little Rock: Understanding the Historical Significance and Relevance of the Six Bridges that Span the Arkansas River At Little Rock". Little Rock: University of Arkansas at Little Rock, 2000.

Rimmer, Martha Williamson. "Charles E. Taylor and His Administration, 1911-1919: Progressivism in Little Rock". Fayetteville: University of Arkansas, 1977.

SPECIAL THANKS TO

A. Tenenbaum Company

Arkansas Education
Association

Capitol Glass Company, Inc.

D. B. Hill Contractor, Inc.

SHARING THE HERITAGE

historic profiles of businesses, organizations, and
families that have contributed to the development
and economic base of Little Rock

Democrat Printing &
Litho Company

Markham House Suites

Refrigeration & Electric
Supply Company

Treadway Electric Company

Welsco, Inc.

TUGGLE SERVICES, INC.

APARTMENT HUNTERS

ARKANSAS SUITES

✧

Above: Cathy Tuggle.

Below: Corporate Suites' living area.

Tuggle Services, Inc. was founded on October 1, 1999 as a "real estate and relocation service" and today includes Apartment Hunters, which offers clients a free service to locate the perfect apartment, duplex, rental house or condominium in their area, and Arkansas Suites, which offers over 100 corporate suites with all-inclusive, furnished apartment packages throughout central Arkansas.

Founders Cathy and Paul Tuggle are natives of Haskell, a small community in Benton, south of Little Rock. Cathy attended the University of Arkansas at Little Rock and quickly established her career in the field of real estate. Today, she is the president and principal broker of Tuggle Services, Inc., dba Apartment Hunters and Arkansas Suites, and Paul is co-owner and president. He also owns a construction company. Cathy's experience in the apartment industry spans fourteen years and includes experience in property management and processing lease applications on new construction. She has also received the National Apartment Association designations of NALP (National Apartment Leasing Professional) and CAM (Certified Apartment Manager).

Tuggle Services, Inc. is headquartered in West Little Rock at the Creekwood Plaza Shopping Center at 1101 South Bowman Road and employs seven leasing and relocation specialists and corporate housing coordinators,

with a large customer base comprised of hospital personnel as well as employees of small businesses and major companies. With increases of at least eighteen percent every year since its opening, the company is set to expand business across the State of Arkansas while promoting relocation efforts and continued growth in the Little Rock area.

Through the Tuggles' one-of-kind apartment location service, Apartment Hunters provides a comprehensive database of apartments in north, west, and southwest Little Rock, Cabot, Conway, and Jacksonville. Each listing includes floor plans, virtual tours, maps and photos, and information about unique amenities, rental costs, deposits, and move-in specials. Professional, local apartment hunters find the perfect apartment to make any moving transition less stressful and more personalized. And Apartment Hunters not only assists those interested in finding just the right apartment, but also carries a wide variety of individually owned properties, such as houses, duplexes, townhouses and condominiums.

Apartment Hunters is compensated by owners of various housing properties, and provides a search that can be narrowly defined to locate the exact apartment available within a given community. Special and employer discounts, and

personal tours for employees relocating to the area are also available for a small fee.

These unique tours were created for anyone who is unfamiliar with the local rental market and, with time at a premium, are offered as either half or full day events to explore the city. Tours consist of a full needs assessment by the rental consultant to determine rental criteria, including area, budget, special needs and commute times; a research and option process, including scheduling of appointments; a scheduled tour, setting appointments and transportation to apartment communities; an area tour and information included with apartment tours; and an extensive follow-up to insure a successful rental process.

Advantages to taking a tour include: saving time and money—the cost of renting a car, extra time in a hotel, and extra time driving around can cost hundreds of dollars, so Apartment Hunters take care of the driving, map out the tour, and set the appointments. This allows the client the unhurried opportunity to enjoy the tour and secure a new apartment; knowing the market—as the leader in apartment locating, Apartment Hunters maintains excellent relationships with hundreds of apartment communities and, with such a large sponsorship, know they can find anyone the perfect apartment; working with all major employers—using professional rental consultants can alleviate the demands of starting a new job and relocating. Local experience and expertise to identify needs and options in a timely fashion take the stress out of the relocation process and the employer may also cover the cost of the tour as part of their relocation benefits package; taking people

where they want to live—whether it's a walk to the River Market or living on the Arkansas River, each associate takes great pride in tailoring every tour to the exact needs of their clients, and services extend from Little Rock to North Little Rock and cover most of the suburban areas.

Additional services offered through tour programs include corporate suite, hotel or airport pick-up, city or neighborhood tours, school and daycare information, furniture rental assistance, social security application, and bank account set-up. With such attention to detail and outstanding, personalized service, it is no wonder that Apartment Hunters have truly become the experts at finding the perfect place to call home.

Corporate lodging has no finer representatives in the area than Arkansas Suites. Created for businessmen and women who find

✧

Above: Front row (from left to right): Diane McCoy, Cathy Tuggle, and Melissa Wooten. Back row (from left to right): Nate Williams, Kathy Greenbaum, Jamie Sanders, and Leah Greenbaum.

Below: Corporate Suites' living area.

themselves relocating to central Arkansas, Arkansas Suites specializes in offering a tailored alternative to an often long and expensive stay in a hotel. Creating a unique "corporate apartment home suite," each location offers elegant furnishings, numerous amenities, extra housewares and linens, basic cable to premium channels, fitness centers and gym memberships, and gourmet-equipped kitchens for weekly, monthly and extended terms—all starting as low as forty-seven dollars per night.

Another unique feature of Arkansas Suites allows clients to choose between basic, deluxe, and executive packages to ensure that every conceivable service is tailored to meet any need. Each package includes floor plans with a large living room, dining room, large bedroom and bathroom, a kitchen, balcony, and storage closet—all designed with fine furnishings such as a chair, sofa, coffee and end tables, lamps, dining table and chairs, dresser and mirror, nightstands, and a queen-size pillow-top bed. Housewares include mealtime place settings, cutlery tray, stainless steel cookware set, cooking utensils, automatic coffeemaker, toaster, mixing bowls, measuring cups and spoon set, kitchen wastebasket, dish towels and potholders, an iron and ironing board, broom and dustpan, a mop, and a vacuum cleaner. Linen and bath accessories include bath towels and washcloths, bed sheet sets, pillows and blankets. Appliances include

a washer and dryer, refrigerator with an icemaker, garbage disposal, dishwasher and microwave. Electronics include a nineteen or twenty-five inch color television with remote, trimline or cordless phones, a video recorder, clock radio, and answering machine. Packages also include complimentary supplies of soap, washing detergent, toilet paper, and paper towels; and utilities include gas and electricity, basic cable and extended basic cable television services, local phone service, and water and trash services. Monitored alarm systems, housekeeping services, and gated communities are also available to clients as optional items.

In offering such a wide range of varied relocation services to customers from around the state, Tuggle Services, Inc. helps to create a highly effective situation for employers and apartment owners and managers alike. Employers are sure to increase their new-hire productivity and more effectively recruit key personnel, while apartment managers and owners enjoy approving applications made by well-informed residents who have chosen their location for very specific reasons, with ease and the invaluable insight and forethought of the Apartment Hunters consulting staff.

The company offers its many years of experience, state-of-the-art systems and software, and a professional, licensed staff—all instrumental in saving any business and personnel time and money, greatly reducing the stress associated with relocating, aiding in recruitment efforts, and making it easier for new employees to concentrate on productivity, instead of searching for an apartment…and all at no cost to the employer.

The Tuggles are members of the Arkansas Apartment Association, of which Cathy serves as its education chairman; IREM (Institute of Real Estate Management), of which Cathy serves as its education chairman; Apartments Nationwide; the ERC Relocation Council; the Little Rock Chamber of Commerce; the North Little Rock Chamber of Commerce; the Arkansas Realtors Association; and the Downtown Little Rock Partnership. Tuggle Services, Inc., also participates in the American Cancer Society's annual Relay for Life fundraising program and the Make A Wish Foundation.

Today, Tuggle Services, Inc. continues its involvement in the growth and expansion of the Little Rock area. In 2004 the company assisted in corporate housing and the relocation of those who participated in the construction and grand opening of the Clinton Library. In 2005, Apartment Hunters assisted BOMA, IREM and the Arkansas Apartment Association in the planning of a Legislative Advocacy meeting consisting of several local State House Representatives.

The company was awarded Best Website through Apartments Nationwide.com in 2003, and received the title "Vendor of the Year" by the Arkansas Apartment Association in 2004.

For more information about reserving a corporate suite or to find the perfect Little Rock apartment, visit the company's outstanding, user-friendly websites at www.arkansassuites.net, www.apthunters lr.com and www.lrapartments.com, or call them locally at (501) 219-APTS (2787) and toll-free at (800) 644-2787.

✧

The staff at Tuggle Services, Inc. is well known for their attention to detail and ability to find the most comfortable living atmosphere for their clients.

BAILEY PROPERTIES, LLC & BAILEY TIMBERLANDS, LLC

❖

Above: Dr. Ted and Virginia Bailey.

Below: The historic Union Station, home of Bailey Properties and Bailey Timberlands.

Virginia Arrington Mitchell and H. A. Ted Bailey were married on June 23, 1945, at First Baptist Church in El Dorado, Arkansas. Virginia was the daughter of Maude and Dr. J. G. Mitchell of El Dorado, Arkansas, and Ted the son of Madeline and Ted Bailey, Sr., of Little Rock, Arkansas. Ted Sr.'s brother, Carl Edward Bailey, served as the thirty-first governor of Arkansas, from 1937 to 1941.

After completing medical training at the University of Arkansas and Tulane University, Dr. Ted served a two-year stint in the U.S. Navy during the Korean War. He and Virginia then returned to Little Rock, where Dr. Ted began his medical practice.

In 1956, Virginia and Ted formed a business venture, Bailey Corporation, a real estate company focused on developments in and around Little Rock. In 2006 the company celebrated its fiftieth anniversary. Initially, Ted served as chairman and Virginia as president. The Bailey Corporation first acquired the historic Packet House and, by 1961, built and established its corporate headquarters in the Capitol Place office building at 1618 West Third Street. Ted opened the Bailey Ear Clinic at 1610 West Third Street in 1960 and became the first physician in the state to limit his practice to surgery and treatment of ears only.

Since that time, several relocations of the corporate offices have occurred. This included offices at the Gaines Place Building at Third and Gaines in 1979, the Riverdale Building in 1983 and the historic Union Station in 1992, where it remains.

Since Bailey Corporation's creation, it has established a successful identity through its quality subdivisions and projects (including Foxcroft, Andover Square and St. Charles), along with its growth and ability to embrace change.

In the early 1990s, the company announced the new officers: President and CEO John S.

Bailey; First Vice President Virginia; Executive Vice Presidents Ted Bailey III, David D. Henry, and Eric W. Stoiber; and Dr. Ted, chairman emeritus. John, Ted III, David, and Eric are licensed Arkansas real estate brokers.

In August 1996 a real estate umbrella partnership was formed as the ownership entity for all the family members' properties. The newly created entity was named Bailey Properties, LLC. In August 2003, through a family restructuring, John and Patti acquired complete interest in Bailey Properties, LLC.

Ted III and David left Bailey Properties to form their own companies—the Multifamily Group and Henry Management, Inc.

The family continued to operate Bailey Timberlands, LLC, holding lands in Arkansas and Louisiana. All of Virginia and Ted's children—Mary Maude Shafer, Ted III, Jo McCray, John, and Madeline Henry—serve on the Bailey Timberlands Board of Managers. They are also members of the Virginia and Ted Bailey Foundation Board, along with Sharon Bailey and Dr. Ted, who serves as foundation president.

A half-century in the real estate business has made the Bailey name synonymous with

quality. The company motto—"Where Our Team Makes the Difference"—gives recognition to the key role of the Bailey Company team.

Today, under John's leadership, Bailey Properties, LLC owns and manages the Union Station and Capitol Place office buildings in Little Rock, a strip shopping center in Blytheville, Arkansas, and over 4,400 apartment homes in 18 apartment communities in Arkansas, Texas, and Louisiana.

Dr. Ted began his practice of medicine in Little Rock in 1953. In 1970, he served as president of the southern section of the American Ear, Nose & Throat Society. In 1971 and 1972, he served as chief of staff of Baptist Medical Center. In 1974, Dr. Ted organized a group of ear, nose, and throat doctors and moved the enlarged practice to the new Baptist Medical Towers Building. In 1990-91 he served as president of the American Otological Society, an organization of ear surgeons; election to membership is based upon significant contributions to the profession. Dr. Ted served as the clinic president and physician administrator until his retirement from medical practice in 1994. Subsequently, he devoted his time to business interests in Bailey Properties, Bailey Timberlands, and

✧

Virginia and Ted Bailey's family members, children, spouses, and twenty-two grandchildren.

Bailey Bluff, a condominium development initiated by Virginia in Cypress Bend Park at Toledo Bend Lake in Louisiana.

Virginia, throughout her business career, was a licensed Arkansas Real Estate Broker and held a degree from Baylor University in Waco, Texas. She was active in many community organizations. She served first as president and then chairman of the Arkansas Arts Center Board from 1976-78. In 1976, she began a three-year term on the Eighth District Federal Reserve Bank Board in St. Louis, Missouri—the first woman to do so. Other boards on which she served included the Florence Crittenden Home, the Visiting Nurse's Association, Parkway Village, and CARTI. Additionally, she was a member of the Little Rock Junior League and Fifty for the Future.

She and Ted received the "Philanthropist of the Year" Award in 1994 from the Arkansas chapter of the National Fundraising Association. Also in 2005, Ted was named the "Individual Art Patron of the Year" by the Governor's Arts Council. Virginia and Ted were both actively involved in UALR volunteer activities. They received the UALR Builders Award in 1989, Ted the UALR Honorary Doctorate of Humane Letters in 1991, and, on June 1, 2002, the new UALR Alumni and Friends Center was named the Bailey Center in their honor. Ted served twelve years on the UALR Board of Visitors and four years as chairman of the UALR Foundation Fund Board. He is currently chairman emeritus of the Foundation Fund Board. Virginia was a founding member of UALR Friends of the Arts and served as the first president.

Dr. Ted's community involvement has included service on the boards of the YMCA, Boy's Club, the United Way, the Little Rock Chamber of Commerce, and as the president of the Baptist Health Foundation in 1985. Additionally, he has served on a number of bank boards, including Union, Worthen, and Boatmen's Banks. He has also served as the president of the Rotary Club of Little Rock. During his term (1987-88), Virginia was among the first nine women to be inducted into the club.

Dr. Ted has a history of service to the sport of tennis. He has served as president of the Arkansas Tennis Association and as chairman of the Arkansas Tennis Patrons Foundation. He has also served as president of the nine-state Southern Tennis Association and has chaired the U.S. Tennis Association's Olympic and Education and Research Committees. He is a member of the Sports Hall of Fame of Arkansas Tennis, Southern Tennis, and UALR. He has also served for eight years as a member of the board of the International Tennis Hall of Fame in Newport, Rhode Island, and presently is a member of the two prestigious tennis organizations, the International Club of the U.S. and the Major Wingfield Club.

Virginia was serving on the Advisory Board of the National Museum for Women in the Arts in Washington, D.C., until the time of her passing on June 1, 2003. Virginia also directed and managed her Louisiana timberlands until her passing.

Ted and Virginia's family includes five children and their spouses, and twenty-two grandchildren: Mary Maude and Robert Shafer, with children Laura, Mary Catherine, Philip, and Sarah; Ted III and Maranda Bailey, with children Ben, Ted IV, Ali, and Barrett; Jo and Kevin McCray, with children Virginia, Jason, Mitchell, Ellianna, Melissa, James, Elizabeth, and Emily; John and Patti Bailey with children Rachael, Erik, Edward, and Rebecca; and Madeline and David Henry with children Mary and John.

On April 23, 2006, Ted and Sharon Shanks were married in a ceremony held at the Country Club of Little Rock. Sharon and Ted met in 1971 while working together at the medical clinic. Their work together included preparing exhibits for national medical meetings, teaching as faculty of the national medical specialty association; serving as one of the original co-investigation teams for the FDA cochlear implant research program; and co-authoring some forty scientific articles for publication in national medical literature.

Sharon served as chief administrative officer of the clinic, Arkansas Otolaryngology Asssociates. She is a past president of the American Medical Audiology Association; a member of the board of trustees of the Arkansas Arts Center; the advisory board of the School of Business at UALR; the Daughters of the American Revolution; and the Rotary Club of Little Rock.

✧

Dr. Ted and Sharon Bailey.

The Quapaw Quarter Association (QQA) is a nonprofit membership-based organization dedicated to historic preservation in Little Rock.

Like many historic preservation organizations in the United States, the QQA grew out of the era of urban renewal and interstate highway construction, a time when thousands of historic buildings and neighborhoods succumbed to the bulldozer. Unlike other preservation groups, however, the QQA can actually trace its roots to an agency which administered urban renewal projects.

In 1961 the Little Rock Housing Authority appointed a five-member "Significant Structures Technical Advisory Committee" to provide advice on the historical and architectural significance of buildings in the MacArthur Park neighborhood, then part of a large urban renewal project. The group determined that a special name for the area was needed to create a positive image for an area that was then in decline. They considered eleven possible names, but eventually decided on the "Quapaw Quarter," derived from the Quapaw Treaty Line of 1819 that runs through the neighborhood. The following year, the group expanded its membership and adopted the name "Quapaw Quarter Committee."

In 1963 the Quapaw Quarter Committee held its first Tour of Homes to acquaint local citizens with the beautiful historic architecture of the area. The Spring Tour of Historic Homes is an event which still continues today. The Committee also began recognizing important historical resources by the presentation of Quapaw Quarter Historic Structure plaques. Trapnall Hall, which had recently been restored by the Junior League of Little Rock, was the recipient of the first plaque.

Organized preservation efforts in Little Rock remained the Quapaw Quarter Committee's province until November of 1968, when several committee members joined with other preservation-minded individuals to incorporate the Quapaw Quarter Association.

Originally the term Quapaw Quarter was defined in the QQA's articles of incorporation as a sixteen-square block area, one quarter of

a township, bounded by Capitol Avenue on the north, Scott Street on the west, Ninth Street on the south, and Bond Avenue on the east. The boundaries of the Quapaw Quarter, while not a legally defined area, have now grown to encompass what would have been the boundaries of Little Rock in 1900. This area extends from the Arkansas River on the north, Fourche Creek on the south, the old Rock Island railroad tracks on the east, and the Central High neighborhood on the west.

The QQA has published the *Quapaw Quarter Chronicle*; it's a bimonthly preservation newspaper, since 1974. The QQA also sponsors preservation workshops, offers technical advice to individuals interested in purchasing and restoring historic homes and buildings, Since 2002, the QQA has been a Local Partner of the National Trust for Historic Preservation. This designation has enabled the QQA to bring the National Trust's technical assistance, grants, and other programs to Little Rock. The QQA also works with city leaders to promote policies that will encourage preservation-based redevelopment of older, historic neighborhoods.

For more information, contact the Quapaw Quarter Association at 501-371-0075 or visit www.quapaw.com on the Internet.

✧

Examples of historic buildings rescued by the QQA's advocacy efforts include Kramer School (ca. 1895) and Curran Hall (ca. 1842). Both were originally slated for demolition but were later rehabbed and given new uses—Kramer School as residental loft apartments and Curran Hall as the Little Rock Visitor Information Center.

CROMWELL ARCHITECTS ENGINEERS INCORPORATED

The subject of two books, both published by the August House of Little Rock, Cromwell Architects Engineers, founded in 1885, is the seventh oldest firm of its type practicing in America today. The firm has provided design services in thirty-seven states and eleven foreign countries in the Eastern and Western hemispheres.

The firm has been known by many names through the years. The firm's genealogy isas follows:

1885	Benjamin J. Bartlett
1888	Bartlett & Thompson
1890	Charles L. Thompson
1891	Rickon & Thompson
1897	Charles L. Thompson
1916	Thompson & Harding
1926	Thompson, Sanders & Ginocchio
1938	Sanders & Ginocchio
1941	Ginocchio & Cromwell
1947	Ginocchio, Cromwell & Associates
1961	Ginocchio, Cromwell, Carter, Dees & Neyland
1962	Ginocchio, Cromwell, Carter & Neyland, Inc.
1969	Cromwell, Neyland, Truemper, Millett & Gatchell, Inc.
1974	Cromwell, Neyland, Truemper, Levy & Gatchell, Inc.
1981	Cromwell, Truemper, Levy, Parker, Woodsmall, Inc.
1988	Cromwell, Truemper, Levy, Thompson, Woodsmall, Inc.
2000	Cromwell Architects Engineers, Inc.

✧

Above: UAMS Jackson T. Stephens Spine and Neuroscience Institute.

Below: Arkansas Children's Hospital.

Because of its growing staff and expanded responsibility of team members, the firm adopted the name Cromwell Architects Engineers in 2000 in honor of its beloved Edwin B. Cromwell, FAIA (deceased in 2001), whose most cherished project was the Capital Hotel. Undoubtedly, the firm will continue to transform in the future, maybe to the point of changing its name again, but for now, it feels it is a good fit.

Ed Cromwell believed, as the firm's current partners do, that no single individual could claim ownership to a design. The partners also believe the best designs are the product of a team effort, which includes owner, user, builder, and others.

Winner of seventy-one awards for design in architecture, engineering, and interior design, the firm is known for its commitment to sustainable design and integrated approach to services it offers to its clients. Cromwell's unique corporate culture, fostered by broad-based employee ownership and a team approach to management, recognizes the inherent talents of its staff as individuals and allows professional development based on strengths and interest.

These principles have allowed the firm to be successful in various conditions of the economy. It also has allowed the firm to develop a broad and diverse practice with specialization in a number of different building types and design services, offering the complete range of all disciplines necessary to design and provide construction phase services.

Cromwell's staff includes architects, civil, structural, mechanical, electrical, and fire protection engineers, interior designers and construction specialists. This holistic or integrated approach to design provides buildings uniquely suited to meet their users' needs.

Being the "largest" and "oldest" firm in Arkansas offers unique opportunities. It also presents formidable challenges. To stay fresh and innovative, the firm is continually recruiting new talent to the staff. Innovation is encouraged, and special attention is given to continuing education and training. The quality assurance/quality control system developed by the firm has been recognized as one of the best in the nation. Personal attention to its clients' needs is demonstrated by repeat project commisions.

Though we have a national and international practice, our favorite place and people to work for are right here in Arkansas. We chose to locate our offices and homes here. We love this state and its people, and if economically practicable, we would work for no other. On the other hand, we are very proud of the economic benefit provided to our state by the firm. Considering the commonly used multiplier of three times budget, the firm contributed over a $40 million benefit to the state in 2004.

The firm's commitment to Arkansas has, and will remain strong. Hopefully for another 120 years.

Profile courtesy of J. Brent Thompson, AIA, ACHA, chairman and chief executive officer, Cromwell Architects Engineers 101 South Spring Street Little Rock, Arkansas 72201 Telephone: 501.372.2900 Fax: 501.372.0482.

References:

Charles L. Thompson and Associates, Arkansas Architects, 1885-1938, by Dr. F. Hampton Roy.

A Century of Service, 1885-1985, by John J. Truemper, Jr., FAIA.

✧

Above: Capital Hotel.

Below: Museum Center Complex River Market District.

WORTHEN BANK & TRUST CO.

✧

Above: The Worthen Bank Building, once the tallest building in the state, was dedicated on January 31, 1970 and stands at 200 West Capitol.

Below: William Booker Worthen founded the bank in 1877 and served as its president from 1902 until his death in 1911.

In his preface to Mary Phyllis Walsh's outstanding book, *In the Vaults of Time* (1976), Edward Penick, former chairman and chief executive officer of Worthen Bank & Trust, reflected on the epic history of this historic institution. "For 100 years, Worthen Bank has been one of the most prominent corporate citizens in the State of Arkansas. During that long period the history of this state and its capital city, the history of banking, and the history of Worthen Bank have been significantly and inextricably woven together. No important question has agitated the banking business or the public conscience that Worthen Bank and its leaders have participated and contributed in appropriate and often illustrious ways."

It all began in the heart and mind of William Booker Worthen. He was born in Little Rock in 1852 and educated in the public school system and St. John's College before taking his first job in the real estate and brokerage business in 1869. At age twenty-one, he joined Colonel Gorden Peay in opening Peay and Worthen, a private banking firm that lasted until the Colonel's death in 1876. Worthen then partnered with Edward Parker to establish Parker and Worthen, Bankers, Brokers and Real Estate Agents on January 1, 1877 in a small space at the northwest corner of Louisiana and Markham.

The partnership continued until 1888, when Worthen bought out Parker's interest in the firm. The *Arkansas Gazette* reported that, "Mr. Worthen has ample capital and his years of experience and the confidence he is held by his host of friends throughout the state cannot fail success…his ability and integrity…richly entitle him to the continued confidence of all…"

Now on his own and in direct competition with his former partner, Edward Parker, and a number of large, "solidly entrenched" institutions such as German National Bank, Exchange National Bank, and First National Bank, the thirty-five year old entrepreneur bravely announced the opening of W.B. Worthen Company, Bankers, Brokers and Real Estate Agents.

In 1889, monthly salaries and year-end bonuses were being paid to three employees. By the end of its second year, Worthen Bank had outgrown its original space, was a leader in savings accounts, and included six employees.

On August 4, 1902, W.B. Worthen Company was incorporated for "general banking business" and included a fully paid capitol stock of $100,000, and only two of the original stockholders did not have family connections. Earnings were on the rise, a surplus account was created and dividends were declared—all as the financial community of the bustling Little Rock-North Little Rock area offered customers the choice of no less than sixteen different banks!

Worthen Bank continued to grow and expand when it was moved to the southeast corner of Markham and Main, the site of the old Metropolitan Hotel in 1904. In February 1911, Worthen happily reported a growing surplus and profit for the bank. Though he died only nine months later on October 23, 1911, "William Booker Worthen had been a man for the times." With consistent virtue and honor, this Little Rock native had successfully established and ensured the progression of an institution that would carry his name throughout the twentieth century.

On May 1, 1914, W.B. Worthen Company was issued a charter as an official State bank, now led by President Gordon Peay and Vice-president George Worthen, W.B.'s only son. In December the bank began a move to the southwest corner of Main and Fifth on the first floor of the Boyle Building.

By 1928 the bank's prosperity required another move, the property at 401 Main Street was bought, and employees moved into the large, modern facility in September of 1929. One month later, the infamous stock market crash known as Black Friday began a downward spiral of financial disasters that would enshroud the entire nation. By the end of 1930, 134 Arkansas banks had closed their doors. The Federal Government had declared a "bank holiday" closing all banks in the country until they could be reexamined. Worthen was the first Little Rock bank to reopen after the bank holiday. This was accomplished by Mrs. W.B. Worthen mortgaging her personal downtown real estate to finance the purchase of additional stock in the bank and a loan from the

Reconstruction Finance Corporation, a Federal institution set up to assist banks in reopening. Meeting the test of these difficult times and reopening first gave Worthen Bank a tremendous influx of new customers during the 1930s.

From 1940 to 1960, the bank enjoyed vast expansion and continued growth across the state. Everything from a nearly undefeatable softball team to 1953's "Snorkel," Worthen Bank's first curbside teller machine, characterized the coming modern age of the historic financial institution. Closed-circuit television cameras were added, and the first bank credit card issued by a bank in Arkansas, called "Worthen Charge," boosted the bank's corporate image among its customers and fellow bankers.

The War Years changed many things in the financial industry. Mainly, women took over most of the jobs of the men who had gone to war. Worthen saw women in all banking officer positions and an entire staff of women tellers. All this proved to the banking world that women's talents and abilities were as good as the men's.

Mary Phyllis Walsh commemorated the years from 1961 to 1976 as nothing short of "phenomenal," particularly in the area of Worthen's growth. New ideas, constantly changing innovations, and increased personnel began to herald a visionary future. Worthen Bank and Trust opened its first banking services branch in June of 1961, ultimately established at Asher and University and known as the Town and Country Office. By September, the East Roosevelt Branch Office was opened for business at 1100 East Roosevelt.

At the close of business in 1962, Worthen held the 330th position among the list of America's largest 400 banks. In the summer of 1964 plans were announced to merge with the Bank of Arkansas and operate under the name of Worthen Bank and Trust Company—with a capital structure of over $7.5 million and resources of more than $110 million. Worthen was now the largest bank in Little Rock and Arkansas. In 1968 a major change occurred with the approval of plans for Worthen Bank and Trust to be owned and operated by First Arkansas Bankstock Corporation (FABCO), a

"one-bank holding company, the first in Arkansas." The main reason for this change was to take advantage of the recently passed Federal Bank Holding Company Act, which authorized bank holding companies to offer a wide range of financial services not authorized to individual banks. Acting under the bank holding company's structure, Worthen acquired nine banks in Arkansas and organized seven bank-services related companies.

Unprecedented growth continued as the bank's new twenty-five story building was dedicated at 200 West Capitol on May 21, 1969—the tallest building in Arkansas at the time. The first six months of 1975 "were the most profitable for any comparable period in the bank's history." At the centennial celebration of Worthen Bank in 1977, it was clear that its many and varied "challenges [were] simply stepping stones to the future...accomplished under the continuous management of the founder's family."

Among the many dedicated individuals who met those challenges were Worthen Bank and Trust's historic roll of presidents: William Booker Worthen (1902 to 1911), Gordon Peay (1911 to 1927), Emmet Morris (1927 to 1940), James H. Penick (1940 to 1961), Edward M. Penick, Sr. (1961 to 1974, and inducted into the Arkansas Business Hall of Fame in 2005) and James H. Penick, Jr. (1974 to 1978).

❖

Above: This stock certificate was issued under the new name, Worthen Bank & Trust Co. in 1947.

Below: The bank's first home was located at Markham at Louisiana.

BALDWIN & SHELL CONSTRUCTION COMPANY

❖

Lafayette Hotel.

Founded as The Baldwin Company in 1946 by Werner C. Knoop, Olen A. Cates and P.W. Baldwin, this Little Rock business has maintained an unswerving devotion to excellence in the building industry for almost sixty years. Recognized as three of the most experienced men in the construction industry at that time, Knoop, the former mayor of Little Rock and an original founder of the Capital Steel Company, brought over twenty years of experience in business management and civil engineering, as well as $25,000 to the company; Baldwin contributed his expertise as a job superintendent, the necessary equipment, and his stature as "the best builder in the South;" and Cates offered his extensive financial insight and ability as the company's chief accountant.

The company's president, Robert J. "Bob" Shell, joined the original Baldwin Company in 1950 after leaving his position as mail clerk at Fones Brothers. As a ten month job ended as Baldwin's timekeeper during the completion of a housing project at Ninth and Picron for the Little Rock Housing Authority, the payroll clerk quit her job, and Shell was given the position and became the company's first male payroll clerk before progressing into Baldwin's accounting and estimating departments. In 1962 he became a board member and officer of the company, and, in 1983, became president of Baldwin and Shell, general contractors.

In the early years, company executives set out to establish a new standard of excellence in the building industry. This philosophy still holds true today and has been proven time and again by the outstanding quality of construction found in every Baldwin & Shell project. The company's central objective has never changed and remains in completing each job with the best qualified personnel, working under the safest conditions, accomplishing the objectives set by the clients, and maintaining an overall prerequisite of pride in a job well done.

Baldwin and Shell's continued success has come because of highly trained, well-qualified professional people who are extremely competent and loyal. The company

has very little employee turnover in the field or office; some superintendents have been with the company for over twenty years. Adherence to a foundational philosophy of assigning a principal member within the firm to direct each project has also been a key to the company's many achievements in the industry.

In the late 1970s, Shell recognized the importance of continuing the company's strong and secure growth into the next century. A young and capable management team was hired and included Scott Copas, Doug Henson, Hank Johns and Jim Wilson. Later, Scott Shell, Bobby Gosser and Patrick Tenney joined the group and brought a wide range of talents that would enable Baldwin & Shell to undertake any construction project that became available. These experienced and devoted professionals have proven themselves many times over and their invaluable work culminated in the completion of the largest building project in Arkansas in 1999—the $55 million Baptist Health Springhill Medical Center in North Little Rock.

Baldwin & Shell continues to maintain a leadership role in the construction field and models an accomplished, smooth running organization that offers both budgeting and management capabilities to provide clients with timely, cost efficient and competitively priced construction. Numerous honors are

held by the company and include the prestigious Motorola "Build America" nomination for its renovation of Old Main, while requests from national corporations support a unique confidence in the company's ability to provide quality projects for an ever-growing list of clients. More than seventy percent of the company's work is repeat business, as employees faithfully complete projects under budget, earlier than expected, and with a quality of workmanship that remains unmatched in the field today.

While working only in Arkansas, Baldwin & Shell has continued to show significant growth over the years. The company is ranked among the third and fourth largest contractors in the state and *Engineering News Record* has named them in its prestigious list of America's Top 400 Construction Companies three of the last ten years. From hospitals to office buildings, educational facilities to churches, industrial plants to financial institutions, historical renovations, or remodeling, Baldwin & Shell provides the highest quality in construction services to every client. Landmark building projects include Murphy Oil in El Dorado, Pine Bluff Convention Center, Riceland Foods in Stuttgart, Arkansas Best Freight in Fort Smith, J.B. Hunt in Lowell, and The Center for Aging at the University of Arkansas Medical Sciences in Little Rock.

The company and its founders have left their mark on downtown Little Rock. Baldwin was the superintendent on Robinson Auditorium and the Frederica Hotel. Baldwin and Shell restored or remodeled a number of buildings, including the Lafayette Hotel, Legacy Hotel, the old State Capitol, Territorial State Capitol, McFadden Building, Main Street Mall between Fifth and Sixth, the old Sears Building at Seventh and Main. They also renovated historic Central High School in 1980 and again in 2004.

The tremendous success that Baldwin & Shell enjoy in the twenty-first century is a result of the resourcefulness and integrity of its 300 knowledgeable professionals coupled with a strict adherence to the philosophy of quality construction developed by its founders. Looking back over his nearly six decades in the construction business, Shell believes that this unique reputation is the company's greatest asset. "We have always been selective in our work. We really enjoy the prestigious jobs, the ones that are difficult and a challenge, the landmarks within the state."

Nominated as Arkansas Business of the Year in 2004, Baldwin & Shell is well known for its involvement in the community and construction industry. Werner Knoop not only served as mayor but also was president of the Chamber of Commerce and the Little Rock school board; and he, Scott Copas, and Bob Shell have all served as state president of the Associated General Contractors and received the prestigious Distinguished Service Award. Knoop and Shell have also served as National Directors and, in 2000 Shell was inducted as a charter member in the Arkansas Construction Hall of Fame.

For more detailed information about this outstanding and decidedly Arkansas company, please visit www.baldwinshell.com.

✧

Main Street Mall.

HADFIELD AGENCY, INC.

Hadfield Agency, Inc., is an independent, multi-line insurance agency with a long history of dedicated service to policyholders. Located in Little Rock, the agency provides insurance coverage to individuals and businesses and has an associated wholesale operation, Smart Choice Agents Program of Arkansas, Inc. Started in 2001, Smart Choice Program of Arkansas, Inc. provides insurance markets and services to independent insurance producers.

Harry P. Hadfield, who worked primarily in real estate, acquired the L.C. Holman Agency in 1944, as payment for a debt. Hadfield's son, Charles, joined his father's firm upon his return from duty as a bomber pilot in World War II and after completing a comprehensive educational program at a Baltimore insurance company's home office. The agency was renamed Hadfield Insurance Agency, and the Hadfields shared a small office and a secretary on the top floor of the Pyramid Life Building on the corner of Second and Center Streets.

After Charles married in 1948, his wife, Marguerite, worked in the business, usually at night, after working a full-time job during the day. Agency personnel sold insurance during the day and typed the policies on manual typewriters at night, using carbon paper for duplication. Through open windows, summer breezes and fans provided cooling in the hot summer months, and operators manned elevators prior to automation.

✧

Above: H. P. Hadfield.

Below: Charles "Charlie" W. Hadfield, III and Charles "Chuck" W. Hadfield, Jr.

In 1967, Charles W. Hadfield merged his agency with one owned by Charles D. Ray, and the business became known as Hadfield and Ray, Inc. The agency moved into an office across from the War Memorial Golf Course on West Markham Street in 1968. Two years later, the owners purchased a building at 1818 South University, where they remained until 1981.

During the 1970s, Hadfield and Ray grew tremendously and became one of the top five agencies in the state, with more than $5 million in written premiums, fourteen employees and three satellite offices in Jacksonville and Dardenelle, Arkansas and Hollywood, California. The company expanded into commercial coverage, including mobile home manufacturing plants, trucking accounts and a nationwide apartment house insurance program.

Hadfield's son, Charles W. Hadfield, Jr., joined the agency in 1980 after graduating with honors from the University of Arkansas with a business degree, majoring in insurance and finance. After Hadfield and Ray, Inc., dissolved in 1981 due to differing operational philosophies, the Hadfields formed a joint venture with insurance provider Craig Williams, operating under the name Hadfield and Williams.

Beginning with a premium base of only $350,000, the agency, with only one customer service representative, relocated to an office on

Rodney Parham. In 1982, Charles, Jr. received the Certified Insurance Counselor designation. Ten years later, Williams retired and sold his portion of the business to the Hadfields. A year later, The Hadfields expanded the business by purchasing the H.C. Johnston Agency.

Charles, Sr., died in 1994, leaving the firm in the hands of the current owner and president, Charles, Jr.

In 2002, Hadfield moved the agency offices to its present location on Pleasant Valley Drive in Little Rock.

The agency has been very much a family operation, with Charles, Jr., his wife and three children working for the agency in recent years. Charles Hadfield, III is the fourth generation to work at the agency. He began his career in the insurance business while in high school, doing everything from filing to emptying the trash. A licensed agent since 1999, he is currently working full-time learning every aspect of the insurance business from his father.

Today, Hadfield Agency, Inc., has thirteen employees with more than 100 years of combined experience in service to policyholders. The agency offers many types of insurance coverage, including auto, homeowners, business, life, health and disability insurance, watercraft and personal umbrella (liability) policies. The agency holds licenses in Arkansas, Georgia, Pennsylvania, Texas, Tennessee, Oklahoma and Missouri, representing Encompass, State Auto, St. Paul Travelers, SAFECO, MetLife, General Casualty, The Hartford, Union Standard, Zurich, Progressive, AIG and Foremost insurance companies. Because of the wide range of companies the agency represents, customers find an abundance of choices to fill their specialized needs for comprehensive insurance coverage.

The agency owner, Charles, Jr., is active in the business community and insurance industry. He is a member of the Sales & Marketing Executives Association, has served extensively, in the past and presently, on the board of directors of the Independent Insurance Agents of Arkansas Association, has been state chairman for Northstar/Encompass Insurance Company's Agent Advisory Panel and as their National Products Chairman over the central

region of the United States and currently serves on Safeco's state advisory council.

Over the years, Hadfield Agency, Inc., has been one of the leading insurance agencies both in the State of Arkansas and in the broader regions of the United States it serves. In 2005 the retail and regional wholesale operations are expected to produce in excess of $15 million in insurance premiums. Both management and staff are involved in continuing education in order to stay abreast of changes in the industry. The agency is committed to providing high-quality insurance coverage that meets and even exceeds customer expectations both in service and in value.

✧

Above: Charles W. Hadfield, Sr.

Below: A Hadfield Insurance Agency newspaper announcement from March 1946.

CHARLES W. HADFIELD

After three years in the Army Air Forces, Charles Hadfield is back in Little Rock, and is now associated with his father, H. F. Hadfield, in charge of the Insurance Department.

Charles attended the United States Fidelity and Guaranty Company's home office school of insurance at Baltimore, Maryland, after he was discharged from the service the first of the year.

HADFIELD INSURANCE AGENCY
FIRE   CASUALTY   FIDELITY
916 Pyramid Bldg.   Phone 2-3461

LITTLE ROCK NATIONAL AIRPORT

Little Rock National Airport is the largest airport in Arkansas, serving both commercial and general aviation customers since 1931, with a history that can be traced back to 1917. Considered a major gateway to the city and state, the airport serves 2.1 million passengers annually with more than 150 daily arrivals and departures.

At Little Rock National Airport, great emphasis is placed on providing exemplary airport service to all its customers. The airport offers nonstop jet service to eighteen cities provided by American Eagle, Continental Express, Delta, Delta Connection, Frontier, Northwest, Northwest Airlink, Southwest and US Airways Express.

The city's first airport, operated by the U.S. Army Signal Corps, opened in 1917 as the Little Rock Intermediate Air Depot. In 1926 the federal government acquired property to be used for support and landing facilities of the Arkansas National Guard's 154th Observation Squadron. Two years later, the first of many aircraft manufacturers established a business adjacent to the airfield. The aircraft manufacture and modification industry is a major presence at the airport site today.

In 1930 the citizens of Little Rock purchased the airfield, and commercial air service began in June 1931 with service by American Airways, now American Airlines.

The airport is officially known as Little Rock National Airport/Adams Field. It is named in honor of Captain George Geyer Adams of the 154th Observation Squadron, Arkansas National Guard, who was killed in the line of duty on September 4, 1937. During his long tenure with the Little Rock City Council, Captain Adams was instrumental in promoting the growth and development of the airport.

Between the two world wars, the facility grew from 40 acres to 640 acres and from one sod runway to three hard-surface runways. It also became a key center for commercial and military air service. The airfield and terminal facilities now cover about 2,200 acres. Throughout World War II, the U.S. War Department operated the airport as a military facility. The City of Little Rock regained responsibility for the airport after the war ended and reestablished daily commercial air service.

Through the years, improvements to both the airfield and terminal facilities have been made on a continuing basis. Major runway improvements were completed in 1953, and the first instrument landing system was installed in 1954. Jet flights began in Little Rock in the 1960s, a new terminal opened in 1972, and a second commercial service runway opened in 1991. During the 1990s and into the new century, more than $180 million in capital improvements were made at the airport.

✧

Below: Balloon Races, April 1926.

A new parking deck opened at Little Rock National in 2001. The parking deck is connected to the terminal by a sky bridge that enables travelers to go from their car seats to their plane seats without being exposed to the weather. This multi-level parking deck was built in response to a 1996 customer survey. By an overwhelming margin, frequent travelers favored building a closed-in parking deck to expanding surface parking with enhanced shuttle service. In addition to the parking deck, long-term parking lots with free shuttle bus service are available and parking slots for the physically challenged are available in the short-term surface lots and on the parking deck. A $3 million renovation to the baggage claim wing has recently been completed.

At Little Rock National Airport, all restaurants, gift shops, and newsstands are located on the concourse level of the terminal. The space devoted to concessions has been expanded to almost twice its former square footage, providing more choices in more locations for airport customers. In the pre-security screening area, for example, the RiverBend Bar and Grill offers full-service restaurant dining and adjacent bar service. The restaurant features an extensive menu with many local favorites and a view of aircraft movement on the west side of the terminal. Directly across from the RiverBend, the Daily News offers a large selection of books, magazines, gifts and other merchandise.

In the post-security screening area, customers may choose foods from Burger King, Pizza Hut, Cinnabon, Carvel Ice Cream, Andina's Coffee, and other vendors located in the food court. The Ouachita Brew House at the north end of the concourse is a full-service bar featuring Arkansas microbrews among its selections. Starbucks is located adjacent to Gate 4. A News Exchange offering books, magazines, and gifts is located next to the food court. Frankly Gourmet, near gate four, features gourmet all-beef hot dogs, sausages and other treats.

Little Rock National offers both high-quality facilities and air service at competitive prices. Not only does the airport serve as a major link in the nation's transportation system, it is an important economic generator. The airport and adjacent aviation-related businesses employ about 3,500 people with total annual payrolls of $40 million, pumping more than $260 million into the economy. The goal at Little Rock National Airport is to continue to well serve the needs of the traveling public.

❖

Top: Swallow Aircraft at Command-Aire factory, 1930.

Below: American Airlines introduced the Boeing 727 to Little Rock in 1965.

AT&T
ARKANSAS

It was 1876 when Alexander Graham Bell transmitted the first complete message using a remarkable new device he called the telephone.

Less than a year later, Little Rock resident John Hamblet brought the first telephone to Arkansas, hoping to impress his fellow townspeople with the power of this strange new instrument. At the time, many considered the telephone a novelty and dismissed its usefulness.

That first impression did not last long, however. On November 1, 1879, Arkansas' first telephone switchboard was installed in Little Rock. Initially a handful of businesses signed up for the service, which cost $5.00 per month. Making a call across town required an operator's assistance and connecting the two parties could take several minutes.

Over the next quarter-century, telephone service spread to other communities and forever changed communications in the Natural State. Today, Little Rock and 101 other local exchanges statewide are served by AT&T Arkansas. But the parent company, AT&T Inc., can still trace its Arkansas roots back more than 125 years to that original Little Rock switchboard and its handful of customers.

The telephone's enduring relationship with Arkansas is marked by a long list of changes, innovations, and new technologies that parallel the state's own social and economic development.

The Western Union Company installed the first Little Rock telephone exchange, utilizing a small room adjoining the Western Union Office at 108-110 Scott Street. The exchange was run by Edward C. Newton and also employed Arthur Adams, who

was the city's first operator. He soon was joined by his sister Kate Adams, who likely was the nation's first female telephone operator.

The first long-distance telephone line in the Southwest was built from Little Rock to Hot Springs in 1880. Until Hot Springs got its own local exchange a year later, customers in that city could place and receive their toll calls from a single telephone installed in Little's Grocery on Central Avenue. Environmental conditions and early technology caused echoes and background noises on the early toll line, leading some to believe it might be haunted.

In 1881, Colonel Logan H. Roots and businessman J. N. Keller created Southwestern Telegraph & Telephone, headquartered in Little Rock, after they acquired exclusive rights to the Bell patents in Arkansas and Texas. Southwestern bought the Little Rock exchange for $3,585.13, a grand sum in those days. Adams stayed with the new company as local manager.

Two years later Erie Telephone & Telegraph, headquartered in Boston, bought Southwestern along with several other Midwest telephone companies. In 1900 the Erie company was dissolved and Southwestern resumed ownership and operation of the Arkansas and Texas properties. By that time, telephone subscribership in Little Rock had grown to 1,503.

Several independent companies competed with Southwestern in the early years. In 1886 three entrepreneurs founded the Independent Telephone Company, but it was disbanded when it was found to have infringed on Bell's patents. After Bell's original patents expired, in 1885, the Little Rock Telephone Company built exchanges in Little Rock and Argenta; that company was purchased by Southwestern in 1912.

Early telephone directories were much thinner than today's; the first Little Rock directory was published in 1880 and had only a few pages. Early listings included now-obsolete businesses such as liverymen, icehouses and coal delivery companies plus a handful of major retailers, bankers and hotels–and an equal number of lawyers and saloons.

The community directory would be updated and reprinted every few months as new subscribers signed up. Because the telephone was unfamiliar to many new customers, early directories had a chapter devoted to proper use of the device. It included tips on party line etiquette and basic instructions like "when you are finished talking, hang the receiver back on the hook."

Over the years, many other independent companies in Arkansas and neighboring states merged with Southwestern Telegraph & Telephone. Those mergers led the company to rename itself Southwestern Bell Telephone Company in 1920, when it served Arkansas, Kansas, Missouri, Oklahoma and Texas.

Southwestern Bell, as it was known for decades, continued to grow. In 1979 the company installed its 1-millionth Arkansas telephone line in then-Governor Bill Clinton's office at the State Capitol. A string of mergers and other advances also led to occasional name changes until the unifying name of AT&T was adopted in 2005.

Today AT&T Inc. is a premier communications holding company in the United States and around the world, with operating subsidiaries providing services under the AT&T brand. AT&T is the recognized world leader in providing IP-based communications services to businesses and the U.S. leader in providing wireless, high speed Internet access, local and long distance voice, and directory publishing and advertising through its Yellow Pages and YELLOWPAGES.COM organizations. As part of its three-screen integration strategy, AT&T is expanding video entertainment offerings to include such next-generation television services as AT&T U-verse℠ TV.

Decade after decade, "plain old telephone service" has evolved to become a fixture in popular culture and a central feature of everyday life. AT&T employees constantly work to provide new technologies, such as high speed Internet access service, that redefine the way customers in Little Rock and the rest of Arkansas live and work.

Today AT&T customers may enjoy an array of products, often bundled for savings and convenience, that provide innovative technology for business and residential use. It was the first to offer Arkansas consumers satellite television, wireless voice and data service, broadband Internet access and local/long distance phone service, all with one call and one monthly bill.

In 2004 the company launched AT&T FreedomLink, a wireless Internet access service for mobile users. The first two wireless hot spots in Arkansas were in Little Rock. By mid-2005, the mobile access service was available at two-dozen local locations, including Little Rock National Airport and Little Rock River Market, plus thousands of locations nationwide.

In Arkansas alone, the company today has 42,000 miles of fiber optic and copper cable–enough to circle the globe 1.7 times. And in a typical twenty-four-hour period, AT&T Arkansas helps complete 29 million calls. Today's telecom environment is far removed from November 1879, when the state's first telephone executive struggled to provide round-the-clock service to his handful of customers in Little Rock.

Ed Drilling, president AT&T Arkansas, said, "Our industry and our state have seen many changes in the 125-plus years since telephone service began here, but one thing that has not changed is the AT&T commitment to Arkansas customers. We know our customers have many choices for telecom services. We are committed to providing quality products, and will continue working to earn the privilege of serving Arkansans for the next 125 years."

Additional information about AT&T Inc. and AT&T products and services is available at www.att.com.

❖

Left: This 1907 photo shows several operators serving local Little Rock customers of Southwestern Telegraph & Telephone. The first local exchange began operations more than 125 years ago, serving nearly forty customers. Today, AT&T Arkansas completes an average of 29 million calls daily, but the company can trace its business roots to that first Little Rock exchange 125 years ago.
COURTESY OF AT&T.

Below: When the Little Rock exchange opened in 1879, it had about forty customers and a one-page telephone directory. This photo shows the first sheet of a somewhat larger Little Rock directory from late 1880, containing numerous names that are still well known in central Arkansas. At the time, local callers often were assisted by Kate Adams, one of the nation's first female telephone operators. Adams was locally renowned for her singing ability, and her "smiling voice" was so popular with early customers that it became the model for generations of telephone operators.
COURTESY OF AT&T.

WOODHAVEN HOMES, INC.

Since 1971 Jack Wilson, president of Woodhaven Homes, Inc. in Sherwood, has been building fine custom homes throughout most of central Arkansas. Building comes naturally to Wilson—he comes from a "family of builders." His grandfather and father-in-law were both involved in the home building industry.

With a degree in Agri-Education and a strong background in engineering, Wilson developed his skills while working with his father-in-law. He built his first custom on home North Fairway in Sherwood over thirty years ago.

"That first house we built for $27,500," says Wilson. "We've come a long way in regards to real estate values and the homebuilding industry."

Wilson, originally from north central Arkansas, has worked diligently and has been actively involved in the Home Builders Association for many years. He is a past president of the HBA of Greater Little Rock, a life director of national, state, and local HBA's, as well as past president of the state HBA.

One of Wilson's greatest challenges has been the development of a cost control system easily understood by prospective clients. The house is basically built on paper, room by room, from start to finish, with a system that allows both Wilson and the homeowner to know exactly where they stand in relation to the budget at any given time. "We want to work with customers on developing a 'best value' concept for their homes," explains Wilson. "We lay out plenty of options and allow the client to customize within the overall budget. We want our customers to be able to get the most for their money." In conjunction with establishment of the budget, Wilson works on customizing the design of the home. Wilson does much of the design process on the computer. With the help of the CAD program, "Softplan," he is able to lay out the exterior design as well as the interior floor plan and incorporate all of the amenities that compose a home's design. "Softplan" allows me to build a complete home on the computer so that the client can see their home practically before their very eyes—even in 3-D. The home plans design are original and limited to the client we are building for—that is a Woodhaven Homes trademark," says Wilson.

Wilson has been an innovator in the area of energy conservation in his homes. During the eighties, he was involved in the design and building of Earth Sheltered Homes, gaining an extensive knowledge of energy sources such as passive and active solar energy as well as how to utilize the natural earth temperatures to the benefit of the completed home.

Structurally, Woodhaven Homes are built on a strong foundation. Wilson offers a ten-year structural warranty on all homes that he

builds. The majority of homes Wilson builds are currently custom homes ranging in price from $150,000 to over $1 million. Of these custom homes, fifty-seven to eighty percent are from satisfied customer referrals. Speculative homes are built in each of his subdivisions to serve as models for customer viewing. Wilson averages approximately forty-five to fifty homes a year, building in areas such as Sherwood, Jacksonville, Cabot, Maumelle, West Little Rock, North Little Rock, Bryant, Conway and England.

In 2000, Wilson, along with two building partners, purchased Country Club of Arkansas in Maumelle. This development is one of central Arkansas' finest and includes nearly 2,000 homes.

Wilson has served as developer of several neighborhoods. These include Foxwood in Jacksonville; Saddlebrook in Cabot; Mound Lake in Scott; and Country Club of Arkansas in Maumelle.

Part of the Woodhaven team of professionals who build, decorate and supervise the construction of many of the beautiful and luxurious homes in and around Pulaski are members of Wilson's immediate family. They include Jack's wife, Mary Ann and youngest daughter, Tracy, and her husband, Keith Childress. "We offer our customers a building team," Jack explains. "Every professional at Woodhaven is responsible for the completion of your home, and we take customer satisfaction very seriously. That is the main reason we have Susan Vaught, customer coordinator for the Woodhaven Homes team. Susan works directly with homeowners to provide building schedules and budget information about their house construction. She is a key person to the Woodhaven team. Along with Susan, Brock Morris works with customers after the close of their new home. On the construction team in the office support division are Donna Killian, Harry Maier and Shanon Price. Subcontractors who have been on the Woodhaven Homes team for numerous years, some for as long as Woodhaven has been building fine homes, perform most of the construction process."

With approximately 1,000 projects completed over the past thirty-one years, Wilson and Woodhaven Homes have had a major impact on home ownership in the central Arkansas area.

When asked to summarize his philosophy of the home-building process, Wilson responds with a smile, "Woodhaven Homes tries to form a partnership with our customers. Everybody pulls in the same direction making the process easy. From plan design to budgeting and cost estimates to actual construction—we have one of the best systems in the business."

FIRST FINANCIAL COMPUTER SERVICES, INCORPORATED

❖

Top: Bob at the bank in the 1960s.

Bottom: Randy Thomason.

Bob Thomason, a former banker with more than twenty years of experience, founded First Financial Computer Services, Inc. (FFCS) in 1985. The goal from the inception was to provide products and services to continuously meet the growing demands of the evolving financial services industry.

About a year after the business began, two of Thomason's sons, Randy and Jon, came to work in the company along with Bob's spouse, Mary. Randy handled the marketing and sales division while Jon headed up the service side. Mary worked with the back office providing records control. This team worked diligently with long hours building a service that was above reproach.

FFCS coupled unique experience and expertise with a wide range of technology, tools, and services needed to deliver tremendous results. Few companies could match the broad array of specialized hardware systems services and expert technicians in areas such as check remittance and lockbox processing, along with equipment sales and refurbishment.

With a division dedicated to IBM® 3890 support, FFCS was the only company

to support new and used transaction processing hardware from all of the major manufacturers. They also sold and serviced mail extraction equipment. FFCS boasted an inventory of more than two million parts, including the largest BancTec parts stock other than the equipment manufacturer, as well as the purchase of financial equipment, including Reader-Sorters, Printers and CPUs.

First Financial Computer Services, Inc. took great pride in creating personalized relationships to assist their clients in every phase of hardware systems support. From 1998, FFCS grew from 1,500 to over 4,000 accounts, and customers included community banks, regional and super regional banks, large financial institutions with multiple capture sites, service bureaus, remittance and lockbox processors, and data-entry services. As a leading proponent of high-touch customer care and planned preventive hardware maintenance, FFCS earned a reputation as the company financial service firms trust most with their mission-critical operations. Their customers included nine of the twenty-one largest financial institutions (in terms of assets) in the United States, and

seventeen of the top fifty. Their trusted service allowed them to achieve record revenues every year since 1998.

Equipment and systems maintenance issues have become one of the primary challenges of operations managers. FFCS developed a robust, single-source suite of equipment services, delivering world-class hardware systems solution to every customer while consistently improving business practices, increasing reliability, and providing extraordinary value.

Its founder recognizes that such historic success rests with their team and much time and energy was spent attracting and retaining highly qualified and motivated people, for talented people were the single most important element of the company's performance. FFCS team members were experts in areas such as used and new equipment sales, installation, de-installation and support, equipment refurbishment and staging, installation support, and equipment purchasing. FFCS blended this broad expertise with an innovative problem solving system to deliver dependable, cost-effective solutions. As a single-source provider, they streamlined support, eliminating the need for multiple vendors. At a time when other companies were laying off proven

professionals, FFCS comprised itself of knowledgeable, customer-focused people empowered to achieve great things. By working hard, respecting co-workers, and having fun, each member of the team gained satisfaction from the day-to-day tasks and shared in the vision of the company.

FFCS technicians were driven, self-motivated, responsible, and most importantly, results-oriented. Over ninety percent of the service team had at least eight years of experience, and more than eighty-five percent of all their personnel were directly involved in field service and customer support.

The environment at FFCS was dynamic and rewarding—dynamic because of constant growth and evolving and rewarding because each team member had a direct impact on the success of the company's clients. They operated on the principles of excellence, integrity, and professionalism to foster tremendous results. They promoted initiative and innovation. This was not just lip service—it was how they grew year after year.

FFCS merged into a public company on November 9, 2004 and is no longer owned by the Thomason's.

✧

Top: Jon Thomason.

Bottom: Bob and Mary Thomason celebrate their Golden wedding anniversary in 2005.

ACE GLASS COMPANY, INC.

Founded upon the principle of the "golden rule" on January 9, 1986, by native Arkansans Newton and Linda Little, ACE Glass Company, Inc., serves customers with outstanding professional experience and dedication in meeting every kind of commercial and residential glass need. The Littles agree that the company's nearly two decades of success are directly related to the continued faithfulness of exceptional personnel. Today the company receives subcontracts exceeding $1 million, while smaller jobs such as re-glazing storm windows, repairing shower doors, and replacing wood windows are handled with the same expert workmanship.

Headquartered near the Clinton Presidential Library and Park site and next to the south entrance of the new Heifer International Building in Little Rock's old Nabisco cookie distribution facility, is 32,000 square feet of fabrication, warehouse and office space. The company offers custom shower doors, glass, mirrors, handrail systems, aluminum composite panels and brake metal, storefronts, entrances, skylights, and curtain wall systems. Each item is also available in our recently consolidated Northwest Arkansas location in Lowell, Arkansas. Originally, ACE Glass was established in Springdale in 1998 and also includes Central Glass and Mirror Company which was purchased in 2004. The Northwest

Arkansas operation continues to offer extensive growth for ACE Glass through numerous high profile projects and full service opportunities.

ACE offers customers easy access to its wide range of sample and model displays and a library of literature and technical information about industry products is always available. State-of-the-art technology provides associates with networked computers and individual-station Internet accessibility, while important industry programs like a cost accounting system, 'Glaspac' glass sales & estimating system, 'Prism' shower door estimating and fabrication system, and several storefront/curtain wall software estimating systems, which include 'PartnerPak,' ensure customers will receive an accurate bid. ACE also utilizes CADD drafting for shop drawings and for ACM/CNC fabrication precision to produce admirable performances. ACE owns many forms of fabrication and installation machinery and communication equipment to enhance its progressive and aggressive pursuit of challenging projects and schedules.

The company's comprehensive Web site, www.aceglass.net, allows customers to access many of the most commonly asked questions about glass thickness, types and colors, shapes and special treatments. This Web site also offers information "about us," project

✧

Above: The University of Arkansas for Medical Sciences' Jackson T. Stephens Spine & Neurosciences Institute.
COURTESY OF TOM CONKLIN.

Below: Arkansas Children's Hospital.
COURTESY OF TIM HURDSLEY.

portfolios and links to industry leaders in ACE's scope of work. Glass is offered in so many applications today that the company provides cutouts, drilled holes, notches, finger pulls, plate grooves, sandblasting and etching to meet these requirements. Whether a customer needs clear glass for a window or a picture frame, heavy glass shelving, tabletops or shower enclosures, ACE surely offers it. Tinted glass and specialty glasses such as low-e, laminated, sandblasted, painted, fire-resistant, ultra-clear and others are also available. Shaped glass cuts include rectangles, boats, triangles, trapezoids, racetracks, hexagons, and octagons. Custom designed shapes can be cut as long as a pattern is provided. Polished and satin edges are available in pencil, ogee, mitered, or elegant beveled forms.

With its many years of expertise in glass and other products' representation, ACE Glass Company has the extraordinary ability to assist clients and designers from Arkansas and from other parts of the nation in discovering new and exciting products available for sale and installation. ACE Glass Company is a 'licensed' subcontractor/installer and has performed work in Arkansas, Mississippi, Louisiana and Florida. ACE furnishes and installs products from major manufacturers of glass, aluminum, steel, wood and related products. The company also carries a superb line of wood windows and door products for new construction, remodeling or replacement needs.

ACE Glass Company is a Drug-Free Workplace. Personnel are instructed in Safety Programs & First Aid Training, Fall Protection, Hazardous Communications, and Ground Fault Assured Electrical Equipment procedures. ACE Glass is an Equal Opportunity Employer and seeks construction-experienced personnel who want to learn its trade. The company is also proud of its cultural diversity, including many Spanish-speaking associates in our crews.

For all of this well-earned success and unmatched workmanship in the field, ACE Glass owner Newton Little insists that it will always be about the people, "They are the key to God blessing our company over the years." Many remarkable men and women have each

played a uniquely important role as the company has moved into a new century of service to Arkansas and the nation.

ACE Glass Company, Inc., remains strong in its commitment to the highest quality sales, installation and representation of their products and services and diligently seeks excellence in performance, appearance, and customer satisfaction. ACE strives to be "clearly the exceptional value" in the marketplace. Keenly aware of the past and thriving in the present, ACE Glass Company is preparing for a bright future.

❖

Above: Custom heavy frameless glass shower enclosure.

Below: The Victory Office Building, located near the Arkansas State Capital.

BAPTIST HEALTH

It was at the Arkansas Baptist State Convention at Immanuel Baptist Church on November 12, 1919, that the convention's standing committee on hospitals recommended "a great, modern, scientific hospital" for downtown Little Rock. Excitement for the project was immediate and a vote by members of the convention to purchase Battle Creek Sanitarium at Thirteenth and Marshall was successful in 1920. Today, Baptist Health is the largest healthcare delivery organization in Arkansas with over 7,000 employees and over 1,000 physicians.

Five major facilities comprise the Baptist Health system:

• Baptist Health Medical Center-Little Rock, a 803-bed tertiary care facility, opened in 1920;

• Baptist Health Medical Center-North Little Rock, a 220-bed facility, opened in 1959;

• Baptist Health Rehabilitation Institute, a 120-bed facility, opened in 1975;

• Baptist Health Medical Center-Arkadelphia, a 25-bed facility, opened in 1983; and

• Baptist Health Medical Center-Heber Springs, a twenty-five-bed facility, opened in 1968.

Hospital officials and board members began with a powerful desire to heal the sick and enhance the lives of people in Arkansas. Today, they deliver healthcare that spans a lifetime, from prenatal services through the golden years. Every aspect of health is addressed, including education, prevention, organ transplantation and more.

Baptist Health is more than just a business, it's a healing ministry based on the revelation of God through creation, the Bible and Jesus Christ. Baptist Health believes in caring for the whole person—body, mind, and soul—and sees its essential mission as an expression and outreach of the Christian faith, allowing staff and medical professionals the opportunity to become instruments of God's restorative power through compassionate and dedicated care.

The ongoing acquisition of cutting-edge medical technology is extensive at Baptist Health and fulfills the continued promise to provide staff members with the best support so they, in turn, can provide patients with the most modern and progressive medical care available. Baptist Health has laid claim to many firsts—including the state's first intensive care unit, the first cancer treatment facility, the first nursing school, the first heart transplant, and the first corneal transplant. They have earned recognition for innovations ranging from the pioneering work in contact laser surgery and orthopedics to the introduction of the area's most

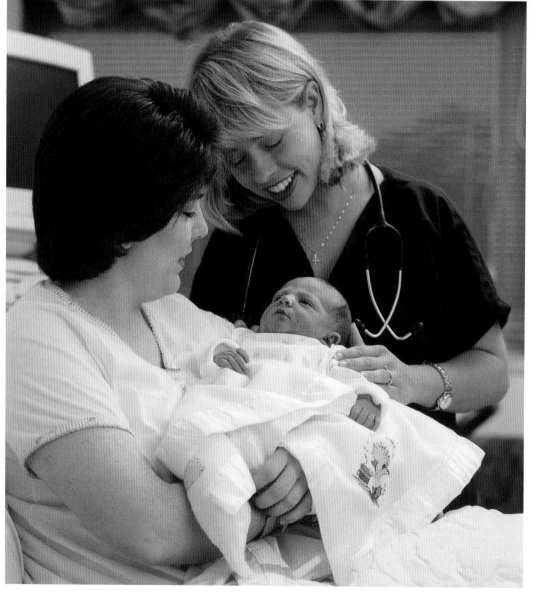

advanced technology for diagnostic testing. And while Baptist Health is honored to claim these milestones, they are equally proud that their achievements will benefit physicians and patients around the world.

A high commitment to quality healthcare is found throughout the organization. From highly trained physicians and caregivers to the comprehensive continuum of services and sophisticated technology, employees who are a close family and comprehensive team at facilities across Arkansas, and hospitals, therapy centers, primary care clinics, retirement community or the home health programs—the Baptist Health quality trademark is evident.

The flagship of Baptist Health, Baptist Health Medical Center-Little Rock, is a licensed 803-bed tertiary care facility located in west Little Rock. It is the largest private, not-for-profit hospital in the state. Since 1920, Baptist Health has become well known for work in the diagnosis and treatment of cardiovascular disease, orthopedic services, women's services, ophthalmology services, and helicopter and fixed-wing emergency transport services. Since 1996 and the past ten consecutive years, the National Research Corporation has conducted a consumer survey that named Baptist Health Medical Center-Little Rock as the top hospital in Arkansas. It also was voted by readers of the *Arkansas Times* as "the best place to have a baby," and has continually been crowned by readers of the *Arkansas Democrat-Gazette* as the top hospital.

Baptist Health continues to grow and build upon the state's most comprehensive healthcare system. In today's environment, that means a truly integrated community care network and requires important partnerships to meet the total health needs of communities. Baptist Health is focused on the future and is taking steps to ensure that the organization will be delivering healthcare to Arkansas well into the twenty-first century. An organized delivery system addresses issues of cost, technology, quality, chronic illness and information management and a quality award was created in recognition of its efforts to ensure continuous quality improvement.

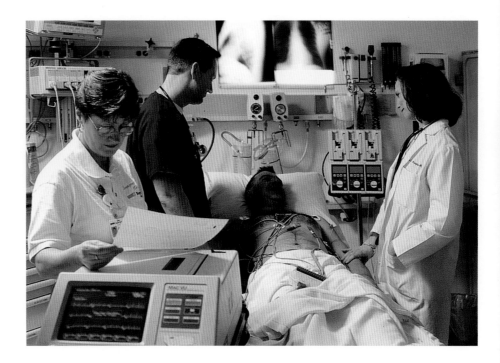

Baptist Health's primary service areas include thirteen counties within Arkansas, comprising approximately eighty percent of the hospital patient discharges in 2000. Currently, it is the fifth largest employer in the state and the third in their primary market. Annually, Baptist Health is directly and indirectly responsible for over $656 million of added value that is returned to the Arkansas economy.

An outstanding relationship within their communities and organizations has always been a valuable component of the mission of Baptist Health. Through its participation on such varied boards as the Arkansas Department of Breast Cancer Advisory Board, Arkansas Center for Health Improvement, and the Arkansas Advocates for Children and Families, unique needs and resources are identified. Listening and talking with communities is also an important role in helping officials identify an area of need and studying it within a strategic framework. Outreach initiatives are extensive and include the Back-To-School Immunization Project, a mobile health unit, the United Way, and Community Wellness Centers and Clinics.

Baptist Health continues its vital efforts to restore the health of Arkansas and make a wide impact upon healthcare today and into the next century. Visit www.baptist-health.com for more information about events and the latest updates in health-related issues.

✦

With nearly seventy percent of cardiac patients requiring a full service hospital to meet all of their medical needs, Baptist Health offers not only state-of-the-art cardiac care through facilities such as this cath lab but also provides quick access to some of Arkansas' best specialists for other health problems.

ROLLER FUNERAL HOMES & CITIZENS FIDELITY

Roller Funeral Homes and Citizens Fidelity were born out of the heart of Denver and Christine Roller.

After serving his funeral apprenticeship in Missouri, Denver and Christine moved to Mountain Home, Arkansas to work for McClure Funeral Home. Although the effects of the Great Depression were still lingering in rural Arkansas, Denver and Christine managed to buy the McClure Funeral Home and soon had a baby daughter, Sue. They practiced the principles of honesty, loyalty and concern for others that built a strong family and would cause their business to prosper.

World War II placed a large burden on Denver, the only mortician in the area, and the whole community worked with the Rollers to care for those who lost their lives during those difficult times. The support from the community earned eternal gratitude from the Roller family, who always try to give back more than they receive.

The Rollers acquired Drummond Funeral Home in Little Rock in the mid-fifties and, in the sixties, Citizens Funeral Home in West Memphis and McNutt Funeral Home in Conway. McNutt Funeral Home's motto, "To serve as we would be served" was established

to guide each local director in the principles of operation. Denver also united his businesses under the symbol of the white dove on a blue background. These attempts to build a caring organization proved successful and soon quality funeral directors around the state were joining under the white dove and the type of service it represented.

Denver was a man of great vision. He established Arkansas' first crematory and created the Assured Peace Funeral Plan, the leading prepaid funeral plan in Arkansas. As of March 2003, over 21,000 people have prearranged and prepaid over $70 million with Assured Peace.

At Denver's death in 1985, there were thirteen funeral homes and five cemeteries operating under the principles he and Christine had established. Christine then took over the position of Chairman of the Board and, with her family, successfully built one of the largest funeral providers in the state.

Now, twenty-seven funeral homes, nine cemeteries and two crematories later, the family remains dedicated to keeping the business a family-owned and family-managed organization. Two generations of the Roller family are now involved in the operation of Roller Funeral Homes. Sue Roller Jenkins,

daughter of Denver and Christine, serves as Chairman of the Board. Other family members involved include: Lynn Jenkins, executive vice president, Renata Jenkins Byler, daughter of Sue and Lynn, secretary/treasurer, and Tim Byler, vice president of Information Systems. Both the owners and officers are committed to transferring the same values and principles established by Denver and Christine to future generations.

The successes of these efforts have been recognized by Arkansas Business, the City of Little Rock and by the readers of the *Arkansas Democrat-Gazette*, voting Roller the best funeral home in Central Arkansas every year since 1999. The organization has been awarded the Hospice Compassion Award by the Hospice Foundation of Arkansas and the Corporate Humanitarian award by the Office of the Governor, Division of Volunteerism.

As Roller Funeral Homes continues to play a vital role in the life of the communities it serves, Citizens Fidelity also remains committed to that characteristic service and care pioneered by the Roller family. It originally began in the 1970s as the public expressed their desire for a form of security to ensure their funeral could be planned and prepaid. Denver fulfilled this need by creating the Assured Peace Funeral Plans. These policies were trust funded to assure the public that their funerals would be paid for. Assured Peace Funeral Plan is now the leading prepaid funeral plan in Arkansas.

In 1981, Roller's daughter, Sue, and her husband Lynn Jenkins, named their growing insurance company Citizens Fidelity Insurance (CFI). This launched the beginning of an incredible growth period for their company. Just four years later, the CFI home office experienced such tremendous growth, they moved to a larger location and one year later they were fortunate to move again. In 1994, CFI moved its home office to 13701 Chenal Parkway in West Little Rock.

CFI became the marketing arm for Denver Roller, Inc., which owns the Roller Funeral Homes and Cemeteries. This has allowed DRI to concentrate on providing the best facilities, equipment and personal service to families experiencing grief. CFI focuses on helping families pay for the cost of memorializing their loved ones. As of March 2003 over 21,000 people have prearranged and prepaid over $70 million with assured peace. CFI offers life insurance and complete pre-paid funeral plan.

St. Vincent Health System

St. Vincent Health System owes its existence to an epidemic that did not occur. In 1878, as yellow fever was ravaging the South, Little Rock had few physicians and no hospital. Citizens such as Mr. and Mrs. Alexander Hager believed that only God could stop the advancing plague and the couple vowed that if Little Rock were spared they would provide funds to build a hospital. Miraculously, the outbreak never occurred and the Hagers kept their promise.

In 1888, Mother General Cleophas and five Sisters of Charity of Nazareth arrived in Little Rock at the invitation of the Hagers. A ten-bed Charity Hospital was founded on East Second Street and was renamed St. Vincent Infirmary in 1889.

As the twentieth century opened, St. Vincent Infirmary moved to a three-story, fifty-bed facility, at Tenth and High Streets. St. Vincent Infirmary School of Nursing, Arkansas' first nursing school, opened in 1906.

By 1920, St. Vincent Infirmary was among the first dozen hospitals in the country to install X-ray apparatus. The hospital staff of physicians had grown to sixteen and it was the first hospital in Arkansas to be certified by the Joint Commission on Accreditation of Hospitals. In 1938 a maternity annex was opened, and later spawned the development of the state's first intensive care nursery in 1972.

With the purchase of forty acres at Hayes (now University Avenue) and Markham Streets, the Diocese of Little Rock transferred ownership of the hospital to the Sisters of Charity of Nazareth. In 1954, St. Vincent Infirmary moved to the nine-story facility that today stands at the heart of St. Vincent's main campus.

The decades of the 1960s and 1970s brought transformation from a small hospital to a major medical center with regional influence. In 1985, The St. Vincent Cardiovascular Care Center opened and The St. Vincent Cancer Center was established.

In 1988, St. Vincent celebrated its centennial anniversary, which culminated with the "Birthday Party of the Century," featuring a 300-foot long birthday cake and hot air balloon rides and the organization's flagship facility was officially renamed the St. Vincent Infirmary Medical Center. The Center for Health Education, featuring a 360-seat auditorium and six fully equipped conference rooms was opened.

As the 1980s concluded, St. Vincent experienced rapid technological change as managed care influences elevated in the 1990s. The Sisters of Charity of Nazareth and St. Vincent responded by creating innovative partnerships to support the healthcare needs of the community. Obstetric services were reinitiated, in 1992, after a fifteen-year lapse, and quickly reestablished St. Vincent as a leading provider of obstetrical care.

In 1994, St. Vincent initiated an operating lease for St. Anthony's Medical Center, in Morrilton. In September 1997, St. Vincent became part of Catholic Health Initiatives, one of the largest Catholic healthcare organizations in the country. This brought a new level of strength to St. Vincent Health System.

In February 1998, St. Vincent acquired the operations of Little Rock's Doctors Hospital and three Family Clinics from Columbia/HCA, significantly expanding St. Vincent's delivery network and clinical capacity.

In September 1999, St. Vincent completed the multi-phased development of St. Vincent Medical Center/North, adding an acute care facility to its growing Sherwood campus.

Today, St. Vincent is a vibrant organization, poised for continued progress. This renewed vitality is evidenced by St. Vincent's inclusion on Solucient's listing of the 100 Top Hospitals®: Performance Improvement Leaders, featured in *Modern Healthcare*.

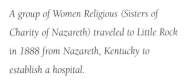

A group of Women Religious (Sisters of Charity of Nazareth) traveled to Little Rock in 1888 from Nazareth, Kentucky to establish a hospital.

William F. Rector was always intrigued by the challenges of the real estate business, even before he partnered with Ernest F. (Fe) Phillips and Byron R. Morse to launch Rector Phillips Morse in 1955. Now, fifty years later, the firm he founded remains a leader in the real estate business in Arkansas.

Real estate gave Rector the opportunity to be more innovative and creative than was possible in his twenty-five-year-old insurance business. That innovation led him to expand his business from residential sales into a full-service real estate company also offering commercial sales, property development, construction and property management. Today, as the company celebrates its fiftieth anniversary, Rector Phillips Morse is the most complete real estate company in Arkansas, with a breadth of services unmatched in the state.

Throughout its history RPM has been a leader, both corporately and through the contributions of its individual employees. The company handled the sale of 1,100 acres in western Little Rock that became the Pleasant Valley subdivision. This transaction was the largest land sale in the county at the time. They also built the very first condominium complex in Arkansas located on Lake Hamilton in Hot Springs, and were involved in developing many major malls and shopping centers. Residential subdivisions developed by RPM include Secluded Hills, Charleston Heights, Treasure Hills, Sturbridge and Marlowe Manor in Little Rock. In addition, RPM has built and continues to construct and sell homes in some of the area's most prestigious neighborhoods including Chenal, Maumelle and the Heights in Little Rock. But, no matter the neighborhood-whether in Little Rock, North Little Rock or Maumelle-RPM's sign "stands out front" listing and selling more homes over the past fifty years than any other Realtor®.

The legacy established over the past fifty years is only as lasting and resilient as RPM's current accomplishments. And future plans. For instance, RPM Management Company provides full-service management

from single-family homes to large, multi-family complexes, shopping centers, warehouses, office buildings and industrial parks. Where multi-family projects are concerned, RPM Management currently oversees over 3,000 units.

RPM owns projects, leases them, locates the right kind of properties for tenants, and manages the assets of others, including the sale of properties to meet the goals and objectives of clients taking advantage of opportunities in a dynamic marketplace.

Commercial real estate, too, continues to live up to the impressive history of RPM. Development of industrial and commercial projects for investors and corporate clients reach statewide. And the assembling, constructing, marketing and management of retail space and office buildings complement RPM's stand-alone position in the industry as a forward-looking company that focuses on increasing value in all types of real estate transactions.

Today, Rector's vision for a full-service real estate company continues to prosper. RPM has more than 250 employees with annual sales volume in excess of $120 million. RPM Chief Executive Officer Pete Hornibrook believes the firm will continue to grow as it prepares for its second half century. "Our industry has to adjust to consumers' ways of doing things," Hornibrook said. "The Internet allows us to be in front of so many more customers than we ever thought possible. This will continue to lead to even greater opportunities for our business."

Rector Phillips Morse: The Strength of Experience is located at 1501 North University in Little Rock and on the Internet at www.rpmrealty.com.

RECTOR PHILLIPS MORSE INC.

❖

Above: C.E.O. Pete Hornibrook.

Below: Founder William F. Rector, Sr.

HILLCREST CAMSHAFT SERVICE, INC.

❖

Hillcrest Camshaft, yesterday and today.

Hillcrest Camshaft Service, Inc. has remanufactured industrial diesel camshafts for the world's finest fleets of trucks, buses, locomotive, stationary and marine engines for over a half-century. Specializing in camshafts, crankshafts, fuel injection camshafts, lifter followers and hard industrial chrome plating, they offer customers the very finest quality in service, dependability, and workmanship.

Originally founded by Fred Schneider in April of 1955, Hillcrest Camshaft was located in a 4200 square foot building at 2904 Kavanaugh in the Hillcrest area of Little Rock. Alex Nesterenko joined Schneider and three other employees on April 26, 1955. Before coming to the United States, Alex received his Professional Instructor Degree in Metal Fabricating from Senai Technical School in San Paulo, Brazil. After his arrival in Arkansas, he began working for the company during the day and while attending evening classes at Little Rock Junior College, where he received a degree in Mechanical Engineering.

When Schneider passed away in 1965, the business was sold to Alex Nesterenko and Joseph Kemp. They became equal partners and, in the late 1970s, moved with eleven employees to a larger 10,000 square foot building at 3517 Asher Avenue. Upon Kemp's death in the early 1980s, Alex purchased the remaining fifty percent of the partnership.

After Tim Nesterenko, Alex's oldest son, worked in the company and received his degree in transportation, he signed on as a general salesman and now serves as Hillcrest Camshaft's vice president.

The company moved to its current location at 5502 West Sixty-fifth in August of 1996 and today includes thirty-nine employees. The building originally had 32,000 square feet but was expanded to 46,000 square feet to include a 7,000 square foot Diesel Machine Shop which was added in October 2004.

Today, Hillcrest Camshaft Service, Inc., services nearly 400 customers from around the world, including the United States, Canada, Mexico, England and Iceland. Well-known names such as Caterpillar Inc., Union Pacific Railroad, Detroit Diesel Remanufacturing, G.E. Locomotives and Mack Trucks are included in its customer base.

The company looks to the future with plans to expand their crankshaft and locomotive camshaft business while continuing to improve upon the camshaft processes and strives to have Arkansas' number one remanufacturing machine shop for diesel engines.

For more information or to contact Hillcrest Camshaft Service, Inc. please visit www.hillcrestcamshaft.com or call 800-832-4859.

Originally founded in 1973 as Arkansas' first indoor tennis facility and formerly known as the Westside Tennis Club, the Little Rock Athletic Club has evolved into a diverse and sophisticated athletic club. From its inception, the LRAC has focused on one goal, improving its members' lives through health and fitness.

Named as one of the forty best health clubs in the United States by *Club Insider Magazine*, the 120,000-square-foot facility, situated on nine acres in West Little Rock, has continually expanded and upgraded its equipment, services and programs, making it Central Arkansas' largest and most popular tennis and fitness facility.

Amenities include nine indoor tennis courts and four outdoor hard courts; three racquetball courts; an indoor track; a six-lane indoor/outdoor swimming pool; a large gymnasium with basketball and volleyball courts; two separate 3,000-square-foot weight rooms featuring Cybex, Free Motion, Hammer Strength and free weight equipment; a group exercise studio; Pilates and group cycling studios; a Cardio Theater with twelve big-screen televisions and seventy-five pieces of cardiovascular equipment such as treadmills, elliptical machines, stair steppers, rowing machines

and stationary cycles. The Little Rock Athletic Club also provides steam, sauna and whirlpools in each locker room, plus massage, fitness testing, personal trainers, a physical therapy clinic, restaurant, pro shop and a smoothie and espresso bar.

Parents of youngsters especially appreciate the LRAC because of the many facilities and services dedicated to children. Chief among these is the 7,000-square-foot activity area known as the Down Under Center for children age fourteen and younger. Here, kids enjoy basketball, soccer, volleyball, and a large indoor playground filled with special "soft play" equipment highlighted by a twenty-seven foot spiral slide. The Down Under Center also offers birthday parties, Parents' Night Out, sports camps and an after-school program that picks up children from school and brings them to the Club.

Additional children's facilities include an outdoor recreation pool, outdoor water playground known as a "sprayground" and a fully staffed childcare room for children four and younger.

Most importantly, the Little Rock Athletic Club is staffed by carefully selected and trained professionals dedicated to helping members improve their fitness and health through proper exercise, program guidance and encouragement. Reputations for excellence and word-of-mouth referrals have helped the Little Rock Athletic Club truly become Central Arkansas' "Club of Choice."

Snell Prosthetic & Orthotic Laboratory

We can trace Snell Laboratory's longevity to a consistent commitment to face a competitive market with honorable and ethical service, dedicated and caring employees, and the most powerful advantage of all: progressive knowledge and willingness to embrace new techniques and technology.

When R.W. "Pop" Snell began his company back in 1911, there were no rules or precedents to guide him. He first began handcrafting each custom-fitted artificial limb relying on his own belief that an important need required him to begin a generations-long search for better solutions.

Pop set his own style, responding proactively and creatively. Patients learned of his skill through word of mouth and referrals. From early limbs fashioned of rawhide and red willow, through the war years and the wave of returning disabled veterans in need of his services, the business prospered.

It was a business to which the family remained committed. From the beginning, the Snells created the benchmark for quality and service in the fields of prosthetics and orthotics. When the first standard tests were established in 1948, Ed Snell was among the first wave of practitioners to qualify as a Certified Prosthetist and Orthotist (C.P.O.).

President Frank Snell, C.P.O., F.A.A.O.P., a great-nephew of the founder, began working alongside his father at age fourteen, developing the skills required for an Orthotist/Prosthetist. When he joined the company full-time in 1972 as a graduate of Northwestern University, he brought with him new marketing and management skills and methods as well as new insights and goals.

His improvements included changing the company's name in 1976 to Snell Prosthetic & Orthotic Laboratory. By the time Ed retired and his son assumed the presidency in 1984, more changes were underway such as construction of the current Little Rock office at 625 North University Avenue, quickly followed by the opening of satellite offices across the state.

At every stage, Snell Laboratory has been in the vanguard of pursuing the latest and best methods and technology to serve patients, and is regarded throughout the state and the O&P industry as a respected leader in quality care. Leading manufacturers bring their newest technology to Snell Laboratory for beta testing, allowing them to offer their patients orthotic and prosthetic solutions not yet widely available. Thanks to a shared concern for quality and determined pursuit of the best ways and means to serve patients, Snell's computerized fabrication capabilities offer an amazing variety of possibilities that enable those with disabilities to lead more active, mobile, and independent lives.

Within the last decade, Snell Laboratory was first in the state to add the latest TracerCAD (Computer-Aided Design) technology, supported by CAM (Computer-Aided Manufacturing) fabrication innovations and improved O&P administrative software programs. Microprocessor-controlled prosthetic knees that "think" and react for their wearer, instant shape-capture technology that replaces the messy, labor-intensive, uncomfortable and lengthy process of plaster casting, and even captures and fits cranial helmets for children with a quick click—all these modern marvels have been promptly adopted. This significant commitment in time, financial investment, energy and effort stand as evidence of our historic belief in the value of equipping ourselves to serve as effectively and successfully as possible—by utilizing the latest in technology and the best in care.

In perpetuating this honored tradition, Snell Laboratory follows a long and honorable history of employing the latest and best methods available to improve its patients' lives, the quality of its service performance, and its overall productivity and support to our community.

In 1919 two young entrepreneurs, George Wittenberg and Lawson Delony, opened a small architectural firm in downtown Little Rock. Hard work and team effort were at the foundation of establishing a group that continues nearly a century later with over forty staff members, each dedicated to the vision of the company's founders. Though many techniques and practices may have changed over the years, the consistent dedication and perseverance by which Wittenberg, Delony & Davidson (WD&D) serves its clients in the twenty-first century holds as strong as it did in the company's first years.

Today, WD&D is a full-service architectural firm with each of their nine principals responsible for a particular area of practice. Forty-two individuals work primarily in the areas of education, municipal facilities, healthcare, correctional, office space and interior design from the firm's offices in Little Rock and Fayetteville. With four LEED™ Accredited Professionals, WD&D is an active participant in the initiative to promote buildings that are environmentally responsible, profitable and healthy places to live and work. In addition to architectural designers, the professional staff includes interior designers, Americans with Disabilities Act compliance specialists, space planners, contract management personnel, and computer aided drafting and design staff. WD&D also provides full contract administration services. As drastic changes both nationally and locally in education and healthcare have occurred, WD&D has met these modern challenges with uniquely trained architects dedicated to each of those areas.

Historically, WD&D has enjoyed a unique role in the state's history. Founder George Wittenberg held the first architectural license in the State of Arkansas and co-founder Julian Davidson was the first architect in Arkansas to be licensed in both architecture and engineering. The firm was architect of record for the nationally famous Central High School and has been active in developing the Little Rock skyline with such landmarks as Regions Center (30 floors); the Stephens Building (25 floors); the former Excelsior Hotel, now the Peabody (19 floors); First Security Center (14

floors); the BlueCross BlueShield Building (11 floors); the USAble Building (11 floors); and the new 670-space RiverMarket Parking Garage.

Wittenberg, Delony & Davidson, Inc. Architects also emphasizes the importance of activism on task forces and legislative committees in efforts to contribute to the overall good of the community. The group's involvement in community and charitable endeavors is varied and includes such organizations as the Alzheimer Arkansas Programs and Services; American Cancer Society; Arkansas Children's Hospital; Arkansas Legislative Task Force on Educational Facilities; Bess Chisum Stephens YWCA; Downtown Little Rock Kiwanis Club; Fifty for the Future; Chambers of Commerce in Little Rock, Fayetteville, Jacksonville, Rogers and Bentonville; Little Rock School District; National Association of Women in Construction; Rotary Club of Little Rock; UAMS Chancellor's Round Table; University of Arkansas School of Architecture Scholarship funds; The Allen School; and Youth Home.

In 2005, WD&D is led by President Thomas R. Adams; Executive Vice President John C. Sloan; Vice President and Secretary/Treasurer Jack F. See, Jr.; VP/Director of Contract Administration Roy E. St. Clair, Jr.; VP/Managing Principal of Health Care Projects Edward E. Peek; VP/Managing Principal of Northwest Arkansas Office Richard K. Alderman; Director of Production Wallie G. Sprick; Chief of Design Chad T. Young; and Project Design Architect Bradley R. Chilote.

❖

Above: The Stephens Building in Little Rock.

Below: Little Rock's historic Central High School.

PULASKI TECHNICAL COLLEGE

✧
Above: Students gather for instruction in the biology lab at Pulaski Tech.

Bottom Pulaski Technical College, 2005.

Pulaski Technical College at North Little Rock is a comprehensive two-year college that serves the educational needs of central Arkansas through technical programs, a university-transfer program and specialized programs for business and industry. The college's mission is to provide access to high quality education that promotes student learning, to enable individuals to develop their fullest potential and to support the economic development of the state.

Pulaski Tech's history dates back to October 1945 when it was established as the Little Rock Adult Vocational School at 601 West Markham Street under the supervision of the Little Rock Public Schools. Its primary mission was to help World War II veterans learn the skills demanded in the post-war economic boom. In October 1969, Arkansas' government leaders saw the need to better prepare Arkansans for the increasing number of industrial jobs that were becoming more plentiful, thanks to successes in courting manufacturing plants to the state. So the administration of the school was transferred to the Arkansas Board of Vocational Education and the school was named Pulaski Vocational Technical School.

Early in the 1970s, 137 acres declared surplus by the Veterans Administration were transferred to the North Little Rock School District and Pulaski was given forty acres for a new school site. Pulaski Vo-Tech moved from Fourteenth and Scott Streets in Little Rock to its present location in January 1976.

New buildings were added in the mid-eighty's, but the school did not begin to truly reach its potential until 1991. When the Arkansas General Assembly created the Arkansas Technical and Community College System in 1991, Pulaski and twelve other vocational-technical schools became technical colleges under the coordination of the Arkansas Higher Education Coordinating Board.

Pulaski Technical College, as it is now known, offers more than forty associate degrees and certificate programs for students who plan to transfer to four-year colleges and universities and/or for career preparation and advancement.

Pulaski Tech serves a large community including Lonoke, Saline, Faulkner, and Pulaski Counties—and that community continues to grow. During the fall 2004 semester, Pulaski Tech's enrollment numbered 7,222 students. To meet its growing enrollment, Pulaski Tech has undertaken a substantial building program, which includes the construction of a 92,000 square foot campus center housing multi-purpose classrooms, community meeting space, lecture halls, a student union, food services, a bookstore and recreation area. The college also plans to expand its existing library by 12,000 square feet, providing additional space for technology, special collections, and group and individual study.

For more information about Pulaski Technical College, please visit www.pulaskitech.edu.

I.C.E., Inc.

Dick Kelley, Bill Denton, and Larry Schmalz founded Industrial Consulting Engineers, Inc. on March 1, 1982. Initially, the business was located in a two-room office downstairs at 501 North University Avenue in Little Rock. The firm's model was to provide structural, mechanical and industrial engineering services to industrial clients. Unfortunately, the country was still in a recession at that time and industrial clients were doing very little in the way of capital expenditures. The next two years were a struggle and the firm added only one employee in the area of drafting.

On February 1, 1985, Ken Jones joined the company with the purpose of expanding the business to include architectural clients. After Bill Denton left in 1986 to pursue other opportunities, the company was reincorporated to become I.C.E., Inc. in 1987 and Ken Jones was made a full partner.

As architectural work increased, services areas were expanded to include structural and mechanical design for commercial, institutional healthcare and educational facilities. By midyear in 1987 the staff had grown to fifteen individuals and the offices were relocated to the second floor of the Prospect Building at 1501 North University Avenue.

Business was good and the staff was steadily increasing as the workload progressed. In 1993 the offices were expanded and relocated to the ninth floor of the Prospect Building, where the group remained until April 2003. During that time the company grew to thirty-nine people and occupied approximately 8,800 square feet on two floors. This growth enabled I.C.E. to expand the staff to include more structural and mechanical engineers and to add electrical engineering to its services.

By the end of 2002 the firm had served more than 600 individual clients and completed more than 5,000 projects throughout the United States, Canada, Mexico, and Taiwan. In 2002 the firm created a marketing department and set out on a mission to brand the firm, first in Arkansas, and hopefully later as a regional firm.

The company's goals were redefined to be able to provide full service engineering, including civil/survey, to clients in order to grow business and the company moved to its present location at Two Financial Center in April 2003. The purpose of this move was not only to provide physical room for growth, but to also provide more visible exposure and to step the company up to the next level.

The strategies for rapid growth, beyond what could be expected organically, included both the possibilities of mergers and acquisitions. In 2002 the company initiated merger talks with Crafton, Tull & Associates, Inc., of Rogers, Arkansas. Crafton, Tull & Associates, Inc., at the time was a 120-person civil/survey/architectural firm with six offices in Arkansas and Oklahoma. While those talks were proceeding, in 2003 ICE acquired Fred Hegi and Associates, Inc., a local five-person structural engineering firm to continue building staff and to bring in new clients. In May of 2004, ICE and Crafton, Tull & Associates, Inc. merged with ICE operating as ICE|A Division of Crafton, Tull & Associates, Inc. until May 2005. Since the merger the firm has grown from the initial combined 160-person firm to over 220 employees in six offices including Rogers, Little Rock, and Russellville, Arkansas; Tulsa and Oklahoma City, Oklahoma; and Birmingham, Alabama.

The Little Rock office has grown from 39 to 50 individuals and now offers full service engineering including civil/survey and landscape architecture design. For further information about the company, please visit wwwicearkansas.com.

CENTRAL ARKANSAS LIBRARY SYSTEM

At various times since 1867 subscription libraries sponsored by a community group had operated in Little Rock, but no municipal library service existed until a pioneering group of Little Rock citizens applied to the Carnegie Corporation in 1909 for funds to build a public library. With a donation of $88,100 from Carnegie, a 23,000 square foot Little Rock Public Library was built at Seventh and Louisiana Streets and opened February 1, 1910 with a collection of 2,150 books. A staff of two women took over 500 library card applications on opening day alone!

For nearly a century now, the library has grown and changed to accommodate the ever-increasing population occurring across the area. A new Main Library was constructed in 1963, adjacent to the original building and, in 1975, the Library's Board of Trustees joined trustees of the Pulaski-Perry Regional Library in merging libraries in Little Rock, Jacksonville, Sherwood, and Perryville, along with the bookmobile services of the Little Rock Public Library and the Regional Library to form the Central Arkansas Library System (CALS).

CALS libraries offer many programs beyond the wealth of books, tapes, compact disks and other audio-visual materials available to patrons. These include the Gateway card program for residents living in nearby central Arkansas counties, as well as book clubs, book sales, DVDs and CD-ROMs. Reference services are available at each library in print and through online access at www.cals.org. Children and teens enjoy a wide array of events including Storytime, a year-round program for children, as well as summer reading programs, volunteer opportunities, and Slam & Jam, a poetry and musical gathering.

In 1997 a new Main Library opened in the renovated Fones Brothers warehouse on Rock Street. In 2001, CALS embarked on a visionary renovation of the Cox Building and transformed the historic warehouse into the Cox Creative Center, with a used bookstore, a meeting room, and two art galleries displaying many Arkansas artists' paintings, sculptures, woodwork, ceramics and art quilts. River Market Books & Gifts is jointly operated by CALS and the Friends of Central Arkansas Libraries (FOCAL), and features "gently read" books and specialty gift items.

In 2004, CALS purchased the Geyer & Adams and Budget Office buildings on President Clinton Avenue as part of a joint venture with the University of Arkansas at Little Rock in the Arkansas Studies Institute. Major components of the collection include papers and artifacts in association with UALR's Ottenheimer Library's Archives & Special Collections, CALS's Richard Butler Center for Arkansas Studies and the Gubernatorial Studies Institute.

Since 1989, CALS has been under the direction of Dr. Bobby Roberts. Named *Library Journal's* "Librarian of the Year" in 1998, Dr. Roberts holds a master's degree in library science from the University of Oklahoma and a Ph.D. in American history from the University of Arkansas and has served as an author, co-author, and co-editor of a number of books detailing the history of the Civil War.

Preserving the heritage and history of the community, CALS is headquartered at the Main Library in Little Rock and includes the Cox Creative Center, seven other libraries in the city, and libraries in Maumelle, Perryville, Jacksonville, and Sherwood.

Little Rock's downtown public library.

KERR PAPER AND SUPPLY INCORPORATED

After twenty-three years with Little Rock Paper Company, Wilcher Kerr decided to start his own paper company in January of 1986. The first base of operation for Kerr Paper and Supply, Inc. was a 6,500 square foot building at 8124 Scott Hamilton. In 1992 the company moved to a 14,000 square foot building at 8100 Scott Hamilton. Five years later, a 26,000 square foot warehouse was completed at 6701 I-30 and today distributes not only paper products, including towels, tissues and napkins, but also retail and industrial packaging products and janitorial supplies and equipment.

Kerr Paper and Supply, Inc. employs twenty people with six outside sales representatives to cover central and southern Arkansas. Among current employees is Barry Kerr, who has been with the company since its formation, and son-in-law, Scott Ginn. The company has over $5 million in annual sales.

For more information or to contact Kerr Paper and Supply, Inc. directly, phone (501) 562-0005.

UNIVERSITY OF ARKANSAS AT LITTLE ROCK

It started in borrowed high school classrooms, offering basic night classes to working men and women lacking the funds to go away from home to college. Nearly eighty years later, the University of Arkansas at Little Rock has evolved into a multi-dimensional, research-intensive institution fully engaged with the community and region, harnessing its intellectual engine to advance economic development and elevating social health and cultural vitality through education, research, and professional outreach.

Founded as Little Rock Junior College in 1927, UALR began as an adjunct to the Little Rock School District. Today, UALR enrolls more than 11,000 students from across the state and the world—all studying a wide range of subjects from opera to nanotechnology.

Once seen as a "commuter school," UALR has been on the front lines in the national movement to reinvent urban campuses as metropolitan universities that do not embody traditional "ivy-covered ivory tower" attitudes. As an early member of the national Coalition of Urban and Metropolitan Universities, UALR embraces an urban version of the rural land grant mission—a commitment to improve the quality of life of the community and state.

The genesis of UALR's long-term success and growth occurred on July 1, 1929, when the junior college became the sole beneficiary of a trust established by former Arkansas Governor George W. Donaghey and his wife, Louvenia. The $2-million gift—at the time the largest single donation to an Arkansas institution—focused statewide attention on the fledgling college and fueled faith in the future of the institution.

By 1957, "Jaycee" had expanded its course offerings and outgrown its downtown campus on the site of the present-day Philander Smith College and became a four-year private liberal arts college—Little Rock University. The growing institution established a new campus on a secluded eighty-acre track of piney woods on Hayes Street—now University Avenue—

donated by Little Rock business executive Raymond Rebsamen.

From its inception and continuing today, UALR has forged strong partnerships with the community, particularly business leaders who understood from the beginning that the future growth of a region's economy is intrinsically tied to the success of its ability to educate its workforce and develop future generations of leaders and innovators.

Whether it's developing courses of study allowing business professionals opportunities to earn MBA degrees on weekends or providing expertise and research for area entrepreneurs through UALR's Small Business Development Center, the University works hand-in-glove with the business community to help provide economic opportunities and grow new jobs.

"By choosing to fit into the metropolitan university model, a university accepts the added responsibility to extend its resources to the surrounding region, to provide leadership in addressing regional needs, and to work cooperatively with the region's schools, municipalities, businesses, and industries," said UALR Chancellor Joel E. Anderson.

UALR also operates an outreach program with the neighborhoods surrounding its campus. The UALR Children International Program addresses the educational, health, and social needs of more than 2,000 at-risk children in Little Rock public schools through tutoring, health assessments, and summer enrichment programs. The initiative includes a partnership with community and health organizations to operate the state's first full-service in-school, dental clinic for children across the district.

In the 1990s, UALR expanded its role as an intellectual resource for the community with the Friday Sturgis Fellows Leadership Program, a scholarship program that exemplifies UALR's service learning emphasis, through which students use classroom knowledge to improve the community.

Episcopal Collegiate School is an independent, coeducational, Episcopal, college preparatory school serving Central Arkansas. Founded in 1997 as The Cathedral Junior High, Inc., the Board of Trustees purchased thirty-one acres at 1701 Cantrell Road as a permanent campus for grades six through eight. Within two months, the name was changed to The Cathedral Middle School, and classes began at the newly named Jackson T. Stephens Campus in August 2000 with grades six through eight. Immediately, plans were made to expand to include an Upper School. With a grade being added each year, the first senior class graduated in May 2004.

The name Episcopal Collegiate School was adopted in July 2003 to reflect the heritage, identity, and mission of the School. Collegiate is a term used by independent schools to articulate the academic mission of a strong college preparatory school, and the word Episcopal conveys the School's religious heritage. Trinity Episcopal Cathedral in Little Rock, Arkansas, endorses the School.

As a school of fewer than 500 students, Episcopal Collegiate School is able to mentor and nurture each individual student to reach his or her full potential by providing small classes and a low student-teacher ratio. Intellectual challenge is the foundation of the liberal arts curriculum. Episcopal seeks to balance the pursuit of academic excellence with the development of character—intellectually, physically, and spiritually. Faculty members are recognized as leaders in their disciplines with over half of the faculty holding advanced degrees.

Episcopal Collegiate School is fully accredited by the Southwest Association of Episcopal Schools and the Arkansas Nonpublic School Accrediting Association. The School is a member in good standing of the National Association of Independent Schools, the College Board, and the National Association of Episcopal Schools.

Episcopal Collegiate School seeks to ensure the appropriate match between a prospective student and the mission of the School. As a school, we respect and affirm the dignity and worth of each individual. Our mission statement is as follows:

An independent, college preparatory school rooted in the Episcopal tradition and affirming all faiths, Episcopal Collegiate School strives to develop in its students respect for all persons, reverence of God, and a sense of moral responsibility. Episcopal Collegiate is dedicated to the pursuit of excellence and joy in learning in a nurturing community that prepares our students to live principled and fulfilling lives of leadership and service to others. The School provides rigorous academic programs to teach each student strong skills of analysis and expression; instills knowledge in the arts, sciences, and humanities; fosters critical, creative, and independent thinking; and inspires intellectual curiosity and passion for learning. Through extensive co-curricular and athletic programs, students will develop strength of body and character and learn discipline, teamwork, and sportsmanship. Episcopal Collegiate seeks and welcomes a vibrant student body, rich in diversity, where students live and honor the School's core values of respect, reverence, and responsibility and carry those values beyond the School community into their futures.

ARKANSAS COMMUNITY FOUNDATION

The Arkansas Community Foundation (ARCF) is a public foundation that works with donors, organizations, companies, and communities to help them reach their charitable objectives through the creation of charitable funds. ARCF invests and manages the funds, from which grants to nonprofit, charitable causes and organizations can be made in perpetuity.

ARCF began in 1976, with leadership and initial funding provided by the Winthrop Rockefeller Foundation. A number of civic and philanthropic leaders from across the state came together to consider the need for a statewide community foundation and the Arkansas Community Foundation (ARCF) was born. The group met several times throughout 1976, forming a board of directors, creating articles of incorporation and bylaws, and hiring an executive director, David Roosevelt, grandson of the late President Franklin Roosevelt.

The building of a statewide organization of this kind was unfamiliar to many Arkansans, and its creation was a daunting task. The five years of grant support from the Winthrop Rockefeller Foundation provided financial stability and was supplemented with a membership campaign.

By the end of the second year, David Roosevelt had left the position of executive director. Norma Wisor, a former program officer at the Chicago Community Trust with expertise in developing program initiatives and seeking foundation grants to support them, proved to be a wise choice for the new directorship. When Wisor left in 1983, the Foundation had developed a considerable reputation as an innovator of programs and initiatives, particularly on the subject of aging. Its assets totaled approximately $2 million and included the establishment of nineteen permanent funds.

Martha Ann Jones, chosen to succeed Wisor in 1983, launched an effort to stabilize the still-struggling Foundation by building an operating endowment and working with donors to create charitable funds. When Jones concluded her work with the Foundation in May 1996, ARCF managed nearly $15 million in assets, distributed among approximately 250 funds.

Chosen in 1996 by the ARCF Board to succeed Jones, Pat Lile had extensive statewide nonprofit experience and had helped to create a community foundation affiliate in Pine Bluff, where she formerly lived. Under Lile's leadership, two multiyear grants from the Winthrop Rockefeller Foundation and Walton Family Charitable Support Foundation were received. The approximately $19 million in these two grants has enabled ARCF to build the capacity to oversee a program to expand affiliate outreach, to build assets, and to focus on growing endowed funds. Each of the twenty-five affiliates has a part-time executive director and an office in its local area. The goal of the program is for each affiliate to have a foundation of at least $1 million within six years while operating within a cost effective model.

By the end of fiscal year 2006, ARCF's assets had reached $100 million, while managing more than 1,000 charitable funds. As Foundation assets increase, ARCF grants now exceed $4 million a year. The Foundation is assured of continuing its impact on the nonprofit sector throughout the state "For good. For Arkansas. For ever."

ARCF central offices are located in the historic Union Station in downtown Little Rock. For more information, please visit www.arcf.org.

The Arkansas Community Foundation, Celebrating thirty years of orchestrating change, through philanthropic impact. 1976-2006.

Situated on the banks of the Arkansas River in North Little Rock, the ALLTEL Arena is a 370,000-square-foot entertainment and convention facility with a seating capacity of 18,000 and 7,000 square feet of meeting room space.

The arena is the home of the Arkansas Twisters Arena football team and hosts attractions such as the Ringling Brothers Barnum and Bailey Circus, Champions on Ice Figure Skating Exhibition, RimRockers Basketball and concerts.

The ALLTEL Arena is one of several attractions located along the Arkansas River that unites the capital city of Little Rock with North Little Rock. The Civic Center Design Team (Burt Taggart & Associates Architects/Engineers, Garver & Garver Engineering and Rosser International of Atlanta) designed the facility. The arena is considered the crown jewel in the development of the riverfront that includes a new central library, a market, the refurbished Old State Territorial Capitol Building, and public parks on both sides of the scenic river. With the addition of the Clinton Presidential Library in Little Rock, the twin cities have become a primary destination for tourists from the state and around the world.

The arena was funded through a combination of local, state and private monies. On the local level, proceeds from a one-year, one-cent sales tax in Pulaski County were dedicated to building the arena. The state contributed $20 million and the sale of suite lease agreements for skyboxes and other private funding netted additional funds. The ALLTEL Corporation contributed $7 million for the naming rights of the arena. When it opened in October of 1999 with a cost of $83 million, the arena was debt free.

The arena is owned by the Multi-Purpose Civic Center Facilities Board for Pulaski County, with Michael Marion as general manager of the facility. Marion, with twenty-five years experience in the entertainment industry, has been highly successful in booking some of the most illustrious names in music, including Elton John, Billy Joel, Britney Spears, Janet Jackson, Cher, The Eagles, Tim McGraw, George Strait, Bruce Springsteen and many more.

In addition to providing a venue for sports and concerts, the arena provides space for meetings, banquets, conventions and exhibitions. Seating capacity ranges from 75 to 2,300. An 80-by-40-foot stage, eight spotlights, a public address system, audio/video equipment and in-house sound system are provided. The arena offers full in-house catering with a complete catering staff and experienced chef.

Since its beginning, ALLTEL has been highly successful in providing people of all ages and backgrounds with the best in entertainment and convention facilities, making it the likely arena of choice in Central Arkansas for generations to come.

The ALLTEL Arena is located at One Alltel Arena Way in Little Rock and on the Internet at www.alltelarena.com.

ALLTEL ARENA

SOL ALMAN COMPANY

Scrap metal recycler Sol Alman Company, 1300 East Ninth Street, originated in 1905 when Charles Alman, a Russian immigrant, founded the business as the Charles Alman Waste Materials Company at 317 West Tenth Street in Little Rock. In 1928, he acquired property and moved the business to a larger location two blocks west at 1000 Arch Street.

Charles' son, Sol, started working at the business as a boy after school hours, Saturdays and during the summer.

Sol's career as a professional jazz musician playing the clarinet and saxophone during the Big Band era was interrupted in 1939 when he began focusing his attention toward helping his ailing father operate the business. In 1942 the doctors declared Charles disabled and Sol legally acquired the business. The company name was changed at the request of Charles to Sol Alman Company in August 1942. Charles died in May 1943.

After the outbreak of World War II, Sol received from the U.S. Government an honorable discharge from Army National Guard military service in order for him to continue supporting the war effort by operating his scrap metal business as a government sanctioned, official salvage depot.

❖

Top: Charles Alman, founder of Charles Alman Waste Materials Company.

Below: Sol Alman.

As an astute, aggressive and hard working businessman, Sol expanded his operation by acquiring six acres of industrial property with railroad facilities in 1947 at 1300 East Ninth Street, three blocks east of Interstate 30. On February 23, 1948, Sol officially opened his scrap metal business at this much larger location.

After over fifty years of being associated with the same company, Sol retired on January 1, 1983. He served as a highly valued and respected consultant to the company until his death in January 1999. During the past twenty-two years, Sol Alman Company has been operating under the leadership of Sol's two sons—Charles and Larry Alman, chairman and president respectively.

Today, Sol Alman Company buys and processes ferrous (steel) and non-ferrous (copper, brass, aluminum, stainless, etc.) metals for recycling and remelting. All scrap metal is segregated and processed according to its specific chemistry and size specification.

The recycling process utilizes a considerable amount of capital equipment including magnet cranes, shears, and balers, along with a fleet of tractors, trailers and container systems. The scrap metal is shipped to mills and foundries via tractor, railroad car or barge, domestically as well as internationally.

Today the largest county society in the state, Pulaski County Medical Society (PCMS) is a professional association for physicians, which includes more than 1,000 Central Arkansas members. It was the first medical organization licensed by the state in 1866 and claims a rich history of service to physicians and to improving the health of the community.

Improving community health during the great cholera epidemics of the 1860s and efforts to defeat poliomyelitis by mass immunizations in the 1950s and 1960s gave the Society its vision. Jerome S. Levy, M.D. served as its president in 1957 and deemed the immunization utilizing the Salk vaccine as the outstanding activity of that year. It was noted as "a clear-cut way to dramatize the profession's public service role and a chance to prove by deed that medicine is a public service profession."

PCMS physicians remain at the forefront of local public health efforts today. Issues ranging from medical legislation to carrier relations provide ample opportunity for involvement in organized medicine.

The Medical Exchange is one of many services offered to the membership of the Society. This includes a 24/7 emergency answering service—the only service in the area exclusive to physicians—and is completely automated and computerized.

The annual PCMS Membership Directory is the preferred resource for locating physicians by name, specialty, and location, and is on the Web at www.pulaskicms.org,

while a monthly newsletter keeps members and clinic administrators abreast of programs and services.

Few organizations have had the privilege of contributing to the betterment and growth of the community, as has the Pulaski County Medical Society. Its mission is to promote and preserve the higher standards of medical care and medical ethics, to conserve and protect the public health of the community, and to foster and guard the professional interests of its members. Dr. Matthew Cunningham, Pulaski County's first physician and the first mayor of Little Rock, set the pace for leadership by the profession.

The PCMS and Medical Exchange headquarters are located in the Doctor's Building at 500 South University Avenue in Little Rock. Growing at an average of nine percent annually, the Society's strategic planning efforts are guided by a membership survey in which members have selected improvement of public health as the most important factor of the twenty-first century.

Pulaski County Medical Society contributes to the future of medicine by providing free stethoscopes annually to Pulaski County freshman medical students at the University of Arkansas for Medical Services. The Society's support of the Arkansas River Trail "Medical Mile" symbolizes the organizations continuing commitment to improving community health.

PULASKI COUNTY MEDICAL SOCIETY

Pulaski County Medical Society Officers
2005 Board of Directors:

Stephen W. Magie, MD, president
R. Lee Archer, MD, president-elect
Jim Ingram, MD, vice president
Kemp Skokos, MD, secretary
Carl Covey, MD, treasurer
Thomas L. Eans, MD, immediate past president.

❖

2005 President Stephen Magie, M.D.

BRAY SHEET METAL COMPANY

Bray Sheet Metal Company, 1508 Scott Street, has served the Little Rock area for more than eighty years. This family owned company consists of three major divisions: sheet metal, roofing and customized fabrication.

William Carson Bray, Sr., founded this family-owned business in 1925 when he opened a small sheet metal shop behind his home at 1512 Scott Street. Bray formed many lasting friendships in the early days in after-hours poker games in his shop. Bray's sons, William Carson Bray, Jr., and John Warren Bray eventually joined the family business, adding a roofing division in the process. Much of the company's work can be seen in the tile roofs that adorn the Little Rock skyline. In later years, Bray built a new home at 1508 Scott Street and moved his business to its present location.

Following the depression of the 1930s, business thrived as Bray Sheet Metal expanded its services to include the paper mill industry. In the following decades, Bray and his crew installed and maintained air systems for paper mills such as International Paper, Arkansas Kraft, and Georgia Pacific.

Mary Simmons, the daughter of Carson Bray, Jr., is the current president of Bray Sheet Metal and operates the business from the Scott Street address that once served as the family home. Simmons represents the third generation to run the family business. Her son, Woody, is the fourth-generation family member to work in the business.

The company's industrial sheet metal division specializes in air systems for the paper mill industry and provides general sheet metal work for a variety of industries. The roofing division specializes in residential, commercial and industrial roofing. Bray installs a variety of roofing systems such as slate, tile and standing seam metal roofs as well as flashing and gutters for a complete roofing system. The customized fabrication division produces products ranging from industrial parts to stainless steel countertops and other specialty items for the home.

Bray Sheet Metal continues to grow, with added facilities and parking space on Scott Street. The company has grown from a one-man operation to thirty-five employees with plans to continue its services to the paper mill industry while expanding its roofing and fabrication divisions. In the midst of change, dedication to quality by the knowledgeable management and staff of Bray Sheet Metal has remained constant through the years, boding well for future success.

For more information and examples of the fine workmanship available to you at Bray Sheet Metal, visit their Web site at www.braysheetmetal.com.

❖

Bray Sheet Metal is located at 1508 Scott Street, east of I-630.

BILLY N.
BRUMBELOW,
LUTCF,
STATE FARM
INSURANCE &
FINANCIAL
SERVICES
AGENT

"Like a good neighbor, State Farm is there." Since April 16, 1970, Brumbelow has seen to it that State Farm's mission of helping customers in "managing the risks of everyday life, recover from the unexpected and realize their dreams" has been available to citizens of Little Rock. Whether through personal, health, or life insurance, or providing banking and financial services, Brumbelow and his staff are dedicated to ensuring the best service possible.

Graduating in 1953 from Benton High School in Benton, Brumbelow went on to join the Air National Guard, where he served for eight and a half years. After attending college at both Little Rock Junior College (presently the University of Arkansas at Little Rock) and Arkansas State Teachers College in Conway (today the University of Central Arkansas), Brumbelow worked for McKesson Wholesale Drug Company, where he was recognized as the Top Salesman for two consecutive years.

The winds of change began blowing in 1970 when Brumbelow became the first appointee made by Don T. Barrow after he became Agency Manager for State Farm Insurance. His first office was located at University and Asher Avenue. After several moves, Brumbelow moved into his present location, a 1,625 square foot office at 13200 West Markham Street. The extra space was necessary as the staff grew from one to four and as the number of policies in force grew into the thousands.

It was during this time that Brumbelow met and married Betty Faye Douglas Herndon. After signing off on his own homeowner's insurance policy, he and Betty moved into their new home and, since that day, have enjoyed raising their family of three children and seven grandchildren.

During his thirty-five years with State Farm, Brumbelow served three years on the Central Arkansas Life Underwriters Association Board. With the help of his staff, he has qualified for numerous State Farm awards, including the State Farm Ambassador traveling club, formerly known as the Millionaire's Club.

Striving to be involved and active with his community, Brumbelow has served among many charitable and service organizations. He was a charter member of the West Little Rock Optimist Club, where he served as its fifth president, earning an award for Distinguished President due to his leadership in growing the group from forty-five to sixty-nine members. He has been active in the Little Rock Chamber of Commerce and has served as co-chairman of the Ambassador Club. He is a member of Immanuel Baptist Church where he has served as a Greeter/Usher for the last twenty-five years. Brumbelow is a Gideon, a Mason with Pulaski Heights Lodge 673, a member of the Arkansas Consistory and a Shriner with the Scimitar Temple.

QualChoice of Arkansas, Inc.

QualChoice of Arkansas, Inc. is a not-for-profit Arkansas-based health services company offering a variety of managed care products and benefit administration services to its members. With over 85,000 members, it is the second largest managed care company in Arkansas and offers a comprehensive line of HMO and POS plans as well and certain third party administration, dental, vision and pharmacy products. QualChoice's membership includes large and small group commercial members and state employees located across the entire state with concentrated membership in large metropolitan markets.

QualChoice of Arkansas, Inc. works to create a sustainable financing vehicle to deliver easily accessible, high quality and affordable healthcare services across the entire commercial and governmental market in Arkansas. The delivery of these services is based upon exceptional support capabilities for all customer constituencies, complimented by a caring environment and effective technology solutions.

Throughout its history, the company has celebrated many milestones. In 1994, after being created by the University of Arkansas for Medical Sciences to offer managed healthcare services to residents of Arkansas, QualChoice opened in November serving 10,000 UAMS members. In 1995, the remainder of the University membership was added, along with members from the state employee benefit plan, and its total membership grew to 40,000. In 1996, QCA Health Plan, Inc., a for-profit affiliate, was formed to provide managed care programs, including HMO, Dual Choice Point of Service and Triple Point of Service, to employees in-state. Between the years of 1998 and 2000, QualChoice invested in more cost-effective business practices, workflow design and new risk management protocol.

The new millennium saw a return on the investment on new technologies and operations. In 2002, QualChoice reported total revenues of $92.6 million and a net income of $2 million on a statutory basis while still offering competitive rate plans for members. The company's first consumer directed health plans were offered to members in 2003. In 2004 the company developed the Chamber Alliance Program with the North Little Rock Chamber of Commerce to provide small and medium size businesses with quality health insurance options. Today there are over forty-two chambers of commerce across the state participating in the Chamber Alliance Program. In 2005 the company worked on expansion of its provider network in compliance with the new Any Willing Provider regulations and entered into new partnerships with local and national financial institutions, offering health saving account functions to compliment its high-deductible health plans.

QualChoice of Arkansas, Inc. is headquartered at 10825 Financial Centre Parkway in Little Rock and on the Internet at www.qcark.com.

Webster University traces its roots to 1812, with the founding of the Sisters of Loretto, one of the first religious communities of women in the United States. Pursuing a mission in education, the women moved westward from Kentucky, founding schools along the way. On November 1, 1915, the cornerstone was laid for a building in Webster Groves, Missouri to honor one of the first Catholic women's colleges west of the Mississippi. The college awarded its first degrees in 1919 to a graduating class of two.

Today, Webster University combines the cultural and intellectual legacies of the past with a pragmatic concern for meeting the challenges of the present and future. In doing so, Webster University creates a student-centered environment accessible to individuals of diverse ages, cultures, and socioeconomic backgrounds and sustains a personalized approach to education through small classes and close relationships among faculty and students. The graduate school offers an accelerated master's program in a nontraditional format. Degrees offered include MBA, MA, and MS.

Webster University recently celebrated the twentieth anniversary of its downtown Little Rock campus. Located at 200 West Capitol, the Little Rock branch includes 350 students led by a staff of four full time employees and one part-time lab technician, academic advisor, and faculty coordinator.

As their historic roots attest, community and charitable activities play an important role in the life of Webster University faculty and students and include donations of time and money to groups such as Riverfest 2005, the Make-A-Wish Foundation, United Way of Pulaski County, and corporate sponsorships with the Arkansas Arts Center. They also serve as partners in education with Robert L. Davis Elementary School.

For more information about the outstanding work and educational excellence of Webster University Little Rock, please visit www.webster.edu/littlerock.

WEBSTER UNIVERSITY LITTLE ROCK METRO CAMPUS

✧

Webster University's metro campus is located at 200 West Capitol, Suite 1500 in Little Rock, Arkansas.

Winrock International, a nonprofit organization headquartered in Little Rock, was created in 1985 through the merger of three organizations originally founded by brothers Winthrop and John D. Rockefeller, III—the Winrock International Livestock Research and Training Center, the Agricultural Development Council, and the International Agricultural Development Service. The combination of these groups has not only secured a valued tradition of education, training, and research, but also formed a powerful mission to improve lives by increasing economic opportunity, sustaining natural resources and protecting the environment.

At Winrock, people make the difference. Twenty years after its founding, nearly 200 people in the United States and more than 500 others working in 65 countries have joined the company. Innovative programs and projects are realized as these men and women forge lasting relationships among those who will carry on the work in communities located around the world.

Lasting improvements and long-term productivity are among Winrock International's most important elements for achieving a balance

WINROCK INTERNATIONAL

between the needs of people and the resources on which the world depends. This balance is most effectively met through the organization's seven main areas of concentration—agriculture; ecosystem services; forestry and natural resource management; leadership development; clean energy; U.S. programs; and volunteer technical assistance. Through a committed staff working together with a sense of unity and dedication to helping others, Winrock International remains a visionary program of lasting impact in the twenty-first century.

Winrock's mission is to help the poor and disadvantaged. Its workplace is the world.

✧

Winrock International's headquarters at 2101 Riverfront Drive in Little Rock. The building was recently awarded the gold rating from the U.S. Green Building Council's Leadership in Energy and Environmental Design program.
COURTESY OF PHOTOGRAPHER CRAIG DUGALL. PHOTO STUDIO: HEIDRICH BLESSING.

T.A.M. Enterprise, Inc.

Tommy Mathieu & Associates was founded in 1995 and has become Arkansas' largest residential real estate appraisal and consulting firm. Growing fivefold in less than a decade, the company has performed thousands of appraisal assignments ranging from REO owned real estate to estates in excess of $4 million. Currently, five full time appraisers with support staff provide the pinnacle of customer service to virtually every bank and mortgage company in central Arkansas. The office at 1300 Westpark serves Pulaski, Saline and Lonoke Counties.

The majority of Mathieu's work experience began in the oil business. For nearly eighteen years he labored in areas ranging from fieldwork to president of Mathieu Oil Company, a family owned independent oil producing company that is still in operation. Upon the death of his father in 1981, Mathieu resigned from Northeast Louisiana University and assumed the leadership in the family business, which involved running ten different corporations

with varied interests in numerous locations throughout the United States.

Today Tommy Mathieu is a member of the Little Rock Chamber of Commerce, the Benton Chamber of Commerce and the Pulaski Heights United Methodist Church in Little Rock.

✧
Tommy Mathieu.

SPONSORS